365 Ways
to Cook Pasta

W9-CSJ-889

365 Ways
to Cook Pasta

For Every Season, for Every Reason,
a Pasta Lover's Paradise

Marie Simmons

A JOHN BOSWELL ASSOCIATES BOOK

Quill
An Imprint of HarperCollins*Publishers*

The recipe for Queenie's Macaroni and Cheese, on page 18, is reprinted with permission from *The Pirates' House Cookbook*, copyright © 1982 by The Pirates' House Restaurant.

365 WAYS TO COOK PASTA. Copyright © 1988 by John Boswell Management, Inc. All rights reserved. Printed in the United States of America. No part of this book may be used or reproduced in any manner whatsoever without written permission except in the case of brief quotations embodied in critical articles and reviews. For information address HarperCollins Publishers Inc., 10 East 53rd Street, New York, NY 10022.

HarperCollins books may be purchased for educational, business, or sales promotional use. For information please write: Special Markets Department, HarperCollins Publishers Inc., 10 East 53rd Street, New York, NY 10022.

First Quill edition published 2004.

Design: Nigel Rollings
Index: Maro Riofrancos

The Library of Congress has catalogued the hardcover edition as follows:
Simmons, Marie.
  365 ways to cook pasta.
  Includes index.
  1. Cookery (Pasta). I. Title. II. Title: Three hundred sixty-five ways to cook pasta.
TX809.M17S57   1988   641.8'22
87-46171
ISBN 0-06-018663-1

ISBN 0-06-058992-2 (pbk.)

  05 06 07 08 RRD 10 9 8 7 6 5 4 3 2

Acknowledgments

I would like to thank Merri Beth Helmes of the
National Pasta Association, the Creamette Company of
Minneapolis, Peggy Stewart of Stewart/Chisholm and Lisa Klinck-
Shea of Ketchum Public Relations for their assistance.

On a more personal note, I am forever grateful to
John and Stephanie for their loyalty and patience, sense of culinary
adventure *and* sense of humor, and their apparently insatiable love
of pasta. This book would have been impossible without the two
of you.

Contents

Take advantage of the bounty of fresh vegetables, and transform that simple jar of olives or can of salmon into a great pasta sauce without lifting a skillet.

A simple technique for creating tempting sauces in less than 30 minutes. Plus suggestions for which pasta shape to choose.

Robust sauces, all flavored with rich meat juices, tomatoes, and herbs.

Nutritious fish and pasta combinations; from mussels to tuna; from sophisticated to homey.

America's favorite food is good for you, too. Just lighten the sauces with our surprisingly simple suggestions and you are on your way to keeping fit and eating well.

Names like Three-Cheese-Stuffed Manicotti with Red Pepper Béchamel Sauce and Sausage-Stuffed Shells with Chunky Pepper-Tomato Sauce get the taste buds going even before you hit the kitchen.

Inspired by Pasta alla Mamma, the house special at Hugo's in West Hollywood, pasta and egg combinations are a nutritious solution to the question "What's for dinner?"

A book on pasta is not complete without recipes for some of our favorite oriental noodle dishes. Feel like sinking your chopsticks into a crispy Noodle Pancake with Beef and Vegetable Stir-Fry?

The ultimate comfort food: rich, creamy, and delicious.

Chapter 1

Italian Classics

Although some form of pasta exists in many parts of the world, when Americans think pasta they usually think Italian. While the lively debate on where pasta originated continues to entertain, the fact is that Italy still leads the worldwide per capita consumption with something like fifty-five pounds per person per year. The seemingly endless variety of pasta shapes and sizes, the romance and poetry of the names of these pasta shapes and dishes, and the folkloric, cultural, and historical significance of many of these dishes are just a few reasons why we should begin our pasta eating journey with Italian classics.

1 SPAGHETTI ALLA PUTTANESCA

Prep: 10 minutes   Cook: 20 minutes   Serves: 4–6

Very loosely translated, Spaghetti alla Puttanesca is spaghetti in the style of the prostitute. According to one of many legends, the ladies would attract their clients with the enticing aroma of this flavorful and gutsy dish. Another legend was that its quick preparation made it popular as a fast snack between clients.

3 tablespoons olive oil
2 garlic cloves, minced
1 can (1 pound 12 ounces) Italian-style peeled tomatoes (do not drain)
¼ cup chopped, pitted, salt-cured black olives
2 teaspoons small capers, rinsed
1 teaspoon crushed dried red pepper, or to taste

½ teaspoon dried oregano
Pinch of coarsely ground black pepper
1 can (2 ounces) flat anchovies, drained, blotted dry, cut into small pieces
2 tablespoons chopped Italian flat-leaf parsley
Salt
1 pound spaghetti

1. Heat oil in a large skillet; add garlic; sauté over low heat about 1 minute; do not brown. Stir in tomatoes with their juice, olives, capers, red pepper, oregano, and black pepper; cook over medium heat, stirring to break up tomatoes until the sauce thickens, about 15 minutes. Stir in anchovies and parsley; simmer 2 minutes. Add salt to taste.

2. While sauce is simmering, cook spaghetti in plenty of boiling salted water until al dente, or firm to the bite, about 5 minutes; drain well. Toss with sauce.

2   PESTO ALLA GENOVESE
Prep: 5 minutes   Yield: 1 cup, or enough for 1 pound pasta

Pesto, the classic Ligurian sauce made with basil, was considered an exotic food to American tastes just a few short years ago. It can now be found, either jarred or frozen, in many supermarkets. In Liguria pesto is made with a mortar, but a blender or food processor makes quick work of what would otherwise be a labor of love. The Genoese serve pesto with a flat noodle called trennete, which is a narrow version of fettuccine. This recipe incorporates some of the boiling pasta cooking liquid, a technique that helps to lighten the rich sauce.

2 cups packed fresh basil
    leaves
⅓ cup pignoli (pine nuts)
1 large garlic clove, chopped

¼ teaspoon salt
½ cup olive oil
⅓ cup grated Parmesan cheese

1. Finely chop the basil, pignoli, garlic, and salt in a food processor. With the food processor running, add the oil in a slow steady stream through the feed tube until mixture is thoroughly blended. Transfer to a bowl; fold in the cheese.

2. Remove ½ cup of the cooking liquid before draining the pasta. Toss pasta immediately with the pesto sauce and the reserved cooking liquid. Serve at once with additional cheese, if desired.

3   SPAGHETTI ALLA CARBONARA
Prep: 10 minutes   Cook: 12 minutes   Serves: 4–6

This is a typically Roman dish that uses Pecorino Romano, a goat's milk cheese, and pancetta, a cured but not smoked bacon. A very lightly smoked American-style bacon can be substituted if pancetta is not available.

2 tablespoons olive oil
2 tablespoons butter
4 ounces pancetta, or 6 slices
    bacon, cut into ¼-inch
    dice
1 pound spaghetti

5 eggs, well beaten
½ cup grated Pecorino
    Romano or Parmesan
    cheese
    Freshly ground black
    pepper

1. Heat the oil and butter in a skillet; add the pancetta or bacon; sauté until golden; lift from fat with a slotted spoon and drain on paper towels.

2. Cook the pasta in plenty of boiling salted water until al dente, or firm to the bite, about 10 minutes; drain.

3. Meanwhile beat the eggs, ¼ cup of the cheese, and pepper in a large serving bowl. Add the pasta; toss. Sprinkle the pancetta or bacon on the top along with the remaining ¼ cup cheese.

4   PAGLIA E FIENO

Prep: 10 minutes   Cook: 10 minutes   Serves: 6

Paglia e Fieno translates as "straw and hay," which is depicted in the mixture of green and natural fettuccine. This recipe is popular in Emilia-Romagna, a rich and fertile region often referred to as the "bread basket of Italy."

6 tablespoons butter	½ cup slivered cooked ham
12 ounces mushrooms, trimmed and cut into ¼-inch dice	Salt and coarsely ground black pepper
½ cup tiny fresh or frozen peas, thawed	6 ounces fresh spinach fettuccine
1 cup heavy cream	6 ounces fresh plain fettuccine
	Grated Parmesan cheese

1. Heat 3 tablespoons of the butter in a large skillet; add the mushrooms; sauté over medium heat until tender and edges begin to brown, about 5 minutes. Add the peas; cover and cook over low heat 2 minutes. Add ½ cup of the cream; heat to boiling; simmer, stirring, until slightly thickened. Add ham and season with salt and pepper. Let stand off heat.

2. Meanwhile, cook the fettuccine in plenty of boiling salted water until al dente, or firm to the bite, about 2 minutes; drain.

3. Heat the remaining ½ cup cream and 3 tablespoons butter in the pasta cooking pan to boiling. Add the drained fettuccine; cook, stirring, until cream begins to thicken. Add half of the mushroom mixture and a sprinkling of grated cheese; toss.

4. Spoon into a serving dish; spoon remaining mushroom sauce on top; sprinkle with cheese and serve at once.

Olive oil

Olive oil is produced in the olive-growing regions along the northern edge of the Mediterranean Sea. Olive oil is exported from Italy, Spain, Greece, France.

Extra-virgin olive oil: A pale green/gold color; very flavorful and the most expensive olive oil. Use on salads or as a condiment to fully enjoy the rich fruit flavor. Less than 1 percent acidity.

Virgin olive oil: A flavorful oil; usually less expensive than extra-virgin oil. Acidity can be up to 4 percent.

Pure olive oil: Least expensive oil; very mild in flavor; readily available. Best used in cooking.

5   PASTA CON SARDE
Prep: 10 minutes   Cook: 15 minutes   Serves: 4

Pasta with Sardines is a classic dish of Sicily. Without the Mediterranean Sea to feed us fresh sardines, and the mountains to supply us with wild fennel, we will have to accept the substitutes offered below. In some versions of this dish saffron threads and tomato paste are simmered in the sauce.

6 tablespoons olive oil
½ cup chopped onion
3 flat anchovies, drained, blotted dry, and finely chopped
¼ cup finely chopped feathery leaves from fresh fennel
¼ cup pignoli (pine nuts)

1 tablespoon raisins, soaked in boiling water 10 minutes, drained
1 can (3¾ ounces) sardines packed in oil, drained and patted dry
12 ounces bucatini or perciatelli
Toasted bread crumbs

1. Heat the oil in a large skillet. Add the onion; sauté over low heat, stirring, until golden, about 5 minutes. Add the anchovies; sauté, stirring, over low heat until dissolved. Add the fennel, pignoli, raisins, and sardines; heat through, stirring gently, about 5 minutes.

2. Cook the pasta in plenty of boiling salted water until al dente, or firm to the bite, about 10 minutes; drain. Spoon into a serving bowl; add sauce; sprinkle with bread crumbs; toss lightly and serve.

6   PASTA ALL'AMATRICIANA
Prep: 10 minutes   Cook: 15 minutes   Serves: 4

This pasta dish is said to have originated in the town of Amatrice, just north of Rome. It is, in its simplest form, a thick spaghetti sauced with a tomato and lean bacon mixture. The cheese of the region would be Pecorino or sheep's milk cheese.

6 tablespoons olive oil
½ cup chopped onion
6 strips lightly smoked lean bacon, minced
2 cans (14½ ounces each) whole peeled tomatoes, drained

Pinch of crushed dried red pepper
Salt
12 ounces bucatini or perciatelli
Grated Pecorino Romano cheese

1. Heat oil in a large skillet; add onion; sauté over low heat, stirring, until golden. Add bacon; sauté, stirring, 2 minutes. Squeeze juice and seeds from tomatoes; chop tomatoes and add to skillet; cook, stirring over medium heat, until softened and sauce is thickened slightly, about 15 minutes. Add the red pepper and salt to taste.

2. Cook the pasta in plenty of boiling salted water until al dente, or firm to the bite, about 10 minutes; drain. Toss with the sauce; sprinkle with cheese and serve.

7 PENNE ALL'ARRABBIATA
Prep: 5 minutes   Cook: 20 minutes   Serves: 4

The name of this recipe translates as "enraged penne." The sauce can be very, very hot, depending on the amount of dried hot pepper you decide to use.

¼ cup olive oil
2 teaspoons finely minced garlic
½ to 1½ teaspoons crushed dried red pepper
1 can (28 ounces) peeled Italian plum tomatoes with juices

Salt
8 ounces penne
2 tablespoons chopped parsley

1. Heat oil in a medium skillet over low heat; add the garlic and red pepper. Sauté, stirring, until garlic turns golden; do not brown garlic.

2. Purée the tomatoes through a food mill. Stir into the oil. Simmer, stirring, until sauce is slightly reduced and thickened, about 20 minutes. Season with salt to taste.

3. Cook the penne in plenty of boiling salted water until al dente, or firm to the bite, about 10 minutes; drain. Toss with the sauce and sprinkle with parsley.

8 SPAGHETTI WITH GARLIC AND OIL
Prep: 5 minutes   Cook: 10 minutes   Serves: 4

This wonderfully simple, but deep-down soul-satisfying dish has a charming melodic-sounding name in Italian: "aglio ed olio."

⅓ cup olive oil
1½ tablespoons minced garlic
12 ounces spaghetti
Salt

Coarsely ground black pepper
2 tablespoons finely chopped Italian flat-leaf parsley

1. Heat the oil in a small skillet over low heat; add garlic, stirring often until the garlic turns golden; be careful not to let it burn.

2. Cook the spaghetti in plenty of boiling salted water until al dente, or firm to the bite, about 10 minutes; drain. Toss with the oil and garlic, salt, pepper, parsley.

Variation:

9 SPAGHETTI WITH GARLIC, OIL, AND ANCHOVIES

Finely chop 1 can (2 ounces) drained and blotted anchovies. Stir into the oil with the garlic, over low heat, until dissolved.

10   FETTUCCINE ALFREDO
Prep: 5 minutes   Cook: 2 minutes   Serves: 4

The true Fettuccine Alfredo, as served in Rome, comprises fresh fettuccine, creamy butter, and fragrant and flavorful Parmigiano Reggiano. Often it is embellished with heavy cream, mushrooms, peas, garlic, and other perfectly good additions, but this is not the real Alfredo.

1 **pound fresh fettuccine**
¼ **pound sweet (unsalted)
    butter, softened**
½ **cup freshly grated
    Parmigiano Reggiano
    cheese**
	**Freshly ground black
	pepper**

1. Cook the fettuccine in plenty of boiling salted water until al dente, or firm to the bite, about 2 minutes; drain.

2. Have ready a large warm bowl with the butter in the bottom, cut into small pieces. Add the fettuccine immediately after draining; add the cheese and toss well. Serve at once. Grind a little black pepper on top.

11   SPAGHETTI WITH FRIED EGGPLANT AND TOMATO
Prep: 15 minutes   Drain: 1 hour   Cook: 20 minutes   Serves: 4

Small bright purple eggplants are a precious Sicilian commodity. This stunning dish can be made with or without the tomatoes.

1 **pound small eggplants**
    Salt
    Vegetable oil
1 **pound spaghetti**
¼ **cup extra-virgin olive oil**
2 **tablespoons chopped Italian
    flat-leaf parsley**
	2 **ripe red tomatoes, peeled,
	    seeded, chopped
	    (optional)**
	**Freshly ground black
	pepper**

1. Cut the eggplant into 2- to 3-inch lengths, each about ¼ inch thick. Toss with salt (about 2 teaspoons) and place in a colander set over a saucer to catch the liquid. Weight the eggplant with a saucer and something heavy. Let stand 1 hour. Rinse off salt; drain and pat dry with paper toweling.

2. Heat about 2 inches of vegetable oil in a heavy skillet. Fry the eggplant "fingers" until lightly browned; drain on paper towels. Place on a heatproof platter and keep warm in an oven set at the lowest setting.

3. Cook the spaghetti in plenty of boiling salted water until al dente, or firm to the bite, about 8 minutes; drain.

4. Toss the spaghetti with the olive oil, eggplant, parsley, and tomatoes, if using. Serve at once with a sprinkling of black pepper.

12 ORECCHIETTE WITH BROCCOLI AND ANCHOVY SAUCE

Prep: 10 minutes   Cook: 10 minutes   Serves: 4

Orecchiette is Italian for "little ears." This sauce is often made with a broccoli rabe, a deliciously bitter green, but regular broccoli can be used.

12 ounces orecchiette	1 can (2 ounces) flat anchovy
2 cups broccoli florets, cut	filets, drained and
with 1-inch stems	chopped
⅓ cup olive oil	Freshly ground black
	pepper

1. Cook the orecchiette and broccoli together in plenty of boiling salted water until al dente, or firm to the bite, about 10 minutes; drain.

2. Meanwhile, heat the oil in a small skillet; stir in the anchovies and cook, stirring, over low heat until the anchovies melt. Toss with the pasta and broccoli; sprinkle with black pepper.

Perfectly cooked pasta every time

SAUCEPAN:

Use a 10-quart pot for 1 pound of pasta, or a pot big enough to hold 8 quarts of water with enough space for the pasta to swim around while cooking.

WATER:

Use lots and lots of water: 6 to 8 quarts per pound; but never less than 4 quarts, even for as little as 2 cups of dried pasta.

SALT:

Add salt *after* the water comes to a rolling boil. For optimum flavor, use 1 tablespoon per pound of dried pasta, but reduce this according to your family's dietary restrictions.

STIR:

Add pasta all at once to the rapidly boiling water and stir *hard* from the bottom of the pot with a long-handled spoon to prevent strands from sticking to the bottom of the pot or to each other.

COOK:

Once the water returns to a full boil, start timing. The times in the recipes are usually minimum cooking times. Use your own judgment , experience, and *taste.* Cook, stirring occasionally to keep the pasta moving about in the water. To determine doneness, scoop up a piece with a slotted spoon; blow on it so you won't burn your tongue and bite into the pasta. You will soon learn to identify the term *al dente*, or firm to the bite. Do not cook pasta to mush; it should have a little texture.

DRAIN:

Place a large colander in the sink. Protect your hands with mitts or towels; *slowly* start to pour out the water, especially if you are working with the maximum amounts. There will be lots of steam so keep your head up high. Do not rinse pasta, unless it is to be used in a salad.

Chapter 2

The American Classic

Like apple pie, macaroni and cheese is an American classic. There are probably as many versions of this old favorite as there are mothers in America. How about Queenie Mae Boyd's version, certainly the Rolls Royce of the lot? What follows are just a few of the best from the best. Sorry if we didn't include your Mom's . . . but we just didn't know.

13 MACARONI AND CHEESE WITH CHICKEN AND MUSHROOMS

Prep: 20 minutes   Bake: 45 minutes   Serves: 8

Sauce

4 tablespoons butter	2 egg yolks
4 tablespoons flour	½ teaspoon salt, or to taste
3 cups chicken broth	⅛ teaspoon black pepper
1 cup heavy cream	

Chicken and Mushroom Filling

4 tablespoons butter	¼ cup thinly sliced scallions
2 boneless and skinless chicken breasts (about 12 ounces), cut into ¾-inch pieces	1 garlic clove, minced
	¼ cup chopped parsley
	Salt and pepper
10 ounces mushrooms, coarsely chopped	Pinch of nutmeg

1 pound elbow macaroni	1 cup coarsely shredded Gruyère or Jarlsberg cheese
1 cup grated Parmesan cheese	

1. For the sauce, melt butter in a saucepan; stir in flour until thoroughly blended; cook, stirring, 2 minutes. Gradually add the chicken broth, stirring constantly, until mixture begins to boil and thicken; add the heavy cream. Cook, stirring, over medum heat until sauce is thickened and smooth, about 10 minutes. Beat the yolks in a small bowl. Gradually beat in some of the hot sauce. Return to the saucepan. Season with salt and pepper.

2. For the filling, melt 2 tablespoons of the butter in a large heavy skillet. Add the chicken and sauté until tender, about 7 minutes. Scrape onto a side dish. Add the remaining 2 tablespoons butter to the skillet. Add the mushrooms; sauté, stirring, until tender and lightly browned. Add the scallions and the garlic; sauté 2 minutes. Return the chicken to the skillet; add the parsley; season with salt, pepper, and nutmeg.

3. Cook the macaroni in plenty of boiling salted water until al dente, or firm to the bite, about 8 minutes; drain. Combine the macaroni, sauce, chicken and mushroom mixture, and grated Parmesan cheese. Spoon into a buttered 9 x 13-inch baking dish. Sprinkle top with the Gruyère.

4. Bake in a preheated 350°F oven until top is browned and bubbly, about 45 minutes.

Remember to undercook pasta just slightly when it is to be used in baked macaroni or other dishes requiring further cooking.

14 YOUR BASIC MACARONI AND CHEESE
Prep: 20 minutes   Bake: 45 minutes   Serves: 6–8

Macaroni and cheese freezes very well: divide this recipe between two small baking dishes and freeze one for later use.

4 tablespoons butter
¼ cup all-purpose flour
4 cups milk, preheated
1 teaspoon prepared mustard
1 teaspoon salt, or to taste
    Pinch of ground red pepper

1 pound elbow macaroni
1 pound sharp Cheddar
    cheese, shredded (about 4
    cups)
    Buttered Bread Crumbs,
    optional (recipe follows)

1. Melt butter in a large saucepan; stir in flour until smooth. Cook, stirring, over low heat, about 3 minutes. Gradually whisk in hot milk until smooth. Cook, stirring constantly, until mixture boils; cook, stirring frequently, over low heat, until thick and smooth, about 10 minutes. Season with mustard, salt, and red pepper.

2. Meanwhile, cook the macaroni in plenty of boiling salted water until al dente, or firm to the bite, about 8 minutes; drain.

3. Combine the sauce, 3 cups of the cheese, and macaroni. Transfer to a buttered 9 x 13-inch baking dish. Sprinkle top with remaining 1 cup cheese and then with buttered crumbs, if using. Bake in a preheated 350°F oven until browned on top and bubbly, about 45 minutes.

Variations:

15 CHUNKY MACARONI AND CHEESE

Increase the amount of cheese to 1¼ pounds; shred half the cheese and crumble or cut remaining cheese into small chunks. Reserve 1 cup of the shredded cheese for topping. Fold remaining shredded and chunks of cheese into the macaroni mixture.

16 MACARONI AND CHEESE WITH BROCCOLI AND PARMESAN

Steam 2 cups of fresh broccoli florets until crisp-tender, about 3 minutes. Fold into mixture with the cheese. Sprinkle the top with an additional ½ cup grated Parmesan cheese.

17 MACARONI AND CHEESE WITH HAM

Add 2 cups shredded fully cooked smoked ham to mixture with the cheese.

18 MACARONI AND CHEESE WITH TOMATOES AND GREEN BEANS

Sauté 1 cup half slices of onion in 2 tablespoons butter until golden; add 1 cup 1-inch pieces fresh green beans, ½ cup fresh or frozen tiny peas, thawed, and 1 garlic clove, crushed. Cook, covered, until vegetables are tender, about 3 minutes. Add 1 cup cut-up peeled and drained fresh or canned whole tomatoes. Combine with the cooked macaroni, sauce, and cheese.

19 MACARONI AND CHEESE WITH BACON

Cook ½ pound thick-sliced bacon until crisp. Drain and cut into ½-inch pieces. Add to mixture with the cheese.

20 MACARONI AND CHEESE WITH TUNA

Add 1 can (6½ ounces) well-drained chunk light tuna to the basic recipe or to Macaroni and Cheese with Tomatoes and Green Beans or Macaroni and Cheese with Broccoli and Parmesan. Fold into mixture with the cheese.

BUTTERED BREAD CRUMBS
Prep: 5 minutes   Cook: 5 minutes   Yield: 1 cup

**3 slices firm white or whole
     wheat bread**

3 tablespoons butter

Tear bread into pieces and make into crumbs in food processor or blender. There should be about 1⅓ cups. Heat butter in a medium skillet over medium heat. When foam subsides, stir in the crumbs. Sauté, stirring, until crumbs are golden and butter has been absorbed, about 4 minutes.

GARLIC BREAD CRUMBS

Stir 1 garlic clove, crushed, and 1 tablespoon minced parsley into the sautéed bread crumbs during the last 1 minute of cooking.

21 QUEENIE'S MACARONI AND CHEESE
Prep: 10 minutes   Bake: 45 minutes   Serves: 8

Many thanks to Kit Traub, a fellow gastronome, for introducing me to this wonderful recipe from Queenie Mae Boyd and to Herb Traub for giving us permission to reprint it here.

1 **pound elbow macaroni**	6 **eggs**
1 **pound mild Cheddar**	2 **cans (13 ounces each)**
cheese, grated	**evaporated milk**
¼ **pound margarine, melted**	**Salt and pepper**

1. Cook macaroni in boiling salted water according to package directions. Drain well and dump into a big bowl. Add grated cheese, reserving ½ cup to sprinkle on top. Stir in cheese until melted.

2. Stir in margarine and eggs—no need to beat first, just stir well to distribute evenly. Add milk and salt and pepper to taste. Mixture will be fairly liquid. Pour into a 9 x 13-inch baking dish, sprinkle reserved cheese on top, and bake in a preheated 350°F oven for 45 minutes, or until set.

22 THREE-COLOR TWISTS WITH MOZZARELLA
Prep: 15 minutes   Bake: 45 minutes   Serves: 6

Pretty short twists of pasta, called rotini or rotelle or fusilli, now come in three colors: green for spinach, pinkish red for tomato, and natural. If smoked mozzarella is available, substitute it for half of the regular mozzarella called for in the recipe. It adds a really delicious smoky flavor to the dish.

3 **tablespoons butter**	1 **can (28 ounces) whole**
3 **tablespoons all-purpose**	**peeled plum tomatoes,**
flour	**drained and coarsely cut**
3 **cups milk, preheated**	**up**
Salt and pepper	½ **cup chopped fully cooked**
12 **ounces three-colored**	**smoked ham**
macaroni twists (see	½ **cup chopped fresh basil**
headnote)	**leaves**
1 **pound mozzarella cheese,**	½ **cup grated Parmesan cheese**
shredded (use half	
smoked mozzarella, if	
available)	

1. Melt the butter in a saucepan; stir in the flour until smooth; cook, stirring, about 3 minutes. Gradually whisk in the milk until boiling; cook, stirring, until thick and smooth, about 10 minutes. Add salt and pepper to taste.

2. Cook the macaroni in plenty of boiling salted water until al dente, or firm to the bite, about 10 minutes; drain.

3. Combine the macaroni with the white sauce, half the mozzarella, the tomatoes, ham, and basil. Pour into a buttered 9 x 13-inch baking dish. Sprinkle the top with the remaining mozzarella and the Parmesan.

4. Bake in a preheated 350°F oven until top is browned and bubbly, about 45 minutes.

23 MACARONI WITH THREE CHEESES

Prep: 20 minutes   Bake: 45 minutes   Serves: 6–8

4 tablespoons butter
¼ cup all-purpose flour
4 cups milk, preheated
½ teaspoon salt
¼ teaspoon Tabasco sauce, or
  to taste
  Pinch of nutmeg
1 pound penne, ziti, or other
  long tubular macaroni
  shape

8 ounces whole milk
  mozzarella cheese,
  shredded (about 1½ cups)
1 container (15 ounces) whole
  milk ricotta cheese
½ cup grated Parmesan cheese
2 tablespoons coarsely
  chopped Italian flat-leaf
  parsley

1. Heat butter in a large saucepan until melted; stir in flour until smooth. Cook, stirring, over low heat until flour is cooked, about 3 minutes. Gradually stir in hot milk until smooth. Cook, stirring constantly, until mixture boils and is thickened. Cook, stirring frequently, over low heat 10 minutes. Stir in the salt, red pepper sauce, and nutmeg.

2. Meanwhile, cook the macaroni in plenty of boiling salted water until al dente, or firm to the bite, about 8 minutes; shake in colander to drain. Transfer back to saucepan.

3. Stir 1 cup of the mozzarella, the ricotta, ¼ cup of the Parmesan, and parsley into the cooked macaroni to blend. Add the white sauce. Taste and correct seasonings.

4. Spoon into a buttered 9 x 13-inch baking dish. Sprinkle the top with the remaining ½ cup mozzarella and ¼ cup Parmesan cheese. Bake in a preheated 350°F oven until browned on top and bubbly, about 45 minutes.

Variation:

24 MACARONI WITH THREE CHEESES AND TOMATO

Fold 1 cup cut-up peeled and drained fresh or canned tomatoes into the pasta with the cheese.

25   BAKED PARMESAN MACARONI
Prep: 15 minutes   Bake: 45 minutes   Serves: 6

3 tablespoons butter
3 tablespoons all-purpose
   flour
3 cups milk, preheated
½ teaspoon salt
   Dash of Tabasco sauce

2 cups elbow macaroni
1 cup grated Parmesan cheese
¼ cup grated Romano cheese
8 ounces mozzarella cheese,
   shredded

1. Heat butter in a saucepan until melted; stir in the flour until smooth. Cook, stirring, over low heat until the flour is cooked, about 3 minutes. Gradually stir in the hot milk until smooth. Cook, stirring constantly, until mixture boils and is thickened. Cook, stirring frequently over low heat, 10 minutes. Stir in salt and Tabasco sauce.

2. Meanwhile, cook the macaroni in plenty of boiling salted water until al dente, or firm to the bite, about 8 minutes; drain.

3. Combine the white sauce, cooked elbow macaroni, Parmesan, and Romano until blended. Pour into a buttered 9 x 13-inch baking dish. Sprinkle the top with shredded mozzarella.

4. Bake in a preheated 350°F oven until top is browned and bubbly, about 45 minutes.

Pasta and cheese

Pasta and cheese are the perfect combination. The following cheeses have dramatic meltability when cooked with pasta.

Cheddar: Varying degrees of sharpness, depending on age; available shredded or in block. Popular domestic cheese.

Fontina: Made in the United States and imported from throughout the world. Purists insist on Italian Fontina from the Val d'Aosta. Noted for its distinctive earthy flavor.

Gruyère and **Emmentaler:** Many countries make these cheeses, the most popular being Switzerland. A popular domestically produced cheese, as well. A moderately mild cheese; excellent as a topping.

Jarlsberg: A Norwegian cheese very similar to Swiss Emmentaler.

Mozzarella: A mild-flavored whole milk or low-fat cheese, available in a block or shredded. Fresh mozzarella, in a variety of sizes, is now available packed in water. Some specialty shops have imported fresh mozzarella made from waterbuffalo's milk and smoked mozzarella.

Monterey Jack: Can be mild or sharp, depending on age. A favorite topping on Mexican dishes. A semisoft cheese; also available shredded.

Muenster: A domestic and imported cheese; the imported is usually sharper.

Chapter 3

Savory Summer Salads

Pasta salads are fun to create and convenient to serve. The variations are endless so let your culinary imagination run wild. The hundreds of wonderful sizes and shapes of pasta—from linguine to fusilli, penne to seashells, couscous to tubetti—adapt perfectly to pasta salad creations. Inspired by summer's bounty, the flavors of the sea, or the flavors of Greece, there is most likely something for every taste in this collection.

Pasta salads are at their best when served at room temperature, or very soon after being assembled. Refrigeration seems to render the pasta bland and ruin its consistency. If you need to refrigerate leftover salad, make sure to bring it to room temperature before serving and *always* taste and add more seasonings.

26 PEPPERONI, MOZZARELLA, AND BROCCOLI PASTA SALAD

Prep: 20 minutes   Cook: 15 minutes   Serves: 6–8

1 pound rigatoni, nocciole, wagon wheels, or medium shells
⅔ cup vegetable oil
¼ cup fresh lemon juice
2 tablespoons red wine vinegar
1 teaspoon salt, or to taste
1 teaspoon dried oregano
¼ teaspoon coarsely ground black pepper
3 cups broccoli florets, steamed until crisp-tender (about 3 minutes)
1 whole pepperoni (about 12 ounces), skinned and cut into ¼-inch pieces

6 ounces mozzarella, cut into ¼-inch pieces
1 medium green bell pepper, cut into ¼-inch pieces
½ cup chopped red onion
½ cup chopped carrot (about 1 medium)
⅓ cup small brine-cured black olives or sliced ripe black olives
¼ cup rough chunks (about ¼ inch) Parmesan, Romano, or other hard sharp cheese (optional)

1. Cook pasta in plenty of boiling salted water until al dente, or firm to the bite, about 10 minutes. Drain; rinse with cool water.

2. Whisk the oil, lemon juice, vinegar, salt, oregano, and black pepper together; set aside.

3. In a large bowl, combine the cooked pasta, broccoli, pepperoni, mozzarella, bell pepper, red onion, carrot, olives, and Parmesan, if using. Add dressing; toss to blend. Taste and add more salt, pepper, or lemon juice, if needed. Serve at room temperature.

Some shapes for salads

Elbows: Everyone's favorite short tubular curve.

Seashells: Perfect for summer; available in a range of sizes, the medium size being the most popular for salads. The outside grooves and inner chamber are perfect for trapping dressings and flavorful juices. Imported seashell-shaped pasta will be called *conchiglie* or *maruzze*.

Fusilli: Two pasta shapes are often given this name. One is a long twisted spaghettilike spiral; the other a short curly spiral, which is also called *rotelle*.

Penne: A moderately fat, tubular pasta with a smooth outside, diagonally cut on both ends to resemble a "pen" or "quill." Very popular for its adaptability to a variety of sauces and ingredients. Similar shapes include *mostaccioli* and *ziti*.

27 TORTELLINI WITH ROAST BEEF AND BROCCOLI IN RED WINE VINAIGRETTE

Prep: 20 minutes   Cook: 15 minutes   Serves: 4

9 ounces fresh or frozen cheese tortellini
2 cups (1-inch pieces) broccoli florets and stems
12 ounces (one ½-inch-thick slice) cooked roast beef (from the deli), cut into ¼ x 2-inch strips
½ cup thin slivers red onion
½ cup thin slivers red bell pepper

¼ cup small brine-cured black olives
2 tablespoons coarsely chopped Italian flat-leaf parsley
⅓ cup olive oil
3 tablespoons red wine vinegar
½ teaspoon salt
¼ teaspoon coarsely ground black pepper
1 garlic clove, crushed

1. Cook tortellini in plenty of boiling salted water until tender, about 10 minutes; drain; rinse with cool water.

2. Steam broccoli over simmering water, covered, until crisp-tender, about 3 minutes; cool.

3. Combine the tortellini, broccoli, roast beef, red onion, red bell pepper, olives, and parsley in a large bowl. Whisk the oil, vinegar, salt, pepper, and garlic until blended. Pour over salad. Let stand 30 minutes at room temperature before serving.

28 CONFETTI ORZO SALAD

Prep: 20 minutes   Cook: 10 minutes   Serves: 4

1½ cups orzo or other small solid pasta such as acini di pepe
⅓ cup light olive oil
3 tablespoons fresh lemon juice
½ teaspoon grated lemon zest
½ teaspoon salt
⅛ teaspoon coarsely ground black pepper
1 garlic clove, crushed

1 medium carrot, cut into ⅛-inch dice
1¼ cups finely diced red, green, and/or yellow bell pepper
½ cup peeled, seeded, finely diced cucumber
¼ cup finely chopped scallions
¼ cup finely chopped red onion
¼ cup finely chopped Italian flat-leaf parsley

1. Cook orzo in plenty of boiling, salted water until tender, 10 to 12 minutes. Drain (in wire mesh strainer); rinse under cool water.

2. Whisk oil, lemon juice, lemon zest, salt, pepper, and garlic until blended. Toss diced and chopped vegetables, orzo, and dressing together. Serve warm or at room temperature.

29 LINGUINE WITH JULIENNE VEGETABLES ORIENTAL STYLE

Prep: 20 minutes   Cook: 15 minutes   Serves: 4

1 medium carrot, pared and cut into thin julienne (⅛ x 2 inches)
1 small zucchini, trimmed and cut into thin julienne (⅛ x 2 inches)
1 small summer (yellow) squash, trimmed and cut into thin julienne (⅛ x 2 inches)
12 ounces linguine
⅓ cup peanut or other vegetable oil
3 tablespoons fresh lime juice

1 teaspoon oriental sesame oil
1 teaspoon grated fresh gingerroot
½ teaspoon salt
½ teaspoon oriental chili oil
1 garlic clove, crushed
2 scallions, white and green parts, trimmed and cut into thin julienne (⅛ x 2 inches)
2 tablespoons coarsely chopped fresh coriander (cilantro)

1. Place steaming rack over 1 inch boiling water; place carrots on rack; steam, covered, 3 minutes. Sprinkle zucchini and summer squash over carrots; cover and steam 1 minute. Remove rack from pan; rinse vegetables with cool water. Set aside.

2. Cook linguine in plenty of boiling, salted water until al dente, or firm to the bite, about 10 minutes; drain; rinse with cool water.

3. Whisk the oil, lime juice, sesame oil, ginger, salt, chili oil, and garlic until blended. Toss the dressing, steamed vegetables, linguine, scallion, and coriander together. Serve at room temperature.

Variation:

30 LINGUINE WITH JULIENNE VEGETABLES AND CHICKEN

Poach 8 ounces boneless, skinless chicken cutlets in 1 inch of chicken broth seasoned with a ¼-inch slice gingerroot and 1 thick slice onion in a covered skillet until tender, about 5 minutes. Cool in broth. Tear chicken into long pieces about ½ inch wide. Add chicken pieces to salad along with ingredients in step 3.

31 WHOLE WHEAT SPAGHETTI WITH BROCCOLI IN TAMARI DRESSING

Prep: 20 minutes   Cook: 20 minutes   Serves: 4

Tamari is a soy-based sauce fermented without wheat. It is similar in flavor to soy sauce.

Tamari Almonds
- 1 tablespoon oriental sesame oil, or as needed
- 1 cup whole unblanched almonds
- 1 teaspoon grated or finely shredded fresh gingerroot
- 1 teaspoon tamari

Dressing
- 3 tablespoons peanut oil
- 2 tablespoons tamari
- 1 tablespoon fresh lemon juice
- 1 tablespoon grated or finely shredded fresh gingerroot
- 2 garlic cloves, crushed
- 2 teaspoons oriental sesame oil
- ½ teaspoon salt

Salad
- 12 ounces whole wheat or plain spaghetti or linguine
- 3 cups (¼-inch slices) fresh broccoli florets plus stems
- ½ cup thinly sliced scallions (white and green tops)
- ½ cup thinly sliced pared seedless or Kirby cucumber, cut into ⅛-inch julienne

1. To make tamari almonds, put just enough sesame oil in a small skillet to coat surface. Heat over very low heat; add almonds; stir to coat. Add ginger and tamari. Sauté, stirring constantly, over low heat until almonds begin to brown slightly, about 8 minutes. Sesame oil has a very low smoking point so care must be taken to use a very low flame.

2. For the dressing, whisk the peanut oil, tamari, lemon juice, ginger, garlic, sesame oil, and salt together; set aside.

3. Cook the spaghetti in a large saucepan of boiling salted water until al dente, or firm to the bite, about 10 minutes; drain well. Rinse with cold water.

4. Steam broccoli, covered, in a steaming basket set over an inch of boiling water until crisp-tender, about 3 minutes. Rinse with cool water; set aside.

5. To serve, toss the tamari almonds, dressing, spaghetti, steamed broccoli, scallions, and cucumber together. Add additional salt to taste.

32 SHELLS WITH TOMATOES, ARUGULA, AND PARMESAN CHEESE

Prep: 15 minutes   Cook: 12 minutes   Serves: 6

Arugula, known to gardeners as rocket, is a small-leaf salad green with a peppery bite, not unlike watercress.

1 **pound medium shells**
5 **tablespoons olive oil**
2 **tablespoons red wine vinegar**
1 **tablespoon fresh lemon juice**
½ **teaspoon salt**
¼ **teaspoon coarsely ground black pepper**
2 **cups small cherry tomatoes, rinsed and stemmed**
1 **cup (about ½ bunch) rinsed, trimmed arugula**

1 **medium green bell pepper, quartered, seeded, and cut into ¼-inch-thick crosswise pieces (about 1 cup)**
½ **cup small chunks (¼ to ½ inch) Parmesan cheese**
¼ **cup coarsely chopped fresh basil leaves**
¼ **cup coarsely chopped Italian flat-leaf parsley**
¼ **cup grated Parmesan cheese**

1. Cook pasta in a large saucepan of boiling salted water until al dente, or firm to the bite, about 10 minutes; drain. Rinse with cold water; drain well, shaking colander to extract excess water.

2. Whisk the oil, vinegar, lemon juice, salt, and pepper to blend; set aside.

3. Combine the pasta, cherry tomatoes, arugula, bell pepper, Parmesan cheese chunks, basil, parsley, and grated Parmesan; toss to blend. Add dressing; toss again.

33 WAGON WHEELS WITH BAKED HAM AND CREAMY MUSTARD DRESSING

Prep: 10 minutes   Cook: 15 minutes   Serves: 4

8 **ounces fresh green beans, trimmed and cut into 1-inch lengths**
2 **cups wagon wheel–shaped pasta**
½ **cup mayonnaise**
¼ **cup olive oil**

3 **tablespoons cider vinegar**
2 **teaspoons grainy mustard**
½ **teaspoon salt**
8 **ounces baked sliced ham, cut into ¼ x 1-inch strips**
½ **cup sliced celery**
½ **cup chopped red onion**

1. Steam green beans in steaming rack set over simmering water, covered, until crisp-tender, about 3 minutes.

2. Cook pasta in plenty of boiling salted water until al dente, or firm to the bite, about 12 to 15 minutes. Drain; rinse and drain again.

3. In a large bowl, stir together the mayonnaise, olive oil, vinegar, mustard, and salt until blended. Add the green beans, wagon wheels, ham, celery, and onion; toss to blend. Serve at room temperature.

34   PENNE WITH GREEN BEANS, TUNA, AND NIÇOISE OLIVES

Prep: 15 minutes   Cook: 11 minutes   Serves: 4

12 ounces penne or other short tubular pasta
 8 ounces green beans, trimmed and halved crosswise
 5 tablespoons olive oil
 3 tablespoons fresh lemon juice
 1 teaspoon salt
 1 garlic clove, crushed
 ¼ teaspoon coarsely ground black pepper
 1 cup small cherry tomatoes, rinsed and stemmed
 1 small red onion, halved crosswise and cut into thin crosswise slices (about ½ cup)

 ½ seedless European or seeded cucumber, pared, cut into thin slices
 ¼ cup niçoise or other small brine-cured olives, preferably pitted
 ¼ cup coarsely chopped Italian flat-leaf parsley
 1 can (6½ ounces) chunk light tuna, well drained
 2 eggs, hard-cooked, shelled, quartered, and cut into ½-inch chunks

1. Cook pasta in a large saucepan of boiling salted water 8 minutes. Stir in green beans; cook until pasta is al dente, or firm to the bite, and the beans are crisp-tender, about 3 minutes. Drain; rinse well with cool water; drain.

2. Whisk oil, lemon juice, salt, garlic, and pepper; set aside. Combine the pasta and green beans with the cherry tomatoes, red onion, cucumber, olives, and parsley. Add dressing and toss well to blend. Add the tuna and egg; toss very gently. Serve at room temperature.

35   CHICKEN AND PASTA SALAD WITH WALNUT PESTO

Prep: 15 minutes   Cook: 15 minutes   Serves: 8

 1 pound penne or other tubular pasta
 1 cup Walnut Pesto Sauce (page 133)
 3 cups torn pieces cooked chicken

 1 container cherry tomatoes, rinsed and stemmed
 ½ cup pitted brine-cured black olives
 1 cup broken walnuts

1. Cook the pasta in plenty of boiling salted water until al dente, or firm to the bite, about 12 minutes; drain. Rinse with cool water; drain again.

2. Toss the pasta with the Walnut Pesto Sauce, chicken, tomatoes, and olives. Add the broken walnuts just before serving. Serve at room temperature.

36 TUBETTI WITH SUN-DRIED TOMATOES AND SMOKED MOZZARELLA

Prep: 15 minutes   Cook: 10 minutes   Serves: 4

Regular mozzarella is a perfectly acceptable substitution if smoked mozzarella is not available. This is more a delicate side-dish salad than a hearty main dish.

2 cups tubetti or other small tubular pasta	Pinch of dried oregano
1 cup chopped (¼-inch pieces) fresh ripe tomatoes	8 ounces smoked mozzarella, cut into ¼-inch dice (about 1 cup)
¼ cup olive oil	6 sun-dried tomato halves packed in oil, drained, blotted dry, and minced (about ¼ cup)
1 tablespoon red wine vinegar	
¼ teaspoon salt	
¼ teaspoon coarsely ground black pepper	
1 garlic clove, crushed	2 tablespoons chopped fresh basil leaves

1. Cook the pasta in plenty of boiling salted water until al dente, or firm to the bite, about 8 minutes; drain and rinse.

2. In a large bowl, combine the fresh tomatoes, oil, vinegar, salt, pepper, garlic, and oregano. Add the tubetti, mozzarella, sun-dried tomatoes, and basil leaves; toss to blend.

37 SUMMER COUSCOUS

Prep: 10 minutes   Cook: 20 minutes   Serves: 4

Couscous is a tiny pasta shape made from wheat and semolina. It is popular in the cooking of North Africa. This simple but pretty salad is a lovely accompaniment to simple summer fare.

1 cup couscous	6 tablespoons olive oil
1½ cups boiling water	2 tablespoons fresh lemon juice
¼ cup finely chopped carrot	
¼ cup finely chopped celery	1 small garlic clove, crushed
¼ cup finely chopped green pepper	½ teaspoon salt, or to taste
	Generous grinding of black pepper
2 tablespoons finely chopped scallions	
2 tablespoons finely chopped parsley	

1. Place the couscous in a medium bowl; add the boiling water; cover and let stand until all the water is absorbed and mixture has cooled slightly, about 20 minutes.

2. Add the finely chopped vegetables. In a small bowl, whisk the oil, lemon juice, garlic, salt, and pepper. Add to the salad; toss to blend.

38 PASTA SALAD WITH GRILLED MARINATED FLANK STEAK, RED AND GREEN PEPPERS, AND CHILI AND LIME DRESSING

Prep: 15 minutes   Marinate: 1 hour   Cook: 15 minutes   Serves: 6

This salad is best with a broad pasta like narrow lasagne noodles, fettuccine, or perhaps a large tubular pasta like rigatoni.

4 tablespoons lime juice
2 teaspoons minced jalapeño pepper
2 teaspoons minced garlic
½ teaspoon salt
¼ teaspoon crushed dried red pepper
1 pound flank steak
1 pound broad pasta or large tubular shape
⅓ cup olive oil

1 red bell pepper, seeded, trimmed, and cut into ¼-inch-thick strips
1 green bell pepper, seeded, trimmed, and cut into ¼-inch-thick strips
1 medium red onion, halved lengthwise, cut into thin lengthwise slices
¼ cup chopped Italian flat-leaf parsley

1. Combine 2 tablespoons of the lime juice and 1½ teaspoons *each* of the jalapeño pepper and garlic; add the salt and crushed red pepper. Rub over the surface of the flank steak, protecting your hand with a rubber glove or a small plastic bag. Marinate, covered and refrigerated, at least 1 hour.

2. Grill or broil flank steak until rare to medium rare, about 5 minutes per side, depending on heat of grill and thickness of meat. Cut into thin diagonal slices; cool slightly.

3. Cook the pasta in plenty of boiling salted water until al dente, or firm to the bite, about 15 minutes. Drain and rinse; drain again.

4. Whisk the olive oil, remaining 2 tablespoons lime juice, and remaining ½ teaspoon jalapeño and garlic.

5. In a large bowl, combine the sliced flank steak, cooked pasta, dressing, red and green bell peppers, onion, and parsley; toss to blend.

What are sun-dried tomatoes?

In the south of Italy where the tomatoes are plentiful and the sun is hot, tomatoes are sprinkled with salt (sometimes) and dried in the sun (as grapes are dried into raisins). They are then preserved in olive oil. Available in small to medium jars in many specialty food stores, imported sun-dried tomatoes, although expensive, are worth it. Remember, because they are dried a little will go a long way. When using for the first time, taste to determine the saltiness; adjust the salt in the recipe accordingly. Mince and add to pasta salads, tomato sauce, and hot pasta dishes; or serve whole as an antipasto with slices of fresh mozzarella and fresh basil leaves.

39   LINGUINE WITH PLUM TOMATOES, CHICKEN, AND TRIPLE CRÈME DRESSING

Prep: 10 minutes   Cook: 10 minutes   Serves: 2–4

This is one of those salads inspired by small amounts of leftovers. In this case it was a half-eaten deli roasted chicken, a few plum tomatoes, and a small piece of St. André triple crème cheese. The variations are endless and a few samples are offered below.

8 ounces linguine
6 tablespoons olive oil
1 ounce St. André or other rich, creamy semisoft cheese such as Explorateur, rind trimmed, cut into small chunks (about ¼ cup)
1 tablespoon red wine vinegar
1 small garlic clove
6 firm ripe plum tomatoes (about 8 ounces), cut into ¼-inch lengthwise slices, each slice cut into a ¼-inch-wide spear

1 cup torn pieces roasted chicken
2 scallions, trimmed, cut into 1-inch lengths, each piece cut lengthwise into ⅛-inch strips
½ medium green bell pepper, seeded, ribs trimmed, and cut into ⅛-inch-wide strips
4 large basil leaves, cut into ⅛-inch lengthwise strips, or
2 tablespoons chopped Italian flat-leaf parsley

1. Cook the linguine in plenty of boiling salted water until al dente, or firm to the bite, about 10 minutes; drain.

2. In a food processor, purée the olive oil, half the cheese, vinegar, and garlic.

3. Combine the linguine, dressing, tomato spears, chicken, scallions, green pepper strips, and basil or parsley; toss and serve at room temperature.

Variations:

40   LINGUINE WITH PLUM TOMATOES, SHRIMP, AND TRIPLE CRÈME DRESSING

Substitute 1 cup cooked small shrimp for the chicken.

41   LINGUINE WITH PLUM TOMATOES, ROAST BEEF, AND BLUE CHEESE DRESSING

Substitute 1 cup (about 6 ounces) thin strips of cooked deli roast beef for the chicken, and 1 ounce blue-veined cheese at room temperature (Bleu de Bresse, Gorgonzola, or Stilton) for the St. André.

42 PASTA SALAD WITH GRILLED MARINATED CHICKEN AND SUGAR SNAP PEAS

Prep: 15 minutes   Marinate: 1 hour   Cook: 15 minutes   Serves: 6

This salad is good with a wide flat pasta like fettuccine, linguine or narrow lasagne noodles. A ridged, wide tubular pasta like rigatoni also works with these ingredients.

12 ounces chicken cutlets, cut into 1-inch strips
3 tablespoons fresh lime juice
⅓ cup plus 1 tablespoon peanut oil
2 tablespoons soy sauce
2 garlic cloves, crushed
1 teaspoon minced or grated fresh gingerroot
¼ teaspoon crushed dried red pepper
6 ounces sugar snap or snow peas, trimmed

12 ounces fettuccine or linguine
1 teaspoon oriental sesame oil
½ teaspoon salt, or to taste
¼ cup thinly sliced scallions, green and white parts
1 teaspoon sesame seeds, toasted 10 seconds in a hot skillet
1 tablespoon fresh coriander (cilantro) leaves (optional)

1. Combine the chicken, 1 tablespoon *each* of the lime juice and peanut oil, the soy sauce, garlic, gingerroot and hot red pepper. Marinate, covered and refrigerated, at least 1 hour, stirring occasionally.

2. Meanwhile, steam sugar snaps in a vegetable steamer set over simmering water, covered, until crisp-tender, about 3 minutes; rinse with cool water; reserve.

3. Cook the pasta in plenty of boiling salted water until al dente, or firm to the bite, about 10 minutes; drain; rinse with cool water; drain again.

4. Whisk the remaining ⅓ cup oil and 2 tablespoons lime juice, sesame oil, and salt together.

5. Grill the chicken cutlets over a hot fire until browned and tender, about 3 minutes per side, or cook 3 minutes per side in a skillet over medium-high heat; cool slightly.

6. Combine the sugar snaps, linguine, chicken strips, dressing, scallions, sesame seeds, and coriander, if using. Serve at room temperature.

43   FUSILLI PRIMAVERA

Prep: 15 minutes   Cook: 15 minutes   Serves: 6–8

Fusilli, a long, corkscrew-shaped pasta is perfect for "catching" sauces. For this dish you can also use rotelle or rotini, a shorter, curlier version of fusilli.

2 cups (½-inch pieces) broccoli florets including stems
1 cup thinly sliced carrots
1 cup (½-inch diagonal pieces) asparagus spears
1 cup (½-inch diagonal pieces) green beans
½ cup fresh or frozen green peas
1 cup (¼-inch slices) zucchini (quarter the slices, if large)
1 cup mayonnaise
¼ cup milk, or as needed
3 tablespoons red wine vinegar

2 tablespoons grated Parmesan cheese
1 garlic clove, crushed
1 pound fusilli
1 cup small cherry tomatoes, rinsed and stemmed
½ cup thinly sliced scallions, white and green parts
¼ cup coarsely chopped Italian flat-leaf parsley
¼ cup pignoli (pine nuts), stirred 1 minute in a hot skillet until toasted

1. Place the broccoli, carrots, asparagus, green beans, peas, and zucchini in the order given in a steaming basket set over simmering water in a wide saucepan. Cover and steam vegetables until crisp-tender, 3 to 5 minutes. Lift rack from water; rinse with cool water; set aside.

2. In a large bowl, whisk the mayonnaise, milk, vinegar, Parmesan cheese, and garlic together.

3. Cook the pasta in plenty of boiling salted water until al dente, or firm to the bite, about 10 minutes; drain. Rinse with cool water; shake colander to drain all excess moisture.

4. Add the pasta to the large bowl with the dressing. Add the steamed vegetables, cherry tomatoes, scallion, and parsley; toss well. Sprinkle with the toasted pignoli. Serve at room temperature. If salad stands, add additional milk to keep the dressing creamy.

A trio of shapes

Wondering what to do with that half box of shells, handful of rotelle, and cupful of penne? Mix them all together! In fact, manufacturers are now creating their own mixtures and selling them under clever trademarks for those not lucky enough to have a little of this and a little of that on hand to mix for themselves. Just make sure the depth and size of the shapes are similar enough for the pasta to cook in exactly the same length of time.

44   PASTA SALAD WITH TOMATOES, SARDINES, AND MUSTARD VINAIGRETTE

Prep: 10 minutes   Cook: 10 minutes   Serves: 4

To sardine aficionados this nutritious food needs no introduction. Recent statistics on the importance of Omega-3 fatty acids in the diet have made this Omega-3 rich little fish even more appealing.

½ cup olive oil
2 tablespoons fresh lemon
   juice
1 tablespoon whole-grain
   mustard
½ teaspoon salt
⅛ teaspoon coarsely ground
   black pepper
1 garlic clove, crushed
2 cups small pasta such as
   tubetti, elbows, or small
   shells

2 cups cubed (½ inch) fresh
   ripe tomatoes (use
   1 yellow tomato, if
   available)
½ cup finely diced red onion
½ cup finely diced green bell
   pepper
¼ cup finely chopped parsley
1 can (3.75 ounces) whole
   imported sardines packed
   in water or oil, well
   drained

1. Whisk together the oil, lemon juice, mustard, salt, pepper, and garlic.

2. Cook pasta in plenty of boiling salted water until al dente, or firm to the bite, about 8 minutes; drain. Toss the pasta with the dressing, tomatoes, red onion, green bell pepper, and parsley. Add sardines; toss once. Serve at room temperature.

45   PENNE WITH PLUM TOMATOES AND CUCUMBERS IN BASIL VINAIGRETTE

Prep: 10 minutes   Cook: 10 minutes   Serves: 6

2 pounds plum tomatoes, cut
   into ½-inch cubes (about
   3 cups)
½ cup olive oil
¼ cup chopped fresh basil
2 tablespoons white wine
   vinegar
½ teaspoon salt
1 pound penne or other long
   tubular pasta

1 small cucumber, pared,
   halved lengthwise, seeds
   removed, and sliced thin
   into half-moons
½ cup chopped red onion
½ cup chopped roasted red
   bell peppers

1. Combine the tomatoes, oil, basil, vinegar, and salt in a large bowl.

2. Cook the pasta in plenty of boiling salted water until al dente, or firm to the bite, about 10 minutes; drain.

3. Combine the pasta, tomato mixture, cucumber, red onion, and red pepper; toss to blend. Serve at room temperature.

46   FUSILLI WITH SHRIMP AND SNOW PEAS IN LIME VINAIGRETTE

Prep: 15 minutes   Marinate: 1 hour   Cook: 20 minutes
Serves: 4

12   ounces medium shrimp, shelled and deveined
⅓   cup plus 1 tablespoon olive oil
3   tablespoons fresh lime juice
1   tablespoon finely chopped fresh coriander (cilantro)
1   garlic clove, crushed
¼   teaspoon crushed dried red pepper

8   ounces fresh snow peas, trimmed
8   ounces fusilli
2   tablespoons fresh coriander (cilantro) leaves
1   teaspoon oriental sesame oil
½   teaspoon salt
¼   cup diagonally sliced scallions (white and green parts)

1. Combine shrimp, 1 tablespoon of the oil, 1 tablespoon of the lime juice, the chopped coriander, garlic, and red pepper; cover and marinate, refrigerated, at least 1 hour.

2. Heat a medium skillet over high heat until a drop of water sputters and evaporates on contact; add the shrimp and marinade; sauté, stirring, until pink and tender, 2 to 3 minutes. Remove from heat.

3. Steam snow peas on a steaming rack set over simmering water, covered, until crisp-tender, about 3 minutes. Lift rack from water; rinse with cool water; let stand.

4. Cook the fusilli in plenty of boiling salted water until al dente, or firm to the bite, 10 minutes; drain. Rinse with cool water; shake colander well to drain thoroughly.

5. In a bowl, whisk the remaining ⅓ cup olive oil and 2 tablespoons lime juice, coriander leaves, sesame oil, and salt. Add the cooked shrimp, snow peas, fusilli, and scallions; toss well. Serve at room temperature.

47   WAGON WHEELS WITH CHICK-PEAS AND CREAMY LEMON-DILL DRESSING

Prep: 10 minutes   Cook: 15 minutes   Serves: 6

12   ounces wagon wheels
1   can (19 ounces) chick-peas, rinsed and drained
½   cup chopped celery
½   cup chopped red onion
½   cup chopped green bell pepper
¾   cup mayonnaise

¾   cup plain low-fat yogurt
¼   cup chopped fresh dill
Juice and grated zest of 1 lemon
1   garlic clove, crushed
½   teaspoon salt
⅛   teaspoon coarsely ground black pepper

1. Cook the wagon wheels in plenty of boiling salted water until al dente, or firm to the bite, about 12 minutes; drain; rinse with cool water; drain again.

2. Combine the pasta, chick-peas, celery, onion, and green pepper in a large bowl. Separately whisk the mayonnaise, yogurt, dill, lemon juice and zest, garlic, salt, and pepper until blended.

3. Fold the dressing into the pasta mixture and serve at once.

---

48 CHICKEN AND PASTA SALAD WITH BASIL MAYONNAISE AND PIGNOLI

Prep: 20 minutes   Cook: 15 minutes   Serves: 8

This salad, large enough to feed a crowd, is flavored with fresh chopped basil, but fresh dill, chives, oregano, or a combination can be used. Start with just 2 tablespoons of the herb and keep adding more to taste as the potency of the herbs will vary considerably.

1 **pound medium shells, radiatore, or mostaccioli**
2 **cups mayonnaise, or 1 cup mayonnaise and 1 cup plain low-fat yogurt**
3 **tablespoons red wine vinegar**
½ **cup chopped fresh basil, or more to taste**
2 **anchovies, drained and chopped**
1 **garlic clove, chopped**
Salt

Freshly ground black pepper
3 **cups cooked cubed chicken**
1 **cup sliced celery**
1 **cup diced red and/or green bell pepper**
1 **cup thinly sliced carrot**
1 **cup small cherry tomatoes, rinsed and stemmed**
⅓ **cup sliced trimmed scallions**
¼ **cup chopped Italian flat-leaf parsley**
½ **cup toasted pignoli (pine nuts)**

1. Cook the pasta in plenty of boiling salted water until al dente, or firm to the bite, about 15 minutes; drain. Rinse with cool water; drain again.

2. In a food processor, purée the mayonnaise (and yogurt, if using), vinegar, basil, anchovies, garlic, and salt and pepper to taste until blended. In a large bowl, combine the mayonnaise with the pasta, chicken, celery, pepper, carrot, cherry tomatoes, scallions, and parsley; toss to blend. Add the nuts just before serving.

49   ELBOW MACARONI WITH SWEET PICKLE MAYONNAISE

Prep: 15 minutes   Cook: 12 minutes   Serves: 4

Another version of the All-American picnic salad.

1 cup mayonnaise
¼ cup drained sweet pickle
   relish
1 tablespoon cider vinegar
1 teaspoon prepared mustard
2 cups elbow macaroni

½ cup diced pared carrot
½ cup diced celery
½ cup chopped red onion
   Salt
1 scallion, trimmed, cut into
   thin diagonal slices

1. In a large bowl, combine the mayonnaise, sweet pickle relish, cider vinegar, and mustard.

2. Cook macaroni in plenty of boiling salted water until tender, 8 to 10 minutes, drain.

3. Combine the macaroni, carrot, celery, and red onion with the mayonnaise mixture in the large bowl. Add salt to taste. Sprinkle with scallions. Serve at room temperature or slightly chilled.

Variation:

50   ELBOW MACARONI WITH SWEET PICKLE AND YOGURT DRESSING

Substitute 1 cup plain low-fat yogurt for the mayonnaise.

51   GREEK-STYLE PASTA SALAD

Prep: 10 minutes   Cook: 10 minutes   Serves: 4

⅓ cup olive oil
1 garlic clove, crushed
1 pita bread
2 cups medium shells
½ pint cherry tomatoes,
   stemmed and halved
1 medium green bell pepper,
   stem and seeds removed,
   cut into ½-inch pieces
1 medium cucumber, pared,
   quartered lengthwise,
   and cut into ½-inch cubes
1 small red onion, cut into
   ½-inch cubes

½ cup sliced celery
3 ounces feta cheese, cut into
   ½-inch cubes
¼ cup pitted, split brine-cured
   black olives
1 tablespoon chopped Italian
   flat-leaf parsley
1 tablespoon chopped fresh
   mint
½ teaspoon dried oregano
   Coarsely ground black
   pepper

1. Combine oil and garlic in a large bowl. Cut around edges of pita and separate into 2 circles; brush lightly with some of the oil; tear into pieces. Toast bread in a nonstick skillet over medium heat, turning to brown evenly.

2. Cook the pasta in plenty of boiled salted water until al dente, or firm to the bite, about 10 minutes; drain.

3. Combine the toasted pita croutons, pasta, tomatoes, bell pepper, cucumber, red onion, celery, feta cheese, black olives, parsley, mint, and oregano with the oil in the large bowl; toss to blend. Add pepper to taste. Serve at room temperature.

52 PENNE WITH TONNATO SAUCE
Prep: 15 minutes   Cook: 10 minutes   Serves: 4

Tonnato is the Italian word for tuna and this sauce is inspired by the classic Italian dish, vitello tonnato, which is thinly sliced veal served cold with a delicately flavored tuna sauce and garnished with capers.

1 can (6½ ounces) imported tuna packed in olive oil, drained	½ cup thinly sliced celery
	¼ cup chopped Italian flat-leaf parsley
½ cup mayonnaise	1 tablespoon capers, rinsed and drained
2 anchovy fillets, drained, blotted, and chopped	1 cup small cherry tomatoes, rinsed and stemmed
1 tablespoon lemon juice	
8 ounces penne or other tubular pasta	¼ cup small brine-cured black olives
½ cup diced (¼ inch) red onion	

1. Purée the tuna, mayonnaise, anchovies, and lemon juice in the bowl of a food processor.

2. Cook the pasta in plenty of boiling salted water until al dente, or firm to the bite, about 10 minutes; drain.

3. Toss the tuna sauce, pasta, onion, celery, parsley, and capers together; spoon into a large serving bowl. Sprinkle the top with tomatoes and black olives.

Variation:

53 PENNE WITH GREEN BEANS AND TONNATO SAUCE

Add 8 ounces trimmed and cooked fresh green beans, cut into 1-inch lengths, to the salad. Garnish salad with tomato wedges.

54   SHELLS WITH ARTICHOKE HEARTS AND SHRIMP IN LEMON-OREGANO VINAIGRETTE

Prep: 30 minutes   Marinate: 30 minutes   Cook: 15 minutes
Serves: 6–8

The artichokes can be marinated at room temperature for as little as half an hour or overnight, if time allows. This is a rather elegant dish and is especially nice as part of a buffet supper.

2 packages (10 ounces each) frozen artichoke hearts, cooked according to package directions
¾ cup olive oil
¼ cup fresh lemon juice
2 tablespoons red wine vinegar
1 teaspoon salt
1 teaspoon grated lemon zest
½ teaspoon dried oregano
2 garlic cloves, crushed
¼ teaspoon coarsely ground black pepper

1 pound medium shells
1 pound medium shrimp, shelled, deveined, and cooked in boiling salted water until tender, cooled
1 cup chopped red onion
¼ cup chopped Italian flat-leaf parsley
1 pint cherry tomatoes, rinsed and stemmed
1 cup pitted California black olives

1. Combine the cooked and drained artichoke hearts, the olive oil, lemon juice, vinegar, salt, lemon zest, oregano, garlic, and pepper in a saucepan. Heat to simmering, covered; let stand off heat 30 minutes, or refrigerate overnight.

2. About 1 hour before serving, cook the shells in plenty of boiling water until al dente, or firm to the bite; drain; rinse in cool water; drain again.

3. Toss the cooked pasta with the artichokes and marinade, the shrimp, red onion, parsley, tomatoes, and olives. Serve at once.

55   CHICK-PEAS, TUBETTI, AND TOMATO SALAD

Prep: 10 minutes   Marinate: 1 hour   Cook: 10 minutes   Serves: 6

Chick-peas and pasta are a popular and nutritious combination. The incomplete proteins in both foods combine to create a nutritious main dish that, when served with a green vegetable, present a balanced meal.

1   can (19 ounces) chick-peas, rinsed and drained
⅓   cup olive oil
2   tablespoons lemon juice
2   tablespoons chopped parsley
½   teaspoon dried oregano
½   teaspoon salt
¼   teaspoon coarsely ground black pepper
2   cups tubetti
2   cups cubed (about ½ inch) fresh tomatoes
1   cup diced (about ¼ inch) celery
½   cup diced red onion

1. Combine the chick-peas, olive oil, lemon juice, parsley, oregano, salt, and pepper in a large bowl; cover and let stand at room temperature 1 hour.

2. Cook the pasta in plenty of boiling salted water until al dente, or firm to the bite, 8 to 10 minutes; drain.

3. Add the pasta, tomatoes, celery, and red onion to the marinated chick-peas; toss to blend. Serve at room temperature.

Chapter 4

Hearty Soups and Stews

Once again the versatility of pasta comes to the rescue. The endless variety of tiny pasta shapes available in the market are a perfect addition to just about any soup you can conjure up. From Fresh Clam Chowder or Fish Soup, both with tiny seashell-shaped pasta, to the simplest Chicken and Stars (or alphabet macaroni), there is a soup to fill the bowl (and busy schedule) of just about everyone. As a side dish with stews, pasta is a natural, especially when the pasta is lapped with an herb butter to complement the flavors in the stew as we have done in Lamb Stew with Herbed Elbows and Veal Stew with Farfalle in Rosemary Butter.

See page 121 for descriptions of some of our favorite tiny pasta shapes.

56   CLASSIC CHICKEN NOODLE SOUP

Prep: 20 minutes   Cook: 2–2½ hours   Serves: 8–10

In this world of fast food service and super-duper markets, if you can find a butcher shop or farm that sells freshly slaughtered chickens with good fresh innards plus the chicken feet all ready for the soup pot, then you are in for a real old-fashioned treat. If you cannot, then just use whatever fresh whole chicken is available. You'll still be in for a pretty delicious pot of soup. By cooking the noodles separately and then adding them to each bowl of soup, the noodles won't swell and absorb too much of the broth. It is also easier to satisfy those who want more noodles and less broth or vice versa.

1　whole chicken, about 3
　　pounds, preferably with
　　neck, heart, and feet
　　included with carcass
12　cups water
1　whole onion, unpeeled and
　　halved
1　whole large carrot, pared
1　parsley sprig
1　bay leaf

1　garlic clove
　　Salt
8　ounces thin egg noodles
　　(look for a short cut very
　　thin noodle called
　　fedelini, "little faithful
　　one")
　　Freshly ground black
　　pepper

1. Rinse the chicken very well, carefully examining the carcass for any clumps of blood. Soak in a large bowl of salted cold water for 20 minutes; drain well.

2. Place the chicken, neck, heart, and feet, if available, in a large saucepan. Add the water, onion, carrot, parsley, bay leaf, and garlic. Heat, over medium heat, uncovered, until water is barely simmering. (For a nice clear broth, the water should not be allowed to boil.) Cook chicken over low heat for 2 hours. Let cool slightly.

3. Line a sieve with a layer of dampened paper towel or a triple thickness of dampened cheesecloth. Set over a large bowl and carefully ladle the broth through the sieve. Discard all the vegetables except the carrot. Let the chicken cool until it can be handled without burning your fingers. Carefully pull the meat from the bones, discarding the skin, bones, and cartilage. Cut the carrot into slices and set aside with the chicken. (At this point the broth can be chilled and the fat lifted from the surface and discarded. The chicken meat and carrot can be covered and refrigerated until ready to use.)

4. Return the broth to the saucepan. Add the chicken meat and the carrot slices. Season to taste with salt. Meanwhile cook the pasta in a saucepan of boiling salted water until al dente, about 5 minutes; drain. Return to the saucepan and add a ladle of the hot broth to keep the pasta warm.

5. To serve, add a generous amount of the pasta to each soup bowl. Add a ladleful of broth, some chicken, and carrot slices. Serve piping hot with freshly ground pepper to taste.

57 PASTA E FAGIOLI
Prep: 15 minutes   Cook: 30 minutes   Serves: 6–8

Pasta and beans is a classic dish with various interpretations. It will continue to thicken upon standing; add additional liquid and seasonings to taste if this happens.

2   **cups medium shells, wagon wheels, or elbow macaroni**
¼   **cup olive oil**
1   **cup chopped red onion**
1   **cup sliced (¼ inch) carrots**
½   **cup sliced celery**
2   **garlic cloves, minced**
8   **ounces fresh green beans, trimmed and cut into ½-inch lengths**

1   **cup frozen Fordhook lima beans**
1   **can (19 ounces) white kidney or cannellini beans, rinsed and drained**
2   **tablespoons chopped Italian flat-leaf parsley**
    Salt
    Generous grinding of black pepper
    Parmesan cheese

1. Cook the pasta in plenty of boiling salted water for 5 minutes (undercooked). Place a colander over a heatproof bowl and drain. Reserve 3 cups of the pasta cooking liquid. Set pasta aside until ready to use.

2. Heat the oil in a large wide saucepan; add the onion, carrots, and celery; sauté until tender, but not browned, about 5 minutes. Stir in garlic; sauté 2 minutes. Add the 3 cups pasta cooking water, green beans and lima beans. Cook, covered, over medium heat, until the vegetables are very tender, about 15 minutes.

3. Stir in the reserved pasta, kidney beans, and parsley. Cover and cook over low heat until pasta is tender and has absorbed enough liquid so that the soup is very thick. Season to taste with salt and pepper. Sprinkle each serving generously with Parmesan cheese.

58 CHICKEN AND STARS
Prep: 5 minutes   Cook: 10–15 minutes   Serves: 2

This is a ridiculously simple soup to prepare. The variations are endless, but just a few are suggested below. To charm young and old, substitute alphabet-shaped macaroni for the stars.

1   **can (10½ ounces) seasoned chicken broth**
1   **cup water**
1   **small carrot, pared and cut into thin coins**

2   **tablespoons stellini (tiny star-shaped pasta)**
    Grated Parmesan cheese

1. Heat the broth, water, and carrot slices to boiling. Simmer, covered, over low heat until carrots are tender, about 5 minutes.

2. Stir in the pasta. Simmer, uncovered, until pasta is tender, 5 to 8 minutes depending on thickness of pasta used. Ladle into bowls and sprinkle generously with cheese.

Variations:

59 CHICKEN SOUP WITH ORIENTAL FLAVORS

Substitute 2 tablespoons orzo for the stellini. After the pasta has cooked, stir in 1 tablespoon thin diagonal slices of scallions, ¼ cup fresh spinach cut into thin chiffonade (⅛-inch strips), 1 teaspoon soy sauce, and ½ teaspoon oriental sesame oil. Omit the Parmesan cheese.

60 CHICKEN SOUP STRACCIATELLE

Coarsely shred the carrot instead of slicing it. Combine the broth, ½ cup water, and the carrot. Cook carrot until tender; add the small pasta (orzo or other small shape); cook until tender. Meanwhile vigorously beat 1 egg with the remaining ½ cup water and 2 tablespoons of grated Parmesan cheese. Heat the soup to a near boil; stir in the egg mixture all at once, stirring vigorously until the soup begins to boil and the egg breaks up into little threads. Serve at once with more cheese, if desired.

61 CREAM OF TOMATO SOUP WITH ACINI DI PEPE
Prep: 10 minutes   Cook: 20 minutes   Serves: 6

This is a perfect soup to chase away those midwinter blahs. It is very quick and easy to put together.

2 tablespoons butter
½ cup diced onion
½ cup diced carrot
1 can (2 pounds 3 ounces) peeled Italian-style tomatoes with their liquid
2 cups seasoned chicken broth
1 cup heavy cream
1 cup cooked acini di pepe or any solid tiny pasta shape (about ⅓ cup raw)
Salt
Freshly ground black pepper

1. Heat butter in a large saucepan. Add the onion and carrot; sauté until tender, about 5 minutes. Set a food mill over the saucepan and purée the tomatoes. Add the chicken broth. Heat to simmering.

2. Heat the cream in a small saucepan until simmering; gradually whisk into the tomatoes; do not boil. Add the acini di pepe and heat through. Add salt to taste.

3. Sprinkle each serving with plenty of black pepper.

62 BEEF AND MUSHROOM SOUP WITH ORZO

Prep: 20 minutes   Cook: 2 hours   Serves: 6–8

This soup can easily be prepared in two installments. Make the broth one day; chill overnight and lift off any fat. The next day, sauté the vegetables and add to the stock along with the orzo.

2 tablespoons olive oil	1 pound mushrooms,
1½ pounds boneless beef chuck	trimmed and coarsely
1 onion, unpeeled, halved	chopped
1 bay leaf	Salt
8 cups water	Freshly ground pepper
1 cup chopped onion	¼ cup chopped parsley
½ cup chopped celery	1 package (10 ounces) frozen
½ cup chopped carrot	mixed vegetables, thawed
1 garlic clove, crushed	¼ cup orzo

1. Heat 1 tablespoon of the oil in a large heavy saucepan. Brown the beef on both sides; add the onion; brown lightly on cut side. Add the bay leaf and water. Heat over medium heat until almost boiling. For a clearer broth, do not let boil. Cook, uncovered, adjusting heat to maintain a gentle simmer, for 2 hours.

2. Strain stock through a sieve lined with dampened paper towels or a double thickness of cheesecloth. Chill overnight, and finish soup next day, or continue with recipe.

3. Pull meat into strings; set aside. Heat the remaining 1 tablespoon oil in a saucepan. Add the chopped onion, celery, and carrot; sauté, stirring, until golden, about 10 minutes. Stir in garlic; sauté 1 minute. Add the mushrooms; sauté, stirring, until golden, about 10 minutes. Season with salt and pepper.

4. Add the shredded meat and broth to the sautéed vegetables; stir in parsley, vegetables, and orzo; heat to boiling. Simmer, uncovered, until orzo is tender, about 15 minutes. Season to taste with salt and pepper.

63 BEEF STEW IN WINE SAUCE WITH SPINACH NOODLES

Prep: 15 minutes   Cook: 2 hours   Serves: 6

Beef Stew
- ⅓ cup all-purpose flour
- ½ teaspoon salt
- ⅛ teaspoon black pepper
- 2½ pounds beef stew meat, trimmed and cut into 1½-inch pieces
- 3 tablespoons olive oil
- 1 cup chopped onion
- 1 cup sliced carrot
- 1 teaspoon minced garlic

- 1 cup red wine
- 1 can (14½ ounces) whole tomatoes with juice, pressed through a sieve or food mill
- 2 tablespoons coarsely chopped sun-dried tomatoes
- 1 bay leaf
- ¼ teaspoon dried thyme

Spinach Noodles
- 6 tablespoons butter
- 10 ounces mushrooms, trimmed and sliced
- 2 tablespoons minced sun-dried tomatoes

- 2 tablespoons chopped Italian flat-leaf parsley
- 1 garlic clove, crushed
  Freshly ground black pepper
- 12 ounces spinach noodles

1. For the stew, combine the flour, salt, and pepper in a plastic bag. Shake the beef cubes in the flour to coat. Heat the oil in a large heavy Dutch oven. Carefully brown the meat in batches on all sides in the oil; do not crowd; remove meat to a plate as it is browned.

2. Add the onion, carrot, and garlic to the Dutch oven; sauté, stirring, over low heat, until tender and onion is golden, about 10 minutes. Spoon onto plate with the browned meat. Add the wine to the Dutch oven. Heat to boiling, scraping the browned bits from the pan. Stir in the sieved tomatoes.

3. Return the meat, sautéed vegetables, and any drippings on the platter to the Dutch oven. Add the sun-dried tomatoes, bay leaf, and thyme. Cover and bake in a preheated 350°F oven 1½ to 2 hours, or until the beef is tender. Season to taste with salt and pepper.

4. For the noodles, heat the butter in a medium skillet. When the foam subsides, add the mushrooms and sauté, stirring until tender and golden, about 10 minutes. Stir in the sun-dried tomatoes, parsley, garlic, and black pepper to taste.

5. Meanwhile, cook the noodles in plenty of boiling salted water until al dente, or firm to the bite, about 8 minutes; drain. Toss the noodles with the mushroom mixture.

6. Spoon the noodles onto a large deep platter. Spoon the stew into the center and spoon juices over top.

64 FRESH TOMATO SOUP WITH ORZO

Prep: 20 minutes   Cook: 45 minutes   Serves: 6

1 tablespoon olive oil
1 cup lengthwise slices large sweet yellow onion
1 inside celery rib with leaves, cut into thin slices
1 small garlic clove, crushed
8 fresh sage leaves
3 to 4 pounds ripe red tomatoes, dipped in hot water and peeled

2 cups homemade light chicken broth, or dilute 1 can (13¾ ounces) broth with enough water to equal 2 cups
1 cup cooked orzo
1 tablespoon salt, or to taste
Freshly ground black pepper

1. Heat oil in a large heavy saucepan; stir in the onions, celery, garlic, and sage leaves; sauté, stirring, over low heat until the onions are coated with oil. Cover and sweat the vegetables over low heat until very soft, about 25 minutes.

2. Meanwhile, place the peeled tomatoes into a sieve set over a bowl. Break tomatoes with hands and squeeze out the juices and seeds. Rinse any seeds off the tomato flesh; coarsely cut up the tomatoes. Press on the pulp left in the sieve to extract as much juice as possible. Discard seeds in sieve. Add the strained juices and the tomato pulp to the onions. Add the chicken broth; heat to simmering.

3. Just before serving, stir in the orzo; season to taste with salt and pepper. Serve piping hot.

65 VEAL STEW WITH FARFALLE IN ROSEMARY BUTTER

Prep: 15 minutes   Cook: 1 hour   Serves: 4

2 tablespoons butter
2 tablespoons olive oil
1½ pounds veal stew meat (cut from shoulder), trimmed and cut into ¾-inch pieces
¼ cup chopped shallots
1 garlic clove, minced
½ cup red wine
1 can (14½ ounces) whole tomatoes with juice, cut up
½ teaspoon dried rosemary

1 strip (¼ x 2 inches) lemon zest, cut into thin slivers
1 package (10 ounces) baby lima beans, thawed
½ teaspoon salt
Coarsely ground black pepper
8 ounces farfalle
3 tablespoons butter
¼ teaspoon crumbled dried rosemary leaves
1 tablespoon chopped Italian flat-leaf parsley

1. Heat the butter and oil in a large heavy skillet. When foam subsides, add the veal, in batches; sauté over medium heat; turn to brown evenly. Add the shallots and garlic; cover and cook until tender, about 10 minutes.

2. Add the wine; heat to boiling; boil, stirring, 2 minutes. Stir in the tomatoes, rosemary, and lemon zest. Cover and cook over low heat until the veal is tender, about 40 minutes. Add the limas, salt, and pepper to taste. Cover and cook until limas are tender, about 5 minutes.

3. Meanwhile, cook the farfalle in plenty of boiling salted water until al dente, or firm to the bite, about 12 minutes. Drain. Heat the butter and rosemary in the same pan until butter is melted. Add the pasta and toss.

4. Spoon the farfalle onto a large platter. Spoon the veal stew over the pasta. Sprinkle with parsley and serve.

---

66 FRESH CLAM CHOWDER WITH TINY SHELLS

Prep: 15 minutes   Cook: 1 hour   Serves: 6–8

1 dozen cherrystone clams, shucked, juices reserved
2 strips bacon, cut into ¼-inch dice
1 cup chopped onion
1 cup sliced carrots
½ cup sliced celery
½ cup *each* diced (¼ inch) red and green bell pepper
2 garlic cloves, minced
1 can (1 pound 12 ounces) Italian-style plum tomatoes with juices
1 cup diced (¼ inch) pared potato
⅓ cup tiny shells or other small pasta such as acini di pepe or coralli

1 tablespoon chopped fresh thyme, or ½ teaspoon dried
1 tablespoon chopped fresh oregano, or ½ teaspoon dried
1 bay leaf
½ teaspoon salt, or more to taste
1 cup corn kernels, fresh or frozen
1 cup cut green beans, fresh or frozen
Coarsely ground black pepper

1. With kitchen shears, cut clams into ¼- to ½-inch pieces; cut out and discard the waste sack from the belly of each clam. Refrigerate clams and juices until ready to use.

2. Sauté bacon in a large wide saucepan over medium-low heat until edges are lightly browned and fat is rendered. Stir in the onion, carrots, celery, and red and green peppers; cover and cook over very low heat until vegetables are tender, but not browned, about 10 minutes. Stir in garlic; sauté, stirring, over medium heat 3 minutes. Add the tomatoes; fill the tomato can with water and add to the saucepan. Stir in the potato, pasta, herbs, and salt; heat to simmering. Cover and cook over low heat 20 minutes, or until vegetables and pasta are very tender.

3. Stir in the clams, corn, and green beans. Heat to simmering, stirring, over high heat. Reduce heat; cook, covered, 10 minutes, or until vegetables are tender and chowder is fragrant. Add more salt to taste and plenty of black pepper.

67   BROCCOLI AND "BUTTERFLY" SOUP
Prep: 10 minutes   Cook: 30 minutes   Serves: 6

Use tiny bow-shaped pasta called farfalline, or "tiny butterflies," in this simple but delicious soup.

½ cup tiny bow-shaped pasta
4 cups homemade chicken broth, or equal parts canned broth and water
1 small bunch (about 1 pound) broccoli, trimmed and coarsely chopped (¼- to ½-inch pieces)

½ cup grated Parmesan cheese
Salt and black pepper

1. Cook the pasta in plenty of boiling salted water until al dente, or firm to the bite, about 12 minutes. Set strainer or colander over a large heatproof bowl and drain the pasta. Reserve 2 cups of the pasta cooking liquid.

2. Heat the chicken broth in a large saucepan; heat to simmering. Add the broccoli; cook, uncovered, over low heat, stirring occasionally, until very tender, about 10 minutes.

3. Add the reserved 2 cups pasta cooking liquid, the cooked pasta, and the grated cheese. Heat through, stirring, over low heat. Add salt, if needed. Sprinkle generously with black pepper.

68   VEGETABLE AND MACARONI SOUP
Prep: 20 minutes   Cook: 1 hour 45 minutes   Serves: 8–10

If you are fortunate enough to be able to buy chunks of Parmesan cheese, be sure to save the hard rinds, tightly wrapped in foil and stored in the freezer. Cut the rinds into half-inch chunks and add to a pot of simmering soup. They will melt and become chewy. A delicious little something extra to find sitting in your bowl.

3 tablespoons olive oil
2 cups chopped sweet white onion
2 cups diced (¼ inch) carrots
1 pound leeks, trimmed, soaked, and rinsed, diced (¼ inch)
8 cups homemade chicken broth, or equal parts canned broth and water

1 can (14½ ounces) whole tomatoes with juices, puréed
1 large russet potato, pared and cut into ¼-inch dice
½ cup small pasta (tiny elbows, anellini, or acini di pepe)
1 cup diced (¼ inch) zucchini
Salt and pepper
Grated Parmesan cheese

1. Heat oil in a large heavy saucepan. Add the onions, carrots, and leeks. Sauté, stirring over low heat, until vegetables begin to wilt. Cover and cook, stirring occasionally, until vegetables are very soft and beginning to turn golden, about 30 minutes.

2. Add broth or broth and water, puréed tomatoes, and potato. Simmer, covered, 1 hour, or until vegetables have flavored the broth. Uncover and simmer 15 minutes.

3. Stir in the pasta; cook, uncovered, until tender, about 10 minutes. Add zucchini and cook until tender, about 5 minutes. Season to taste with salt and pepper. Serve with plenty of grated cheese.

69 GREEN MINESTRONE
Prep: 20 minutes   Cook: 45 minutes   Serves: 4–6

2 tablespoons olive oil
1 strip bacon, finely diced
2 scallions, white and green parts, finely chopped (about ½ cup)
1 medium leek, trimmed and washed, white part finely chopped
6 cups homemade light chicken broth, or half canned broth and half water
2 cups packed coarsely chopped trimmed and rinsed spinach
2 cups packed coarsely chopped trimmed and rinsed dark outside leaves of romaine lettuce or escarole

1 cup drained and chopped canned peeled tomatoes
1 cup trimmed and diced green beans
1 cup trimmed and diced yellow wax beans
¾ cup diced (¼ inch) potatoes
⅓ cup broken egg noodles or tiny elbow macaroni
1 teaspoon salt, or more to taste
2 tablespoons chopped Italian flat-leaf parsley
1 can (19 ounces) cannellini beans, rinsed and drained
Grated Parmesan cheese
Coarsely ground black pepper

1. Heat oil in a large wide saucepan. Add bacon and sauté 1 to 2 minutes; do not brown. Add scallions and leek; sauté, stirring, over low heat until tender, about 10 minutes.

2. Add the chicken broth; heat to simmering. Stir in the spinach and the romaine or escarole; cook, covered, 10 minutes. Add the tomatoes, green beans, wax beans, potatoes, and noodles or macaroni; add salt. Cook, uncovered, over low heat until the vegetables and pasta are tender, about 15 minutes. Stir in the parsley and cannellini beans. Stir in cheese and black pepper to taste.

70 LENTIL AND "PEPPERCORN" SOUP
Prep: 15 minutes   Cook: 2 hours   Serves: 8

The "peppercorns" are tiny little nuggets of pasta called acini di pepe. This is a hearty, nourishing soup, and with the addition of coarsely shredded Parmesan cheese, becomes a meal of complete proteins.

2 tablespoons olive oil
2 cups chopped onions
2 cups diced (¼ inch) carrots
½ cup chopped celery
1 teaspoon minced garlic
8 cups homemade chicken broth, or equal parts canned broth and water
1½ cups dried lentils

1 can (14½ ounces) whole tomatoes in juice, pressed through a sieve or food mill
¼ cup finely chopped Italian flat-leaf parsley
⅓ cup acini di pepe, cooked (about 1 cup cooked)
Salt and pepper
Coarsely shredded Parmesan cheese

1. Heat the oil in a large saucepan. Sweat the onions, carrots, celery, and garlic, covered, over low heat, until tender, about 20 minutes.

2. Add the broth or broth and water; heat to boiling. Stir in the lentils; heat, stirring occasionally, until boiling. Stir in the sieved tomatoes and the parsley. Cook, covered, over low heat until the lentils are tender, 1½ to 2 hours.

3. Just before serving, stir in the cooked pasta. Season with salt and pepper to taste. Serve with plenty of coarsely shredded Parmesan cheese.

71 FISH SOUP WITH TINY SEASHELLS
Prep: 10 minutes   Cook: 15 minutes   Serves: 4

A tiny seashell-shaped pasta, imported from Italy and called conchigliette piccole, is the shape I have in mind for this soup, but any small pasta shape such as ditalini, orzo, or acini di pepe can be used. With a salad and a hearty loaf of Italian whole wheat bread this makes a terrific supper menu.

2 tablespoons olive oil
½ cup chopped red onion
1 teaspoon finely chopped garlic
1 cup dry white wine
1 pound ripe plum tomatoes, chopped (about 3 cups)
2 tablespoons chopped basil
1 bay leaf
Salt and pepper to taste
⅓ cup tiny seashell-shaped pasta, cooked

½ pound sea scallops, cut into 1-inch pieces if large
½ pound boneless and skinless mildly flavored firm fish fillets (red snapper, tilefish, or cod), cut into 1-inch pieces
¼ pound (about 8) small shrimp, shelled and deveined
Basil leaves, cut into long thin strips

1. In a large wide saucepan, heat the oil; add the onion; sauté until tender, about 5 minutes; add the garlic; sauté 2 minutes. Add the wine; heat to boiling; boil 2 minutes. Stir in the tomatoes, chopped basil, and bay leaf. Simmer over low heat 5 minutes. Season with salt and pepper.

2. Stir in the cooked pasta and the scallops, fish, and shrimp. Cover and cook over low heat 5 minutes, or until fish is tender. Ladle into bowls and garnish each with a few strips of basil.

---

72 MINESTRONE
Soak: overnight or 1 hour   Prep: 30 minutes   Cook: 1 hour   Serves: 8

This is just one more version to add to the collection of "but that's not how I make my minestrone recipe" stories. The beans can be soaked overnight and drained before using; or cover with water, heat to boiling, and let stand 1 hour before draining and using. If you have any pesto around, stir a tablespoon into each bowl of steaming hot minestrone.

1 cup dried pinto beans, soaked overnight in water, drained (see headnote)
2 cups packed trimmed and rinsed Swiss chard
2 cups packed trimmed and rinsed escarole
2 tablespoons olive oil
1 cup chopped sweet yellow onion
1 tablespoon finely chopped garlic
2 slices prosciutto, finely diced
1 cup diced celery
1 cup diced carrot
1 pound ripe tomatoes, chopped (about 3 cups)
2 tablespoons chopped Italian flat-leaf parsley

1 teaspoon fresh marjoram leaves, or ½ teaspoon dried
1 teaspoon fresh oregano leaves, or ½ teaspoon dried
1 teaspoon salt
⅛ teaspoon coarsely ground black pepper
6 to 8 cups light chicken or beef broth (if using canned, use half broth and half water)
½ cup small pasta, traditionally ditalini or other tiny tubular shape
1 cup chopped cabbage
1 cup sliced (¼-inch pieces) fresh green beans

1. Cook the beans in plenty of water until almost tender, about 1 hour; drain.

2. Blanch the Swiss chard and escarole in plenty of boiling salted water until tender, about 15 minutes; drain.

3. Heat the oil in a large wide saucepan; add the onion and garlic. Cover and cook over very low heat until the onion is very soft, about 25 minutes. Stir in the prosciutto, celery, and carrot. Sauté, stirring, over low heat, until the onion begins to caramelize, about 10 minutes. Stir in the tomatoes and herbs; cook, stirring, until tomatoes cook down slightly, about 10 minutes. Add salt and pepper.

4. Add 6 cups of the broth and the beans; heat to simmering. Cook, uncovered, over low heat 1 hour. Stir in the pasta, cabbage, and green beans; cook until tender, about 10 minutes. Adjust seasoning.

73 LAMB STEW WITH HERBED ELBOWS

Prep: 20 minutes   Cook: 2 hours   Serves: 6

The simple elbow accompaniment is a pleasant surprise to the sophisticated flavors of the stew. The fresh mint, if available, adds an extra sparkle to the herb mixture. Couscous, cooked according to package directions and then tossed with the herbed butter, is also a lovely pasta accompaniment to the lamb.

2 pounds boneless lamb shoulder, cut into 1-inch pieces	4 tablespoons butter
½ pound lean neck of lamb, cut into 1-inch pieces	12 small white onions, peeled
	1 teaspoon sugar
	1 medium white turnip, peeled and diced (½ cup)
3 tablespoons all-purpose flour	1 cup fresh or frozen tiny green peas
2 tablespoons oil	2 cups elbow macaroni
1 cup chopped onion	2 tablespoons finely chopped parsley
½ cup diced carrot	
6 garlic cloves, peeled, left whole	1 teaspoon fresh thyme leaves, or ½ teaspoon dried
Salt and pepper	
Pinch of dried thyme	1 teaspoon fresh oregano leaves, or ¼ teaspoon dried
1 bay leaf	
1 can (14 ounces) whole peeled tomatoes with juice, cut up with scissors	Few fresh mint leaves, if available (optional)
2 cups light homemade chicken broth, or equal parts canned broth and water	

1. Wipe the pieces of lamb with a paper towel. Place in a plastic bag; shake to coat lightly with the flour. Heat the oil in a large Dutch oven. In small batches, lightly brown the lamb on all sides; transfer to a side dish. Add the onion, carrot, and whole garlic to the Dutch oven; sauté, stirring, over low heat until golden, about 15 minutes. Add the browned lamb to the Dutch oven; sprinkle with salt, pepper, and thyme. Add the bay leaf, cut-up tomatoes, and the chicken broth. Heat to simmering.

2. Cover the Dutch oven and place in a preheated 350°F oven. Bake 1 hour. Meanwhile, heat 2 tablespoons of the butter in a medium skillet; when the foam subsides, add the onions. Sauté, stirring gently to coat with butter; sprinkle with sugar. Sauté, stirring, until golden. Add onions and turnip to the lamb, poking down into the sauce. Cover and bake 30 minutes. Add the peas; bake 15 minutes, or until the peas are tender. Taste and correct seasonings.

3. Cook the elbow macaroni in plenty of boiling salted water until al dente, or firm to the bite, about 10 minutes; drain. Add the parsley, the fresh or dried thyme, oregano, and mint, if using, together. Melt the remaining 2 tablespoons butter in a skillet; add the elbows and the herbs; toss.

4. Serve the stew with the elbows on the side.

74 ZUCCHINI AND LEEK SOUP WITH PASTINA

Prep: 10 minutes   Cook: 30 minutes   Serves: 4

Make this soup when zucchini, tomatoes, and basil are at their best. It is nourishing enough to be a main course.

2 tablespoons olive oil
1 strip thick-sliced lightly smoked lean bacon, finely diced
1 medium leek, greens and roots trimmed, well washed, and finely diced (about 1 cup)
2 tomatoes, peeled, seeded, and coarsely chopped (about 1 cup)

12 ounces small, tender zucchini, trimmed and diced (about 2 cups)
2 to 3 cups light chicken broth or water
Salt and freshly ground black pepper
3 tablespoons pastina
1 egg
Grated Parmesan cheese
6 large basil leaves, torn into pieces

1. Combine the oil, bacon, and leek in a large heavy saucepan; sauté, stirring over low heat until coated with oil. Cover and cook over low heat until the leek is very tender, about 20 minutes. Stir in the tomatoes, zucchini, and 2 cups of the broth; sprinkle with salt and pepper; stir in the pastina.

2. Cook, covered, until the zucchini is very soft, about 15 minutes. If the soup is very thick, add a little more broth or water.

3. Beat the egg in a small bowl with 1 tablespoon of the cheese. With the soup over low heat, stir the egg into the soup in a slow steady stream. Just before serving, stir in the basil. Serve with additional cheese sprinkled on the top.

Chapter 5

Spaghetti in the Pantry

Spaghetti is truly the quintessential food. Long before the word "pasta" was added to the American vocabulary, we had been eating and enjoying spaghetti and meat balls. Spaghetti is a pure convenience food. With a minimum of fuss and the simplest sauce, dinner can be on the table in the time it takes to boil the water and melt the butter. The recipes run from a pure and simple tossing with freshly grated Parmesan cheese and melted butter to a Spaghetti Frittata with Three Onions and Tuna. Spaghetti frittatas are fun to create and to serve: the configuration of the spaghetti in a slice of frittata is sure to keep even the most impatient little diner occupied while devouring dinner.

A spaghetti primer

Spaghetti: A long and thin solid round strand of pasta.
Spaghettini: Same as spaghetti, but thinner.
Vermicelli: Very thin strands of pasta, often sold in clusters.
Capellini: Means "fine hairs," very delicate round noodles; sometimes called capelli d'angelo, or "angel's hair."
Bucatini: A long round thin spaghetti with a pierced hollow down the center.
Perciatelli: A fatter version of bucatini.
Fedelini: Thin spaghetti cut into short curved lengths.

75   SPAGHETTI WITH OLIVE SAUCE
Prep: 20 minutes   Cook: 10 minutes   Serves: 4

The combined fruity and nutty flavors of the olives contribute to the success of this dish. Look for imported or domestic brine-cured olives. Popular black varieties are Gaeta, Kalamata, and niçoise; green varieties include Spanish, Californian, and Sicilian.

¼ cup olive oil
⅓ cup pitted and finely chopped brine-cured black olives
⅓ cup pitted and finely chopped brine-cured green olives
¼ cup finely chopped red onion
1 tablespoon minced drained anchovies
1 tablespoon finely chopped Italian flat-leaf parsley
1 garlic clove, crushed
1 teaspoon finely shredded orange zest
½ teaspoon dried oregano
¼ teaspoon coarsely ground black pepper
Salt
12 ounces spaghetti, bucatini, or perciatelli

1. Combine the oil, olives, red onion, anchovies, parsley, garlic, orange zest, oregano, black pepper, and salt to taste.

2. Cook spaghetti in plenty of boiling salted water until al dente, or firm to the bite, 7 to 10 minutes. Toss spaghetti with room-temperature sauce.

76   SPAGHETTI WITH SALAMI AND PEAS
Prep: 10 minutes   Cook: 10 minutes   Serves: 4

1 pound spaghetti, bucatini, or perciatelli
1 package (10 ounces) frozen peas, thawed
¼ cup olive oil
4 tablespoons butter
2 garlic cloves, crushed
3 ounces (about 8 slices) Genoa or other hard salami, cut into ¼-inch-wide strips
Grated Parmesan cheese

1. Cook spaghetti in plenty of boiling salted water for 4 to 7 minutes. Stir in the peas; cook 3 minutes, or until peas are tender and pasta is al dente, or firm to the bite; drain.

2. Wipe out saucepan; heat oil and butter over low heat until butter melts; stir in garlic; sauté 1 minute. Remove from the heat; add the spaghetti, peas, and salami; toss to blend. Serve with grated cheese.

77   SPAGHETTI WITH BROCCOLI, TOMATO, AND ROASTED RED PEPPERS

Prep: 10 minutes   Cook: 15 minutes   Serves: 4

1   pound spaghetti
1   bunch broccoli (about 1 pound), trimmed and cut into 1-inch lengths; thick stems sliced thin
⅓   cup olive oil
2   garlic cloves, crushed
¼   teaspoon crushed dried red pepper

1   medium tomato, cored and chopped (about 1 cup), or canned tomatoes, drained and chopped
1   jar (7 ounces) roasted red peppers, rinsed, drained, and cut into ⅛-inch-wide strips
Grated Parmesan cheese

1. Cook spaghetti in plenty of boiling salted water for 3 minutes; add the broccoli; cook until spaghetti is al dente, or firm to the bite, and the broccoli is tender, about 7 to 10 minutes; drain.

2. Heat the oil in a medium skillet; add the garlic and dried red pepper; sauté 1 minute. Stir in the tomato; sauté 5 minutes. Add the red peppers and heat through.

3. Toss sauce with spaghetti and broccoli. Serve with grated cheese.

78   SPAGHETTI WITH WALNUTS AND PARMESAN

Prep: 10 minutes   Cook: 10 minutes   Serves: 4

12   ounces spaghetti or spaghettini
6   tablespoons olive oil
1   garlic clove, crushed

½   cup finely chopped walnuts
¼   cup grated Parmesan cheese
3   tablespoons finely chopped parsley

1. Cook the spaghetti in plenty of boiling salted water until al dente, or firm to the bite, about 7 to 10 minutes; drain.

2. Heat oil in a small skillet; stir in garlic; sauté 1 minute. Add walnuts; sauté 2 minutes, stirring.

3. Toss the walnut sauce, spaghetti, cheese, and parsley together. Serve immediately.

Variation:

79   SPAGHETTI WITH WALNUTS AND BLUE CHEESE

Substitute 3 ounces blue-veined cheese, crumbled (Stilton, American blue, Gorgonzola, or Roquefort), for the Parmesan cheese.

80 SPAGHETTI WITH PARSLEY BUTTER SAUCE

Prep: 10 minutes   Cook: 10 minutes   Serves: 4

12 ounces spaghetti,
   spaghettini, or vermicelli
6 tablespoons butter

1 garlic clove, crushed
¼ cup very finely chopped
   parsley (curly or flat leaf)

1. Cook the spaghetti in plenty of boiling salted water until al dente, or firm to the bite, 7 to 10 minutes; drain.

2. In a skillet, melt butter; when foam subsides, stir in the garlic; sauté 1 minute.

3. Toss spaghetti with the garlic butter and parsley; serve at once.

81 SPAGHETTI FRITTATA WITH ZUCCHINI, TOMATO, AND MOZZARELLA

Prep: 10 minutes   Cook: 25 minutes   Serves: 6

3 tablespoons olive oil
½ cup chopped onion
1 cup diced (about ¼ inch)
   trimmed zucchini
1 cup diced (about ¼ inch)
   plum tomatoes
1 garlic clove, crushed
6 eggs
1 cup shredded mozzarella
   cheese

4 tablespoons grated
   Parmesan cheese
1 tablespoon chopped fresh
   basil, or ½ teaspoon dried
½ teaspoon salt
⅛ teaspoon coarsely ground
   black pepper
8 ounces cooked spaghetti
   (about 3 cups)

1. Heat 2 tablespoons of the oil in a 10-inch nonstick skillet; add onion and sauté until tender, about 5 minutes. Stir in the zucchini, tomatoes, and garlic; cook, stirring, until juices cook down and sauce is thick, about 10 minutes; remove from heat. Reserve sauce; cover to keep warm.

2. In a large bowl, beat the eggs; stir in the mozzarella, 2 tablespoons of the grated Parmesan, the basil, salt, pepper, and cooked spaghetti; stir to blend.

3. Wipe out skillet; add the remaining 1 tablespoon oil; heat over low heat. Add the egg mixture; cover and cook 5 minutes; shake pan to discourage sticking. Cook, covered, until egg is set and frittata is well browned, 10 to 15 minutes longer. Uncover and sprinkle with remaining 2 tablespoons grated Parmesan cheese.

4. Cut into wedges and serve from the skillet, or invert frittata by setting a large platter on top of the skillet and, protecting hands with mitts, invert the skillet onto the plate. Season reserved sauce with salt and pepper, to taste; serve sauce with the frittata.

> ## Spaghetti for one, two, three, or more
>
> A simple rule of thumb is: 1 pound of spaghetti will feed 4 very hungry appetites or 6 normal appetites. But, consider the sauce: if it is rich and hearty, 12 ounces of spaghetti should satisfy 4 normal appetites.

82 SPAGHETTI FRITTATA WITH THREE ONIONS

Prep: 10 minutes   Cook: 25 minutes   Serves: 6

A frittata is an omelet, Italian style, and is a great way to use up leftover spaghetti. Eight ounces of spaghetti equals about three cups cooked, which is just enough for this recipe. The variations can be endless. Save any small amounts of leftover cooked vegetables, meats, or small chunks of cheese and put your culinary imagination to work when concocting your own version of spaghetti frittata. A 10-inch nonstick skillet makes turning the frittata out a cinch.

2 tablespoons olive oil
½ cup *each* chopped red and Spanish (sweet/white) onions
¼ cup thinly sliced trimmed scallions, green and white part
1 garlic clove, crushed
6 eggs

4 tablespoons grated Parmesan cheese
2 tablespoons chopped parsley
½ teaspoon salt
⅛ teaspoon coarsely ground black pepper
8 ounces leftover cooked spaghetti (about 3 cups)

1. Heat the oil in a 10-inch nonstick skillet; add the onions and sauté until tender, about 5 minutes. Stir in the scallions and garlic; sauté 2 minutes.

2. In a large bowl, beat the eggs; add the sautéed onion mixture, 2 tablespoons of the cheese, parsley, salt, pepper, and leftover spaghetti; stir well to combine.

3. Reheat the nonstick skillet over low heat until a drop of water sizzles and evaporates immediately upon contact. Add the spaghetti mixture. Cover and cook over low heat 5 minutes. Shake pan to discourage sticking. Cook, covered, until egg is set and frittata is well browned, 10 to 15 minutes longer. Uncover and sprinkle with remaining 2 tablespoons cheese.

4. Cut into wedges and serve from the skillet or invert frittata by setting a large plate on top of the skillet and, protecting hands with mitts, invert the skillet onto the plate.

Variation:

83 SPAGHETTI FRITTATA WITH THREE ONIONS AND TUNA

Add 1 can (6½ ounces) chunk light tuna, well drained, to the egg mixture in step 2.

84 SPAGHETTI WITH LEMON BUTTER

Prep: 10 minutes   Cook: 10 minutes   Serves: 4

12 ounces spaghetti,
   spaghettini, or vermicelli
4 tablespoons butter

2 teaspoons finely shredded
   lemon zest
2 tablespoons fresh lemon
   juice

1. Cook pasta in plenty of boiling salted water until al dente, or firm to the bite, 7 to 10 minutes; drain.

2. Meanwhile, melt butter in a skillet, over low heat, stirring until creamy. Stir in lemon zest and juice.

3. Toss lemon sauce with hot pasta and serve at once.

Variations:

85 SPAGHETTI WITH LEMON BUTTER AND TUNA

Add 1 can (6½ ounces) chunk light tuna, well drained, and 2 tablespoons coarsely chopped Italian flat-leaf parsley to the lemon sauce. Heat gently 1 minute before tossing with hot pasta.

86 SPAGHETTI WITH LEMON BUTTER AND PEAS

Add 1 cup frozen tiny peas to the butter. Heat, stirring, over low heat until peas are tender, about 3 minutes. Add the zest and lemon juice; toss with hot pasta.

87 SPAGHETTI WITH LEMON BUTTER AND SHREDDED ZUCCHINI

Shred 2 small (about 6 ounces) trimmed zucchini; add to the butter. Heat, stirring, until crisp-tender, about 3 minutes. Add the lemon zest and juice; toss with the hot pasta.

88   SPAGHETTI WITH SPINACH AND CREAM SAUCE

Prep: 10 minutes   Cook: 15 minutes   Serves: 4

1½ cups heavy cream
12 ounces spaghetti
2 tablespoons butter
3 ounces prosciutto, cut into short, thin slivers
6 ounces fresh spinach, stems trimmed, leaves stacked, and cut into julienne strips

2 tablespoons pignoli (pine nuts), stirred in a hot skillet until lightly toasted, about 2 minutes
Grated Parmesan cheese

1. In a saucepan, gently boil the cream until it is reduced by half, about 5 minutes.

2. Cook spaghetti in plenty of boiling salted water until al dente, or firm to the bite, about 7 to 10 minutes; drain.

3. Meanwhile, melt butter in a skillet; add prosciutto; sauté 1 minute. Add spinach; sauté, stirring, until spinach is wilted, about 3 minutes.

4. Toss spaghetti, cream, and spinach mixture together. Sprinkle with pignoli. Sprinkle grated cheese on top.

Variation:

89   SPAGHETTI WITH PROSCIUTTO, PEAS, AND CREAM

Substitute 1 cup frozen tiny peas for the spinach. Sauté peas with prosciutto until tender, about 3 minutes. Use spaghetti or spaghettini.

90   SPAGHETTI WITH BUTTER AND PARMESAN

Prep: 5 minutes   Cook: 10 minutes   Serves: 4

12 ounces spaghetti, spaghettini, vermicelli, or capellini
¼ pound butter

½ cup grated Parmesan cheese
2 tablespoons finely chopped parsley (optional)

1. Cook spaghetti in plenty of boiling salted water until al dente, or firm to the bite, 7 to 10 minutes; drain.

2. Melt butter in a small skillet.

3. Toss spaghetti with melted butter, cheese, and parsley, if using. Serve hot.

91 SPAGHETTI WITH GARDEN VEGETABLES
Prep: 15 minutes   Cook: 10 minutes   Serves: 4

12 ounces spaghetti
6 tablespoons butter
1 carrot, pared and shredded (about ⅔ cup)
1 small (about 3 ounces) zucchini, trimmed and shredded
2 scallions, trimmed and cut into 1½-inch lengths and ⅛-inch julienne

1 garlic clove, crushed
Salt and pepper
2 tablespoons finely chopped parsley (curly or flat leaf)
1 tablespoon chopped fresh dill
Grated Parmesan cheese

1. Cook the spaghetti in plenty of boiling salted water until al dente, or firm to the bite, about 7 to 10 minutes; drain.

2. Heat butter in a large skillet; when foam subsides, add the carrot, zucchini, and scallions. Sauté over medium heat, stirring, until vegetables are crisp-tender, about 3 minutes. Stir in garlic; sauté 1 minute. Add salt and pepper to taste.

3. Toss spaghetti with the vegetables, parsley, and dill. Serve at once with cheese sprinkled on top.

92 SPAGHETTI WITH CREAMY TOMATO AND GOAT CHEESE SAUCE
Prep: 10 minutes   Cook: 10 minutes   Serves: 4

Fresh domestic goat cheese, as opposed to aged imported goat cheese, is really the best product for this dish. The fresh goat cheese is sweet and flavorful with just a little tang and has a smooth creamy consistency.

3 tablespoons olive oil
1 garlic clove, crushed
2 cups chopped fresh tomatoes
12 ounces spaghetti, bucatini, or perciatelli

4 ounces fresh goat cheese, broken into chunks with a fork
2 tablespoons chopped Italian flat-leaf parsley
Coarsely ground black pepper

1. Heat oil in a skillet; stir in garlic; sauté 1 minute. Add the tomatoes; simmer until reduced to a thick mixture, about 10 minutes.

2. Meanwhile, cook the spaghetti in plenty of boiling salted water until al dente, or firm to the bite, 7 to 10 minutes.

3. Add the goat cheese to the tomato sauce; heat, stirring, over low heat until fairly smooth. Toss the hot pasta with the tomato sauce, parsley, and black pepper.

93 SPAGHETTI WITH GARLIC BREAD CRUMBS AND ANCHOVY OIL

Prep: 10 minutes   Cook: 10 minutes   Serves: 4

12 ounces spaghetti
¼ cup olive oil
4 tablespoons butter
2 garlic cloves, finely chopped
1 can (2 ounces) anchovy
   fillets, drained, blotted,
   and finely chopped

2 tablespoons coarse dry
   bread crumbs made from
   day-old Italian bread
1 tablespoon finely chopped
   parsley

1. Cook spaghetti in plenty of boiling salted water until al dente, or firm to the bite, about 7 to 10 minutes; drain.

2. Heat oil and butter in a medium skillet; add garlic; sauté 1 minute. Stir in anchovies; heat, stirring, until dissolved, about 2 minutes. Add bread crumbs; sauté, stirring, until browned and crisp. Pour over spaghetti; toss. Sprinkle with parsley.

94 SPAGHETTI WITH BASIL CREAM SAUCE

Prep: 10 minutes   Cook: 10 minutes   Serves: 4

This dish is a must at least once during the height of basil season. It makes an especially nice first course, followed by grilled beef and a tomato salad.

1½ cups heavy cream
2 tablespoons julienned basil
   leaves
1 teaspoon fresh lemon juice

Pinch of salt
12 ounces spaghetti,
   spaghettini, vermicelli, or
   capellini

1. In a saucepan, gently boil the cream until it is reduced by half, about 10 minutes. Stir in the basil, lemon juice, and salt.

2. Meanwhile, cook the pasta in plenty of boiling salted water until al dente, or firm to the bite, about 7 to 10 minutes; drain. Toss with the cream sauce and serve at once.

Variation:

95 SPAGHETTI WITH BASIL CREAM AND PLUM TOMATOES

Peel, halve, and scoop seeds and juice from 8 ounces fresh plum tomatoes. Cut the tomatoes into ¼-inch lengthwise strips; add to hot cream with the basil, lemon juice, and salt and toss with the hot spaghetti.

96 SPAGHETTI BAKED WITH TOMATO SAUCE AND TWO CHEESES

Prep: 10 minutes   Bake: 20 minutes   Serves: 4

3 cups leftover cooked
    spaghetti (8 ounces dried)
1½ cups prepared Quick
    Chunky Tomato Sauce
    (page 142)

1 cup shredded mozzarella
    cheese
¼ cup grated Parmesan cheese
4 ounces mozzarella cheese,
    cut into thin slices

1. Combine the spaghetti, tomato sauce, shredded mozzarella, and Parmesan in a lightly buttered 1½-quart shallow baking dish. Lay the sliced mozzarella evenly over the top.

2. Bake in a preheated 350°F oven until hot and bubbly, about 20 minutes.

97 SPAGHETTI WITH SAUSAGE, PORCINI, AND TOMATO SAUCE

Prep: 10 minutes   Soak: 20 minutes   Cook: 25 minutes   Serves: 4

½ ounce dried porcini (about
    ¼ cup)
1 cup water
8 ounces Italian-style sausage
    (sweet and/or hot)
1 garlic clove, crushed
1 can (15 ounces) Italian-style
    plum tomatoes with juice
1 tablespoon tomato paste

½ teaspoon salt
¼ teaspoon dried fennel (omit
    if sausage is heavily
    seasoned with fennel)
⅛ teaspoon coarsely ground
    black pepper
12 ounces spaghetti, bucatini,
    or perciatelli
Grated Parmesan cheese

1. Combine porcini and water in a small saucepan; heat to boiling; let stand 20 minutes. Meanwhile, start sauce.

2. Remove sausage from casings and crumble into a skillet. Sauté, stirring, until lightly browned, about 10 minutes. Drain off excess fat. Add the garlic; sauté 1 minute.

3. Purée the tomatoes in a food processor or through a food mill; add to skillet. Stir in the tomato paste, salt, fennel, if using, and pepper. Heat to a slow simmer.

4. Drain the porcini through a very fine sieve or a sieve lined with a double layer of dampened cheesecloth; reserve the liquid. If the porcini are gritty, rinse clean under running water. Chop the porcini and add to the tomato sauce along with the reserved liquid.

5. Simmer the sauce until slightly reduced and thickened, about 15 minutes, stirring often.

6. Cook the spaghetti in plenty of boiling water until al dente, or firm to the bite, 7 to 10 minutes; drain. Toss with half the sauce. Serve the remaining sauce on the side to spoon over spaghetti as desired. Pass grated cheese to sprinkle over the spaghetti.

98 SPAGHETTI WITH CHOPPED BROCCOLI AND PIGNOLI IN BROWNED GARLIC OIL

Prep: 10 minutes   Cook: 15 minutes   Serves: 4

⅓ cup olive oil
1 tablespoon thin crosswise slivers of garlic
2 cups fresh or frozen chopped broccoli (slightly thawed, if frozen)

12 ounces spaghetti
2 tablespoons pignoli (pine nuts), stirred in a hot skillet 2 minutes, or until toasted
Grated Parmesan cheese

1. Heat oil in a medium skillet over low heat; stir in garlic. Sauté, stirring, just until edges begin to turn golden, about 3 minutes. Add the broccoli; cover and cook over low heat until tender, about 5 minutes.

2. Cook the spaghetti in plenty of boiling salted water until al dente, or firm to the bite, about 7 to 10 minutes; drain.

3. Toss with broccoli and garlic oil; sprinkle with pignoli and grated cheese before serving.

99 SPAGHETTI WITH TOASTED ALMOND SAUCE

Prep: 10 minutes   Cook: 10 minutes   Serves: 4

½ cup unblanched almonds, coarsely chopped
¼ cup olive oil
¼ cup packed Italian flat-leaf parsley
2 garlic cloves, chopped
1 teaspoon salt

12 ounces spaghetti
¼ cup lightly packed torn fresh basil leaves
1 tablespoon slivered drained and blotted sun-dried tomatoes packed in olive oil

1. In a medium skillet, toast the almonds over low heat, stirring constantly about 3 minutes; transfer to a small bowl.

2. Combine ¼ cup of the almonds, the oil, parsley, garlic, and salt in the bowl of a food processor; process until almonds are finely chopped.

3. Cook spaghetti in plenty of boiling salted water until al dente, or firm to the bite, about 7 to 10 minutes; drain.

4. Toss spaghetti with reserved ¼ cup toasted almonds, almond and oil mixture, the basil leaves, and sun-dried tomatoes.

Spaghetti for a crowd?

What better way to feed a crowd than to boil up a pot or two of spaghetti. We say two, since spaghetti needs lots of water and not every pot is large enough. It is safer to handle two 10-quart pots of water than to tackle a stockpot or canning pot filled with boiling water and hot spaghetti.

Chapter 6

Elbows on the Table

Elbows, like spaghetti, are a familiar and friendly type of pasta known to Americans simply as elbow macaroni. Macaroni and cheese, of course, has been filling American bellies for years, and has in fact already filled a chapter in this book (see Chapter 2/The American Classic). But this adaptable shape can also be sauced and used in omelets, soups, and salads. In this chapter there are several versions of a classic Italian pasta and bean soup called Pasta e Fagioli—Elbows with Ham, Limas, and Caramelized Onions; Elbows with Cannellini Beans, Bacon, and Red Onion; and Elbows with Chick-Peas and Escarole. The Elbows with Four Cheeses and Elbows with Sausage and Mushrooms, Carbonara Style are two hearty renditions guaranteed to please the most gargantuan appetite. And there is lots more; so let's get those *elbows on the table*.

100   ELBOWS WITH HAM, LIMAS, AND CARAMELIZED ONIONS

Prep: 10 minutes   Cook: 15 minutes   Serves: 4

2   cups elbow macaroni
1   package (10 ounces) frozen
        Fordhook lima beans
1   medium carrot, pared and
        sliced thin
4   ounces fully cooked ham,
        cut into thin slivers about
        1 inch long

3   tablespoons olive oil
1   medium onion, quartered
        and cut crosswise into
        thin slivers
    Coarsely ground black
        pepper
    Grated Parmesan or
        Romano cheese

1. Cook the macaroni in plenty of boiling salted water for 5 minutes; add the limas and carrots; cook, stirring occasionally, until tender, about 8 minutes longer. With a ladle, remove ½ cup of the macaroni cooking liquid; reserve. Drain macaroni and vegetables.

2. While the macaroni is cooking, sauté the ham in the oil over medium-high heat until the edges begin to brown, about 5 minutes. Stir in the onion; sauté over medium-low heat, stirring until onion is golden and edges begin to brown, about 8 minutes.

3. In a large bowl, combine the elbows, vegetables, the ½ cup reserved cooking liquid, and the sautéed ham and onion; toss to blend. Sprinkle with black pepper. Spoon into wide-rimmed shallow soup bowls and sprinkle generously with grated cheese.

101   ELBOWS WITH CANNELLINI BEANS, BACON, AND RED ONION

Prep: 5 minutes   Cook: 12 minutes   Serves: 4

2   cups elbow macaroni
6   strips thick-cut bacon, cut
        into ½-inch pieces
2   tablespoons olive oil
1   cup diced (¼ inch) red onion
        (about 1 cup)
¼   cup finely chopped green
        bell pepper

1   can (19 ounces) cannellini
        beans, rinsed and drained
¼   teaspoon coarsely ground
        black pepper
    Salt
    Grated Parmesan or
        Romano cheese

1. Cook macaroni in plenty of boiling salted water until al dente, or firm to the bite, about 12 minutes. With a ladle, remove ½ cup of the macaroni cooking liquid; reserve. Drain macaroni.

2. While macaroni is cooking, sauté the bacon in a medium skillet until crisp; drain on paper towels. Discard all but 1 tablespoon of the bacon drippings in the skillet; add the olive oil to the skillet. Add the red onion and green pepper; sauté until crisp-tender, and onion is still red in color, about 1 minute. Over low heat, stir the cannellini beans just until heated through. Add the bacon, black pepper, and salt; stir to blend.

3. In a large bowl, stir the macaroni and reserved cooking liquid together. Add the bean mixture; toss and serve at once in wide-rimmed shallow soup bowls with plenty of grated cheese on the side.

---

102   BAKED ELBOWS WITH LATE SUMMER VEGETABLE SAUCE

Prep: 15 minutes   Cook: 35 minutes   Bake: 20 minutes   Serves: 4

¼ cup olive oil
1 cup chopped Spanish or other sweet onion
1 small green bell pepper, stemmed and seeded, cut into ½-inch pieces (about 1 cup)
1 pound small zucchini (½- to 1-inch diameter), cut into ½-inch slices (about 2 cups)
1 garlic clove, crushed
1 pound ripe tomatoes, cored and cut into 1-inch chunks (about 2 cups)

1 tablespoon chopped fresh basil, or 1 teaspoon dried
1 tablespoon fresh oregano leaves, stripped from stems, or ½ teaspoon dried oregano
Salt
⅛ teaspoon coarsely ground black pepper
2 cups elbow macaroni
½ cup grated Parmesan cheese
Garlic Bread Crumbs (recipe follows)

1. Heat oil in a wide saucepan; add onion and sauté until golden, about 8 minutes. Stir in green pepper, zucchini, and garlic; sauté until crisp-tender, about 5 minutes. Stir in tomatoes, basil, and oregano; cook, covered, over low heat until vegetables are tender, about 20 minutes. Season with salt and pepper to taste.

2. Cook macaroni in plenty of boiling salted water until slightly under-cooked, about 10 minutes; drain.

3. Heat oven to 350°F. Combine the cooked macaroni, cooked vegetables, and grated cheese. Scrape into a lightly oiled 2-quart baking dish. Sprinkle the top with Garlic Bread Crumbs. Bake 20 minutes, or until top is lightly browned.

GARLIC BREAD CRUMBS

1 garlic clove, crushed
3 tablespoons olive oil

1 cup coarse crumbs from day-old Italian or French bread

Sauté garlic in oil in a small skillet over low heat 1 minute. Stir in bread crumbs. Sauté, stirring, over medium heat until the crumbs are golden, about 5 minutes.

103   ELBOWS WITH CAULIFLOWER, SUN-DRIED TOMATOES, AND GARLIC OIL

Prep: 10 minutes   Cook: 15 minutes   Serves: 4

2 cups elbow macaroni	½ teaspoon crushed dried red
1 medium head cauliflower	pepper (or less to taste)
(about 1½ pounds),	1 tablespoon chopped sun-
trimmed and broken into	dried tomatoes packed in
florets (about 4 cups)	oil, or 1 tablespoon
¼ cup olive oil	tomato paste
1 tablespoon finely chopped	1 tablespoon chopped parsley
garlic	or fresh basil leaves

1. Cook macaroni in plenty of boiling salted water until al dente, or firm to the bite, about 12 minutes. Using a ladle, remove ½ cup of the macaroni cooking liquid; reserve. Drain macaroni.

2. Meanwhile, steam cauliflower on a rack set over gently boiling water in a covered saucepan until tender, about 8 minutes.

3. Heat oil in a small skillet; add garlic. Sauté over low heat until garlic is softened but not brown, about 5 minutes. Add red pepper; sauté 30 seconds. Stir in sun-dried tomatoes or tomato paste to blend. Remove from heat.

4. In a large bowl, stir the macaroni and resrved ½ cup macaroni cooking liquid together. Add the cauliflower and garlic oil mixture; sprinkle with parsley. Serve at once in wide-rimmed shallow soup bowls.

104   ELBOWS WITH TUNA, RED PEPPER, AND CREAM SAUCE

Prep: 10 minutes   Cook: 15 minutes   Serves: 4

2 cups elbow macaroni	½ cup heavy cream
1 jar (7 ounces) roasted red	1 can (6½ ounces) Italian-style
peppers, rinsed well and	tuna in oil, drained
drained	1 tablespoon chopped, pitted
¼ cup olive oil	brine-cured black olives
⅓ cup chopped onion	1 tablespoon chopped Italian
2 teaspoons minced garlic	flat-leaf parsley

1. Cook macaroni in plenty of boiling salted water until al dente, or firm to the bite, about 12 minutes; drain.

2. Meanwhile, purée the roasted red peppers in a food processor until smooth. Heat the oil in a wide saucepan; sauté the onion until tender but not browned, about 5 minutes; add the garlic; sauté 2 minutes. Add the red pepper purée and the heavy cream; heat to a simmer over low heat. Simmer, stirring, until slightly thickened, about 5 minutes. Stir in the tuna; heat through.

3. Toss the cooked macaroni with half the sauce; spoon onto a platter and spoon remaining sauce down the center. Sprinkle with the olives and parsley.

---

105   PASTITSIO
Prep: 30 minutes   Bake: 50 minutes   Serves: 8

This is a classic Greek pasta dish. It makes a good-size pan and is rich and special enough to serve to a fairly large group of people. Like lasagne, it can be prepared ahead and baked just before serving, which is another reason it works so well as a party dish.

Meat Sauce

4 tablespoons butter	1 teaspoon salt
2 cups chopped onion	1 bay leaf
1 pound lean ground beef	½ teaspoon dried oregano
1 pound lean ground lamb	½ teaspoon ground cinnamon
2 garlic cloves, crushed	¼ cup chopped Italian flat-leaf
2 cups tomato sauce	parsley

Béchamel Sauce

4 tablespoons butter	⅛ teaspoon salt, or to taste
¼ cup all-purpose flour	⅛ teaspoon coarsely ground
3 cups milk	black pepper
6 eggs	Pinch of nutmeg

1 pound elbow macaroni	1 cup grated Romano cheese

1. To make meat sauce, melt butter in a large skillet; add onion; sauté until golden. Add beef and lamb; sauté until browned. Add the garlic, tomato sauce, salt, bay leaf, oregano, and cinnamon; heat to simmering. Cover and cook over low heat, stirring occasionally, 30 minutes. Stir in the parsley.

2. While meat sauce is cooking, prepare the béchamel sauce. Melt the butter in a saucepan; gradually stir in the flour until a smooth paste forms. Sauté, stirring constantly, over low heat 3 minutes. Gradually stir in the milk; whisk over medium heat until sauce is thickened and smooth and comes to a boil. Beat the eggs thoroughly in a large bowl; gradually add the hot sauce to the eggs, whisking thoroughly. Add the salt, black pepper, and nutmeg.

3. Cook the elbow macaroni in plenty of boiling salted water until slightly undercooked, about 10 minutes; drain.

4. Heat oven to 350°F. Select a 3-quart or 14 x 10-inch baking dish. Generously butter dish. Add half the cooked macaroni. Sprinkle with half the cheese. Top with all of the meat sauce. Spoon remaining macaroni over sauce. Pour béchamel sauce over top and sprinkle with remaining cheese.

5. Bake until custard is set and top is browned and bubbly, about 50 minutes. Let stand about 15 minutes bfore cutting into squares and serving.

106 THREE-HERB PESTO WITH ELBOWS AND CHERRY TOMATOES

Prep: 15 minutes   Cook: 12 minutes   Serves: 6

This elbow dish is especially pretty if very small red and yellow cherry tomatoes are in season. It is served hot, but also makes a terrific room-temperature salad.

⅔ cup packed Italian flat-leaf parsley with tender stems
⅔ cup packed dill sprigs with tender stems
⅔ cup packed basil leaves with tender stems
1 cup coarsely chopped walnuts
¼ cup sliced trimmed scallions
2 tablespoons fresh lemon juice
2 garlic cloves, cut into pieces
½ teaspoon salt, or to taste
⅔ cup olive oil
3 tablespoons grated Parmesan cheese
3 cups elbow macaroni
1 pint small cherry tomatoes, stems removed (use half red and half yellow, if available)

1. Coarsely chop the parsley, dill, basil, ½ cup of the walnuts, scallions, lemon juice, garlic, and salt in the bowl of a food processor. With motor running, add the oil in a slow steady stream through the feed tube. Add the Parmesan cheese. Transfer to a large serving bowl.

2. Cook the elbows in plenty of boiling salted water until al dente, or firm to the bite, about 12 minutes. With a ladle, carefully remove ½ cup of the macaroni cooking liquid; add to pesto. Drain macaroni. Add immediately to pesto. Stir to coat. Stir in the remaining ½ cup walnuts and the cherry tomatoes. Serve while still hot or at room temperature.

107 ELBOWS WITH EGGPLANT AND GROUND BEEF SAUCE

Prep: 15 minutes   Drain: 1 hour   Cook: 20 minutes   Serves: 6

1 firm eggplant, about 1 pound, pared and cut into ½-inch cubes
2 tablespoons salt
½ pound lean ground beef
¼ cup olive oil
½ cup chopped onion
2 garlic cloves, crushed
½ teaspoon salt
¼ teaspoon coarsely ground black pepper
½ teaspoon dried oregano
1 can (14 ounces) Italian plum tomatoes, with juices
3 cups elbow macaroni
¼ cup grated Parmesan cheese
2 tablespoons chopped Italian flat-leaf parsley

1. Toss eggplant and salt in a large colander. Set over a shallow bowl and place a saucer or other small dish on the eggplant to weight it down. Let stand 1 hour. Rinse eggplant under running water; drain and squeeze out water with hands or press with the back of a large spoon. Transfer to a clean kitchen towel and wrap and twist to extract as much water as possible; set aside.

2. In a 10-inch nonstick skillet, cook beef, crumbling with the side of a spoon, until browned, about 5 minutes. Drain in a sieve. Wipe out skillet. Heat the olive oil in the skillet over medium heat. When hot enough to sizzle one piece of eggplant, add all the eggplant and fry over medium-high heat, stirring often and turning pieces, until lightly browned, about 8 minutes. Stir in the onion; sauté over medium-high heat until edges begin to brown, about 5 minutes. Stir in the garlic; sauté 1 minute. Add the browned beef; season with salt, pepper, and oregano. Stir in the tomatoes; heat to boiling. Cook over low heat 15 minutes.

3. Meanwhile, cook the elbows in plenty of boiling salted water until al dente, or firm to the bite, about 12 minutes; drain. Toss with the hot sauce. Add 2 tablespoons of the cheese. Transfer to a serving platter; sprinkle with remaining cheese and the parsley.

---

108 ELBOW FRITTATA WITH SAUSAGE, BROCCOLI, AND MOZZARELLA

Prep: 20 minutes   Cook: 25 minutes   Serves: 6

2 cups broccoli florets and stems (cut stems into ¼-inch slices)	1 garlic clove, crushed
	6 eggs, beaten
1½ cups elbow macaroni	1 cup shredded mozzarella cheese (about 6 ounces)
8 ounces Italian sausage, removed from casing and crumbled	1 cup half-and-half
	2 tablespoons grated Romano cheese
¼ cup chopped onion	

1. Steam the broccoli on a rack set over boiling water in a covered saucepan until tender, about 8 minutes.

2. Cook macaroni in plenty of boiling salted water until al dente, or firm to the bite, about 12 minutes; drain.

3. Meanwhile, brown the sausage in a 10-inch nonstick skillet, about 8 minutes; drain off all but about 1 teaspoon of the fat. Add the onion; sauté over low heat until tender, about 5 minutes. Stir in the garlic; sauté 1 minute.

4. Stir the cooked macaroni and the broccoli into the skillet with the sausage mixture until blended. Heat over medium heat until sausage is sizzling. Stir the eggs, mozzarella, half-and-half, and grated cheese together. Pour the egg mixture evenly over the macaroni mixture; stir gently to blend.

5. Cook, covered, over medium to medium-low heat until the frittata is set in the center and the underside is nicely browned, 20 to 25 minutes. To serve, loosen edges of frittata from skillet with a small spatula. Place a large round platter over the skillet. Protect hands with mitts and carefully invert the skillet over the platter. Cut frittata into wedges.

109 ELBOWS WITH SAUSAGE AND MUSHROOMS, CARBONARA STYLE

Prep: 10 minutes   Cook: 20 minutes   Serves: 4

8 ounces sweet Italian sausage, removed from casing and crumbled
2 tablespoons olive oil
½ cup chopped onion
½ cup chopped red or green bell pepper
2 cups diced (½ inch) trimmed mushrooms (about 6 ounces)

2 garlic cloves, crushed
½ teaspoon salt
¼ teaspoon coarsely ground black pepper
3 eggs
¼ cup grated Romano cheese
2 cups elbow macaroni
2 tablespoons chopped Italian flat-leaf parsley

1. Brown sausage in a medium skillet, about 8 minutes; transfer to a sieve to drain off the fat; reserve sausage.

2. Add olive oil to the skillet; heat over medium heat. Sauté the onion, red or green pepper, and mushrooms in the oil, stirring frequently until vegetables are tender and lightly browned. Add the garlic; sauté 1 minute. Add the sausage; season with salt and pepper. Keep warm over low heat.

3. Beat the eggs and the cheese in a large serving bowl; set aside.

4. Cook the elbows in plenty of boiling salted water until al dente, or firm to the bite, about 12 minutes. Drain.

5. Add the hot elbows, the sausage mixture, and the parsley to the beaten eggs. Stir slowly until blended and creamy. Serve with extra cheese to sprinkle on each serving.

110 ELBOWS WITH TOMATO-MEAT SAUCE AND FOUR CHEESES

Prep: 10 minutes   Cook: 12 minutes   Serves: 4

2 cups elbow macaroni
1 container (15 ounces) ricotta cheese
1 cup Tomato Sauce with Ground Beef (page 154) or store-bought sauce
Pinch of ground cloves

1 cup shredded mozzarella cheese (about 6 ounces)
¼ cup grated Parmesan cheese
2 tablespoons grated Romano cheese
2 tablespoons chopped Italian flat-leaf parsley

1. Cook elbows in plenty of boiling salted water until al dente, or firm to the bite, about 12 minutes. Drain.

2. Meanwhile, heat the ricotta in a wide saucepan over low heat; stir in the tomato-meat sauce and cloves. Heat through, stirring over low heat.

3. In a large bowl, stir the drained elbows, warm ricotta mixture, mozzarella, Parmesan, Romano, and parsley together. Serve at once with additional grated cheese, if desired.

111   ELBOWS WITH FOUR CHEESES
Prep: 15 minutes   Cook: 15 minutes   Serves: 4

4 tablespoons butter
1 garlic clove, crushed
1 container (15 ounces) ricotta cheese
¼ cup grated Parmesan cheese
2 tablespoons grated Romano cheese
2 tablespoons chopped fresh Italian flat-leaf parsley

2 tablespoons chopped fresh basil
¼ teaspoon ground nutmeg
Pinch of ground cloves
2 cups elbows
1 cup shredded mozzarella cheese (about 4 ounces)

1. Heat butter in a medium skillet; add garlic; sauté 1 minute. Stir in ricotta, Parmesan, Romano, parsley, basil, nutmeg, and cloves. Cook, stirring over low heat, until heated through. Let stand on low heat to keep warm.

2. Meanwhile, cook the elbows in plenty of boiling salted water until al dente, or firm to the bite, about 12 minutes. Drain.

3. In a large serving bowl, fold the elbows with the ricotta mixture and the mozzarella until blended.

112   ELBOWS WITH CHICK-PEAS AND ESCAROLE
Prep: 10 minutes   Cook: 30 minutes   Serves: 4

8 ounces escarole, trimmed and cut into 1-inch crosswise pieces
1 cup water
6 tablespoons olive oil
1 tablespoon finely chopped garlic
1 tablespoon tomato paste

1 can (19 ounces) chick-peas, rinsed and drained
½ teaspoon salt
¼ teaspoon coarsely ground black pepper
2 cups elbow macaroni
Grated Romano or Parmesan cheese

1. Combine escarole and water in a saucepan. Cook, covered, over low heat until escarole is tender, about 20 minutes. Do not drain; set aside.

2. In a 10-inch skillet, heat the oil; stir in garlic; sauté over low heat until soft and fragrant without browning, about 5 minutes. Stir in the tomato paste until blended. Add the chick-peas; stir to coat with oil. Mash about one quarter of the chick-peas with the back of a spatula. Add salt and pepper. Remove from heat.

3. Cook the macaroni in plenty of boiling salted water until al dente, or firm to the bite, about 12 minutes. Drain. Briefly reheat the escarole mixture. Combine with the elbows. Serve with plenty of grated cheese sprinkled on the top.

113 EGGPLANT, TOMATO, AND ELBOW CASSEROLE

Prep: 30 minutes   Bake: 30 minutes   Serves: 4

1 eggplant (1¼ pounds)
2 tablespoons olive oil
1 egg, beaten
1 pound ground beef
½ cup chopped onion
1 garlic clove, minced
   Salt
   Coarsely ground black
     pepper

¼ teaspoon ground cinnamon
1 cup elbow macaroni
1 can (8 ounces) tomato sauce
¼ cup grated Parmesan cheese
2 tomatoes, sliced thin
¼ teaspoon dried oregano
1 cup shredded mozzarella
   cheese (4 ounces)

1. Pierce the flesh of the eggplant with a fork. Bake at 400°F until very soft, about 30 minutes. When cool enough to handle, peel off the skin. Mash the flesh in a bowl. Stir in olive oil and egg; set aside.

2. Meanwhile, brown the beef in a skillet; stir in onion and garlic; sauté until tender, about 5 minutes. Season with ½ teaspoon salt, ⅛ teaspoon black pepper, and cinnamon.

3. Cook elbows in plenty of boiling salted water until slightly undercooked, about 10 minutes; drain.

4. Lightly butter a 2-quart casserole dish. Fold the eggplant, ground beef, and elbows together; add the tomato sauce and Parmesan. Spoon the mixture into the casserole. Top with an overlapping layer of sliced tomatoes. Sprinkle with oregano and the mozzarella.

5. Bake in a preheated 350°F oven until browned and bubbly, about 25 minutes.

114 ELBOWS WITH BUTTER, PARMESAN, AND PEAS

Prep: 5 minutes   Cook: 15 minutes   Serves: 4

2 cups elbow macaroni
1 package (10 ounces) frozen
     peas

6 tablespoons butter
1 garlic clove, crushed
½ cup grated Parmesan cheese

1. Cook elbows in plenty of boiling salted water 8 minutes; add the peas. Cook until elbows are al dente, or firm to the bite, and peas are tender, about 5 minutes. Ladle out ½ cup of the macaroni cooking liquid; reserve. Drain macaroni.

2. Meanwhile, melt the butter in a medium skillet; stir in the garlic and sauté over low heat until fragrant, about 2 minutes; do not brown.

3. Combine the elbows and peas, the reserved ½ cup macaroni cooking liquid, the butter, and the Parmesan cheese. Serve in shallow wide-rimmed soup bowls.

115 ELBOWS WITH SCALLION AND HERB BUTTER

Prep: 10 minutes   Cook: 15 minutes   Serves: 4

2 cups elbow macaroni
4 tablespoons butter
1 garlic clove, crushed
Pinch of dried oregano

Pinch of dried tarragon
¼ cup thinly sliced trimmed scallion
1 tablespoon minced parsley

1. Cook pasta in plenty of boiling salted water until al dente, or firm to the bite, about 12 minutes; drain.

2. Meanwhile, melt butter in a small skillet; stir in garlic, oregano, and tarragon; sauté 1 minute. Off heat, stir in the scallion and parsley. Add the cooked pasta; toss and serve.

116 BAKED ELBOWS WITH ZUCCHINI, TOMATO, AND PARMESAN

Prep: 10 minutes   Cook: 15 minutes   Bake: 20 minutes   Serves: 4

2 cups elbow macaroni
2 tablespoons butter
½ cup chopped onion
8 ounces small zucchini, sliced
1 cup cubed (½ inch) fresh ripe tomatoes
½ cup chopped Italian flat-leaf parsley

1 garlic clove, crushed
1 container (15 ounces) whole milk ricotta cheese
½ cup milk
2 tablespoons grated Romano cheese
2 tablespoons grated Parmesan cheese

1. Cook the macaroni in plenty of boiling salted water until just slightly undercooked, about 6 minutes; drain.

2. Meanwhile, melt butter in a wide skillet; add onion; sauté 5 minutes. Add zucchini; sauté 5 minutes more. Stir in tomatoes, parsley, and garlic; simmer, uncovered, 5 minutes. Stir in ricotta, milk, Romano cheese, and 1 tablespoon of the Parmesan cheese.

3. Combine the cooked elbows with the sauce. Pour into a buttered 1½-quart shallow baking dish; sprinkle the top with the remaining 1 tablespoon Parmesan cheese.

4. Bake in a preheated 350°F oven until top is lightly browned, about 20 minutes.

Chapter 7

Lasagne

Scholars speculate that *lasagna*, a dish known in ancient Rome, was the origin of lasagne. Today, everyone agrees that lasagne is a favorite way to cook ahead, feed a crowd, or create leftovers. Convenient and versatile, lasagne is one dish that improves when allowed to stand overnight, which makes it a natural for entertaining or cooking ahead. In this baker's dozen assortment of recipes there is something for everyone from an elegant Lasagne with Five Cheeses or the subtly sophisticated Spinach and Porcini Lasagne to the whimsical September Lasagne or typical Everyone's Favorite Lasagne. If the lasagne is prepared a day ahead: cool to room temperature, wrap with plastic, and refrigerate. To reheat: remove the plastic, cover with foil, and bake in a 325°F oven 25 minutes. Uncover and bake at 350°F until top is browned and bubbly and lasagne is cooked through.

117 PESTO LASAGNE

Prep: 30 minutes   Bake: 50 minutes   Serves: 6–8

Folding pesto into ricotta and layering in between lasagne noodles is another wonderful use for this rich sauce.

2 cups Quick Chunky Tomato Sauce (page 142) or Fresh Tomato Sauce with Garden Herbs (page 149)

Pesto

½ cup pine nuts
1 garlic clove
1 cup packed basil leaves

Salt
⅓ cup olive oil
½ cup grated Parmesan cheese

12 spinach or plain lasagne noodles
2 containers (15 ounces each) ricotta cheese
2 eggs

¼ teaspoon coarsely ground black pepper
8 ounces Italian Fontina or mozzarella cheese, shredded (about 2 cups)

1. Make the tomato sauce of your choice; set aside.

2. To prepare pesto, finely chop the pine nuts and garlic in a food processor; add the basil and salt; finely chop. With the motor running, add the oil in a thin drizzle through the feed tube until incorporated. Scrape the pesto into a small bowl; fold in the cheese; set aside. (The pesto can be made 1 or 2 days ahead, covered tightly, and refrigerated until ready to use.)

3. Cook lasagne noodles in plenty of boiling salted water until al dente, or firm to the bite, about 12 minutes; drain. Let noodles sit in a bowl of cool water until ready to use.

4. In a bowl, beat ricotta, eggs, and pepper until blended; fold in the pesto until blended.

5. Heat oven to 350°F. Select a 9 x 13-inch shallow baking pan. Lift the noodles from the water individually and blot dry on paper toweling. Arrange 4 noodles in a slightly overlapping layer in the bottom of the dish.

6. Spread half of the ricotta mixture over the noodles. Sprinkle with ½ cup of the shredded Fontina cheese. Arrange a second layer of 4 slightly overlapping lasagne noodles on top of the ricotta mixture. Spread the remaining ricotta mixture on top; sprinkle with ½ cup of the Fontina. Arrange a top layer of 4 slightly overlapping lasagne noodles. Spoon the tomato sauce over the top and sprinkle with the remaining 1 cup shredded Fontina cheese.

7. Bake until top is browned and bubbly, about 50 minutes. Let stand at least 15 minutes before serving.

118   SEPTEMBER LASAGNE

Prep: 30 minutes   Drain: 1 hour   Bake: 50 minutes   Serves: 8

This lasagne uses all the vegetables at their best in September: tomatoes, corn, zucchini, eggplant, and peppers. It is rich and flavorful, a perfect vegetarian dish. The eggplant and the zucchini are both salted and weighted for at least 1 hour to extract as much moisture as possible before browning in olive oil.

1 **medium eggplant, about 1 pound, pared and cut into ¼-inch lengthwise slices**
1 **pound zucchini, trimmed and cut into ¼-inch lengthwise slices**
   Salt
12 **spinach and/or plain lasagne noodles**
1 **container (15 ounces) ricotta cheese**
½ **cup chopped fresh basil**
6 **tablespoons grated Parmesan cheese**
   Coarsely ground black pepper
6 **tablespoons olive oil, or as needed**
1 **large green bell pepper, chopped**

1 **large red bell pepper, chopped**
1 **large onion, halved lengthwise and cut into vertical slices**
2 **garlic cloves, chopped**
2 **ears corn, husks removed and kernels cut from the cobs (about 1 cup)**
¼ **cup chopped pitted brine-cured black olives, such as Gaeta or Kalamata**
2 **cups chopped fresh tomatoes with their juices (about 1 pound)**
1 **pound mozzarella cheese, shredded (about 4 cups)**

1. On a large tray, arrange a double layer of paper towels; top with a single layer of eggplant and zucchini; sprinkle with ½ teaspoon salt. Lay a double layer of paper towels over the vegetables and arrange a second layer of eggplant and zucchini slices; sprinkle with ½ teaspoon salt. Continue layering until all the vegetables have been salted. Top with a double layer of paper towels; place a tray on top and weight with a 5-pound bag of sugar or other heavy object. Let stand at least 1 hour.

2. Meanwhile, cook the lasagne noodles in plenty of boiling salted water until al dente, or firm to the bite; drain. Place noodles in a large bowl of cool water until ready to use.

3. Stir the ricotta, ¼ cup of the basil, 2 tablespoons of the Parmesan, and ⅛ teaspoon black pepper until blended; set aside.

4. Heat 2 tablespoons of the oil in a large skillet. Add the red and green bell peppers, onion, and garlic. Cook, covered, over low heat, stirring occasionally, until the peppers are tender, about 10 minutes. Uncover; sauté over medium-high heat until edges begin to brown, about 5 minutes. Stir in the corn, black olives, and the remaining ¼ cup basil. Season with salt and pepper; set aside.

5. When eggplant and zucchini are ready, wrap tightly in the paper towels and squeeze to extract as much moisture as possible. Heat 2 tablespoons of the oil in a large skillet over medium-high heat and fry as many vegetables as will comfortably fit in the skillet at one time, turning to brown evenly. Transfer to a tray lined with paper towels to absorb excess oil. Add additional oil to dry skillet, 2 tablespoons at a time, and heat before adding the zucchini and eggplant. Continue frying until all vegetables are browned.

6. Heat oven to 350°F. Select a 9 x 13-inch shallow baking dish. Spoon ½ cup of the chopped tomatoes onto the bottom of the dish. Lift the lasagne noodles individually from the water and blot dry on paper toweling. Arrange a single layer of 4 overlapping noodles on the bottom of the dish.

7. Top with a single layer of half the zucchini and the eggplant. Top with half the pepper and corn mixture. Sprinkle with 1 cup of the mozzarella and 2 tablespoons of the grated Parmesan.

8. Arrange a second layer of 4 lasagne noodles in a single overlapping layer. Spread with the ricotta mixture. Arrange a single layer of the remaining zucchini and eggplant slices; sprinkle with 1 cup of the mozzarella.

9. Arrange a third layer of the remaining 4 lasagne noodles in a single overlapping layer. Top with the remaining pepper mixture and the 1½ cups chopped tomato. Sprinkle with the remaining 2 cups mozzarella and 2 tablespoons grated Parmesan.

10. Bake until cheese is bubbly and edges browned, about 50 minutes. Let stand 15 minutes before cutting and serving.

Pasta for a crowd

Pasta is economical, popular, easy on the cook, and fun to serve—great for entertaining. We suggest trying the following recipes next time you have to feed a crowd. You will want to double some of the recipes.

119   VEGETARIAN LASAGNE
Prep: 35 minutes   Bake: 1 hour   Serves: 8–10

12 whole lasagne noodles
(about 12 ounces)
1 small bunch broccoli (about
12 ounces) stalks
trimmed, washed
4 tablespoons olive oil
½ cup chopped onion
2 teaspoons chopped garlic
2 containers (15 ounces each)
ricotta cheese
2 eggs, beaten
4 tablespoons grated
Parmesan cheese
4 tablespoons chopped Italian
flat-leaf parsley
Freshly ground black
pepper
Pinch of nutmeg

2 large carrots, trimmed,
peeled, and coarsely
chopped
2 cans (15 ounces each) whole
tomatoes with juices, cut
up with scissors
1 tablespoon chopped fresh
basil leaves
Salt
8 ounces large mushrooms,
wiped clean and coarsely
chopped
1 green or red bell pepper,
coarsely chopped
1 tablespoon fresh lemon
juice
2 cups shredded mozzarella
cheese (8 ounces)

1. Cook lasagne noodles in plenty of boiling salted water until al dente, or firm to the bite, about 12 minutes; drain. Let noodles sit in bowl of cool water until ready to use.

2. Steam the broccoli in a rack set over 1 inch simmering water, covered, until crisp-tender, about 5 minutes. Cool; coarsely chop; set aside.

3. Heat 2 tablespoons of the oil in a medium skillet; add onion; sauté until tender. Add 1 teaspoon of the garlic; sauté 1 minute.

4. In a bowl, combine the chopped broccoli, half the sautéed onion, the ricotta, eggs, 2 tablespoons of the Parmesan cheese, 2 tablespoons of the parsley, and a pinch each of black pepper and nutmeg; set aside.

5. Add the chopped carrots to the onion remaining in the skillet; sauté, stirring, over medum heat until crisp-tender; stir in the tomatoes. Cook, stirring, until boiling gently. Boil, stirring, until sauce is thickened, about 10 minutes; stir in 1 tablespoon of the remaining parsley, the basil, and salt and pepper to taste. Transfer to a small bowl. Wipe out skillet.

6. Heat the remaining 2 tablespoons oil in the skillet; add the mushrooms. Sauté, stirring, over medium heat, until liquid has evaporated, about 5 minutes. Add green or red bell pepper; sauté until crisp-tender, about 3 minutes. Stir in the remaining 1 teaspoon garlic; sauté 1 minute. Stir in the remaining 1 tablespoon parsley and the lemon juice; season with salt and pepper.

7. Heat oven to 350°F. Select a shallow 4-quart baking dish approximately 10 x 14 inches. Spoon about ½ cup of the tomato sauce over the bottom of the dish. Lift the lasagne noodles from the water individually and blot dry on paper toweling. Arrange a single layer of noodles in dish.

8. Spread the mushroom layer over the noodles; sprinkle with 1 cup of the mozzarella and 1 tablespoon of the remaining Parmesan. Top with a second layer of noodles. Spread with the ricotta and broccoli mixture; sprinkle with ½ cup of the mozzarella. Top with a third layer of noodles. Spread with the tomato sauce. Sprinkle with the remaining 1 tablespoon Parmesan and the remaining 1 cup shredded mozzarella.

9. Bake until cheese is melted and bubbly, about 40 minutes. Let stand at least 15 minutes before serving.

---

120   SEAFOOD LASAGNE
Prep: 45 minutes   Bake: 50 minutes   Serves: 6–8

This lasagne is much lighter and a little less rich than the typical lasagne. To allow the delicate seafood flavors and the flavor of the fresh basil to predominate, a mildly flavored mozzarella is the only cheese used.

2 **tablespoons olive oil**
1 **medium leek, white part only, rinsed well and finely chopped**
1 **can (28 ounces) Italian-style plum tomatoes with juices**
1 **tablespoon tomato paste**
   Salt and pepper
8 **ounces shrimp, shelled, deveined, and coarsely chopped**
8 **ounces medium-size sea scallops, sliced thin**

1 **pound boneless and skinless fish fillet (haddock, sole, or snapper), cut into 1-inch pieces**
12 **fresh basil leaves, torn in half**
15 **spinach and/or plain lasagne noodles**
1½ **pounds mozzarella cheese, coarsely shredded or sliced thin**

1. Heat the oil in a medium skillet; add the leek; sauté until tender, about 10 minutes. Stir in the tomatoes and paste. Cook, stirring and breaking tomatoes with the side of a spoon, until mixture boils. Simmer, uncovered, until the sauce is slightly thickened, about 20 minutes. Season with salt and pepper.

2. Stir in the shrimp, scallops, and fish fillet; add a few pieces of the torn basil leaves. Cover and cook over low heat 10 minutes. Do not boil or overcook.

3. Meanwhile, cook the lasagne noodles in plenty of boiling salted water until al dente, or firm to the bite, about 12 minutes; drain. Place noodles in a large bowl of cool water until ready to use.

4. Heat oven to 350°F. Select a 9 x 13-inch shallow baking dish. Spoon ½ cup of the sauce into the bottom of the dish. Lift the lasagne noodles individually from the water and blot dry on paper toweling. Arrange a single layer of 5 overlapping noodles on the bottom of the dish.

5. Spoon a third of the sauce and seafood over the noodles. Sprinkle with a third of the basil and top with a third of the mozzarella. Repeat with the next two layers.

6. Bake until the cheese is bubbly and edges browned, about 50 minutes. Let stand 15 minutes before cutting and serving.

121   CHICKEN AND BROCCOLI LASAGNE IN PARMESAN CUSTARD

Prep: 40 minutes   Bake: 50 minutes   Serves: 6–8

Parmesan Custard

- 4 tablespoons butter
- 4 tablespoons all-purpose flour
- 2 cups milk
- 1 cup chicken broth or stock

- 3 whole eggs
- ½ cup grated Parmesan cheese
- ½ teaspoon salt, or to taste
- Pinch of ground red pepper and ground nutmeg

- 15 plain lasagne noodles
- 2 tablespoons butter
- 1 cup chopped onion
- 1 garlic clove, minced
- 2 whole skinless and boneless chicken breasts (about 1¼ pounds), cut into ¼-inch strips
- 1 bag (1¼ pounds) frozen broccoli cuts or chopped broccoli

- ½ cup shredded carrot
- ¼ cup chopped Italian flat-leaf parsley
- Salt and pepper to taste
- 1 pound mozzarella cheese, cut into thin slices
- ¼ cup grated Parmesan cheese

1. To make the Parmesan custard, melt the butter in a medium saucepan; stir in the flour, over low heat, until smooth and golden, about 3 minutes. Stir in the milk; whisk over medium heat until smooth, about 5 minutes. Stir in chicken broth. Cook, whisking, until mixture boils and is thick and smooth, about 10 minutes. Beat the eggs in a separate bowl; gradually whisk sauce into the eggs; return to saucepan and let stand, off heat. Stir in cheese; season with salt, red pepper, and nutmeg.

2. Cook the lasagne noodles in plenty of boiling salted water until al dente, or firm to the bite, about 12 minutes; drain. Let noodles sit in a bowl of cool water until ready to use.

3. Melt the 2 tablespoons of butter in a large skillet. When foam subsides, add the onion; sauté until golden, about 5 minutes. Stir in the garlic; sauté 1 minute. Add the chicken strips and sauté over medium heat until cooked through, turning as needed. Stir in the broccoli and carrot; cook, covered, over medium heat just until vegetables are tender, about 5 minutes. Add parsley and season with salt and pepper.

4. Heat oven to 350°F. Select a 9 x 13-inch shallow baking dish. Spoon about ½ cup of the Parmesan custard into the bottom of the dish. Lift the noodles from the water individually and blot dry on paper toweling. Arrange 5 noodles, slightly overlapping, on the bottom of the dish.

5. Arrange half the chicken and broccoli mixture over the noodles. Drizzle with ½ cup of the Parmesan custard. Add a layer of one third of the mozzarella slices. Sprinkle with 1 tablespoon of the Parmesan. Arrange a second layer of 5 slightly overlapping lasagne noodles on top. Add the remaining chicken and broccoli mixture, half of the remaining mozzarella, 1 tablespoon of the grated Parmesan, and ½ cup of the Parmesan custard.

6. Top with the remaining 5 lasagne noodles in a slightly overlapping layer. Arrange the remaining mozzarella slices on top and carefully pour the remaining Parmesan custard over the top, pulling away the noodles along the sides of the dish so that the sauce can seep down. Sprinkle with the remaining grated Parmesan.

7. Bake until the top is browned and bubbly, about 50 minutes. Let stand at least 15 minutes before serving.

---

122   EVERYONE'S FAVORITE LASAGNE
Prep: 2 hours 30 minutes   Bake: 50 minutes   Serves: 6–8

¼ cup olive oil	¼ teaspoon pepper
1 pound lean ground beef	15 plain or spinach lasagne
½ cup chopped onion	noodles
2 garlic cloves, crushed	1 container (15 ounces) ricotta
2 cans (28 ounces each) Italian-style plum tomatoes, drained with juices	cheese
	½ cup grated Parmesan cheese
	¼ cup chopped Italian flat-leaf parsley
1 can (8 ounces) tomato sauce	1 egg, beaten
1 can (6 ounces) tomato paste	1 pound mozzarella cheese,
1 teaspoon dried basil	sliced thin or shredded
½ teaspoon oregano	
½ teaspoon salt, or to taste	

1. Heat the olive oil in a large wide saucepan; add the ground beef, onion, and garlic. Sauté, stirring, over medium heat until the meat is browned, about 10 minutes. Add the tomatoes, tomato sauce and paste, basil, and oregano. Cook, stirring occasionally, over medium-low heat until sauce is cooked down and thickened, 1½ to 2 hours. (There should be about 4 cups sauce.) Season with salt and pepper.

2. Cook the lasagne noodles in plenty of boiling salted water until al dente, or firm to the bite, about 12 minutes; drain. Let noodles sit in a bowl of cool water until ready to use.

3. Beat the ricotta, Parmesan cheese, parsley, and egg together; set aside.

4. Heat the oven to 350°F. Select a 9 x 13-inch shallow baking dish. Add about ½ cup of the tomato sauce to the bottom of the dish. Lift the noodles from the water individually and blot dry on paper toweling. Arrange a slightly overlapping layer of 5 noodles on the bottom of the dish.

5. Dot the noodles with half the ricotta mixture; add about a third of the remaining sauce and arrange a layer of a third of the mozzarella slices on top. Arrange a second layer of 5 slightly overlapping lasagne noodles. Dot with the remaining ricotta, half of the remaining tomato sauce, and half of the remaining mozzarella.

6. Top with the 5 remaining lasagne noodles in a slightly overlapping layer; add the remaining sauce and a layer of the remaining mozzarella.

7. Bake until cheese is melted and mixture is bubbly, about 50 minutes. Let stand at least 15 minutes before serving.

123 LASAGNE WITH SAUSAGE AND THREE-COLOR PEPPERS

Prep: 30 minutes   Bake: 50 minutes   Serves: 6–8

If pretty yellow bell peppers are not available, substitute an additional red and green bell pepper. Make your own favorite tomato sauce or choose a good quality prepared all-tomato or tomato-and-meat sauce.

2 cups Tomato Sauce, Bolognese Style (page 160), Quick Chunky Tomato Sauce (page 142), or a good quality store-bought sauce

1 pound sweet Italian sausage, removed from casings and crumbled

8 ounces hot Italian sausage, removed from casings and crumbled

1 large onion, halved lengthwise, and cut into thin vertical slices

2 red bell peppers, cut into ½-inch strips

2 green bell peppers, cut into ½-inch strips

2 yellow bell peppers, cut into ½-inch strips

3 garlic cloves, cut into thin slices

¼ cup chopped Italian flat-leaf parsley

½ teaspoon salt

⅛ teaspoon coarsely ground black pepper

12 lasagne noodles

1 pound mozzarella cheese, shredded (4 cups)

3 tablespoons grated Parmesan cheese

1. Make the Bolognese or Quick Chunky Tomato Sauce.

2. Crumble the sausage into a large skillet; cook, covered, over low heat until cooked through, stirring occasionally. Uncover; drain off fat. Over high heat, sauté meat, stirring, until lightly browned, about 3 minutes. Add the onion, peppers, and garlic; cook, covered, over low heat, stirring occasionally, until vegetables are very tender and beginning to brown, about 20 minutes. Stir in parsley and season with salt and pepper. Set aside.

3. Cook lasagne noodles in plenty of boiling salted water until al dente, or firm to the bite, about 12 minutes; drain. Let stand in a large bowl of cool water until ready to use.

4. Heat oven to 350°F. Select a 9 x 13-inch shallow baking dish. Spoon about ½ cup of the tomato sauce on the bottom of the dish. Lift the noodles from the water individually and blot dry with paper toweling. Arrange a single layer of four slightly overlapping noodles. Top with half the sausage mixture; sprinkle with 1 cup of the mozzarella and 1 tablespoon of the Parmesan.

5. Cover the sausage mixture with a single layer of 4 more slightly overlapping lasagne noodles. Top with the remaining sausage mixture, 1 cup of mozzarella, and 1 tablespoon of the Parmesan.

6. Top with the 4 remaining noodles in a single slightly overlapping layer. Top with the remaining 1½ cups tomato sauce, 2 cups mozzarella cheese, and 1 tablespoon Parmesan cheese.

7. Bake until top is browned and bubbly, about 50 minutes. Let stand at least 15 minutes before serving.

Variations:

124 LASAGNE WITH SAUSAGE, MUSHROOMS, AND THREE-COLOR PEPPERS

Add 8 ounces trimmed and sliced mushrooms to the skillet with the peppers, onion, and garlic.

125 BÉCHAMEL-TOPPED LASAGNE WITH SAUSAGE, MUSHROOMS, AND THREE-COLOR PEPPERS

Omit the tomato sauce and prepare 2 cups Béchamel Sauce (page 86). Use Béchamel Sauce in place of tomato sauce.

126   LASAGNE WITH FIVE CHEESES

Prep: 30 minutes   Bake: 50 minutes   Serves: 6–8

The smoked mozzarella adds a haunting flavor to this rich lasagne rendition, but you can use regular whole milk mozzarella instead. This dish is especially pretty when made with pale green spinach lasagne noodles, but they are sometimes hard to find, so regular lasagne noodles can be substituted.

Béchamel Sauce

- 6 tablespoons butter
- 6 tablespoons all-purpose flour
- 2 cups milk

- 1 cup seasoned defatted chicken broth
- 1 teaspoon salt, or to taste
- ¼ teaspoon ground nutmeg

- 12 lasagne noodles, preferably spinach
- 1 container (15 ounces) ricotta cheese
- ¼ cup chopped Italian flat-leaf parsley
- 5 tablespoons grated Parmesan cheese
- ⅛ teaspoon coarsely ground black pepper

- 4 ounces sweet Gorgonzola cheese, crumbled
- 1 cup shredded mozzarella cheese (4 ounces)
- 4 ounces smoked mozzarella cheese, sliced
- 4 ounces Italian Fontina cheese, shredded

1. To make béchamel sauce, melt butter in a medium saucepan; add flour; stir over low heat until smooth and golden, about 3 minutes. Stir in milk; whisk over medium heat until smooth, about 5 minutes; add chicken broth. Cook, whisking, until mixture boils and is thick and smooth, about 10 minutes. Add ½ teaspoon salt, or to taste, and ⅛ teaspoon nutmeg. Let stand, off heat, until ready to use.

2. Cook lasagne noodles in plenty of boiling salted water until al dente, or firm to the bite, about 12 minutes; drain. Let noodles sit in a bowl of cool water until ready to use.

3. Heat oven to 350°F. Select a 9 x 13-inch shallow baking dish. Spoon about ½ cup of the béchamel sauce into the bottom of the dish. Lift the noodles from the water individually and blot dry on paper toweling. Arrange a slightly overlapping layer of 4 noodles on the bottom of the dish.

4. In a bowl, stir the ricotta, parsley, 2 tablespoons of the Parmesan cheese, ½ teaspoon salt, or to taste, the black pepper, and ⅛ teaspoon of the remaining nutmeg until blended. Spread in a layer over the noodles.

5. Arrange 4 more noodles in an overlapping single layer over the ricotta. Sprinkle with the crumbled Gorgonzola and the shredded mozzarella. Top with remaining 4 lasagna noodles arranged in a slightly overlapping single layer. Arrange a single layer of smoked mozzarella slices over the noodles; sprinkle with the shredded Fontina cheese. Pour the remaining béchamel sauce over the top. Sprinkle with the remaining 3 tablespoons of Parmesan.

6. Bake until top is browned and bubbly, about 50 minutes. Let stand at least 15 minutes before serving.

Variation:

127 LASAGNE WITH FIVE CHEESES AND PROSCIUTTO

Cut 4 ounces prosciutto, rolled tightly, into thin crosswise slices. Sprinkle evenly over the second layer of cheese (Gorgonzola and mozzarella). Then proceed with recipe.

128 RICOTTA, TOMATO, AND SPINACH NOODLE LASAGNE

Prep: 30 minutes   Bake: 45 minutes   Serves: 6–8

This delicate lasagne is a small masterpiece. Use fresh plum tomatoes to make the sauce if they are in season; otherwise canned will do. Fresh basil is a *must*.

3 tablespoons olive oil
1 garlic clove, bruised
3 pounds ripe plum tomatoes, peeled and seeded, or 1 can (28 ounces) Italian-style plum tomatoes with juices
  Salt and pepper
16 spinach lasagne noodles

1 container (15 ounces) ricotta cheese
¼ cup grated Parmesan cheese
1 egg, beaten
  Pinch of ground nutmeg
½ cup loosely packed torn fresh basil leaves
1 pound mozzarella cheese, coarsely shredded

1. Heat the oil in a medium skillet; add the garlic and sauté until golden; remove and discard garlic. Purée the tomatoes through a food mill into the skillet; heat to simmering. Cook, stirring, over medium heat until sauce is thickened and reduced, about 20 minutes. Season with salt and pepper to taste.

2. Cook the lasagne noodles in plenty of boiling salted water until al dente, or firm to the bite, about 12 minutes; drain. Let noodles sit in a bowl of cool water until ready to use.

3. Combine the ricotta, Parmesan, egg, and nutmeg; whisk to blend.

4. Heat oven to 350°F. Select a 9 x 13-inch shallow baking dish. Spoon just enough of the tomato sauce into the dish to lightly coat the bottom. Lift the lasagne noodles individually from the water and blot dry on paper toweling. Arrange a layer of 4 slightly overlapping lasagne noodles on the bottom of the dish.

5. Spoon one quarter of the tomato sauce over the first layer of noodles; sprinkle with a few basil leaves. Top with a second layer of 4 slightly overlapping noodles. Spread this layer with the ricotta; sprinkle with a few basil leaves. Top with a third layer of 4 slightly overlapping lasagne noodles. Sprinkle evenly with the mozzarella cheese and a few basil leaves. Top with the fourth and last layer of slightly overlapping noodles. Spread the remaining tomato sauce on the top.

6. Bake 45 minutes. Let stand 15 minutes before serving.

129   SPINACH AND PORCINI LASAGNE
Prep: 45 minutes   Soak: 30 minutes   Bake: 50 minutes
Serves: 8–10

2 cups Light Red Sauce (page 174), Quick Chunky Tomato Sauce (page 142), or your favorite tomato sauce recipe

1 ounce dried porcini

Porcini-Béchamel Sauce
3 tablespoons butter
¼ cup all-purpose flour
1 cup milk

Salt
Freshly ground black pepper

1 pound lasagne noodles
2 packages (10 ounces each) frozen chopped spinach, cooked, thawed, drained and squeezed until very dry
2 containers (15 ounces each) ricotta cheese
2 eggs, beaten
8 tablespoons grated Parmesan cheese

½ cup chopped Italian flat-leaf parsley
Nutmeg
2 tablespoons olive oil
1 cup chopped onion
1 tablespoon chopped garlic
1 pound fresh mushrooms, wiped clean, trimmed, sliced
1 pound mozzarella cheese, sliced thin

1. Make the tomato sauce of your choice; set aside.

2. Combine the dried porcini and 1½ cups water in a small saucepan. Heat to boiling; let stand, covered, off heat 30 minutes; drain; reserve the liquid. Rinse the porcini carefully if they feel gritty; drain and pat dry with paper towels. Coarsely chop; there should be about ½ cup; set aside.

3. To make the porcini-béchamel sauce, melt the butter in a small saucepan; stir in the flour and sauté, stirring, 5 minutes. Gradually add the milk; whisk until smooth. Add the porcini liquid (there should be about 1 cup); whisk over low heat until mixture boils and is thick and smooth, about 8 minutes. Season with salt and pepper; set aside.

4. Cook the lasagne noodles in plenty of boiling salted water until al dente, or firm to the bite, about 12 minutes; drain. Let stand in a large bowl of cool water until ready to use.

5. In a bowl, combine the spinach, ricotta, eggs, 3 tablespoons of the Parmesan, ¼ cup of the parsley and nutmeg and pepper to taste; set aside.

6. In a skillet, heat the oil; add the onion and sauté, stirring, until tender but not browned, about 5 minutes. Stir in the garlic; sauté 1 minute. Add half of this mixture to the spinach and ricotta mixture.

7. Add the fresh mushrooms to the onion remaining in the skillet; sauté over medium heat until tender and all the moisture has evaporated, about 10 minutes. Add the reserved chopped porcini, the remaining ¼ cup parsley, 2 tablespoons of the Parmesan, and black pepper to taste.

8. Heat the oven to 350°F. Select a 4-quart shallow baking dish or one approximately 10 x 14 inches. Lift the lasagne noodles from the water individually and blot dry with paper towels. Arrange a single layer of lasagne noodles in the baking dish. Spread with the ricotta and spinach mixture. Top with a third of the mozzarella slices placed at random on top of the ricotta. Top with a second layer of lasagne noodles. Spoon the tomato sauce in a thin layer over the noodles. Top with a third of the mozzarella slices. Spoon the mushroom layer over the noodles; arrange the remaining mozzarella slices, at random, over the mushrooms. Top with the final layer of noodles.

9. Carefully spoon the porcini-béchamel sauce over the top and sprinkle with the remaining Parmesan cheese. Bake in preheated oven until the top is puffed and browned, about 50 minutes. Let stand 15 minutes before serving.

What are dried porcini?

Porcini (a charming diminutive meaning "piglet") is the Italian word for a popular wild mushroom called *boletus edulis*. In France the same mushroom is called *cepe*. As exotic mushrooms become more popular and amateur mycological associations are popping up all over the country, this mushroom is now being popularly referred to as a "bolete." Dried porcini are available loose and in small packages. Anywhere from ½ to 1 ounce is plenty to add a wonderful woodsy, mushroom flavor to a pasta dish or sauce.

Soak dried porcini in very hot water (I usually bring the water and the mushrooms to a simmer over low heat, covered) for 15 to 30 minutes. Drain through a fine sieve lined with a dampened paper towel or double layer of damp cheesecloth; *save* the precious and flavorful liquid. Run your fingers over the porcini to make sure there isn't any grit still clinging to the reconstituted slices. Rinse briefly under cool water if you find any grit. Then chop the porcini and they are ready to use. Don't forget to include the porcini liquid; or freeze it and use later in soups, stews, or sauces.

Chapter 8

From Fettuccine Ribbons to Angel's Hair

At one time every broad flat pasta was simply called *noodle*. Now we have everything from fettuccine, which translates as "small ribbons," to capelli d'angelo, or "angel's hair," the very thin pasta now popular as a first course in trendy restaurants. The Italian language has played an important part in romanticizing pasta with its charming diminutive terms. As Americans become more and more of a culinary transcultural people, the authentic names (and the charming translations) have become the familiar. Fettuccine and capelli d'angelo are often available fresh in the refrigerated section of many supermarkets. The following recipes give fresh and dried measurements and cooking times.

130 FETTUCCINE WITH MUSHROOMS AND TOASTED ALMONDS

Prep: 15 minutes   Cook: 20 minutes   Serves: 4

2 tablespoons coarsely chopped unblanched almonds
4 tablespoons butter
8 ounces mushrooms, trimmed, quartered, and sliced
1 garlic clove, crushed
Salt
2 cups half-and-half
1 teaspoon fresh lemon juice
12 ounces fresh or 8 ounces dried fettuccine
1 tablespoon chopped parsley
Coarsely ground black pepper

1. Heat a large skillet over low heat; add almonds; toast, stirring, until lightly browned and fragrant, about 2 minutes. Scrape into a small dish; reserve.

2. Melt the butter in the skillet over medium heat. When the foam subsides, stir in the mushrooms. Sauté over medium-high heat, stirring, until tender and lightly browned, about 10 minutes. Stir in the garlic; season to taste with salt.

3. Add the half-and-half; heat to boiling. Boil until liquid is reduced by half and sauce is slightly thickened, about 10 minutes. Stir in the lemon juice.

4. Meanwhile, cook the fettuccine in plenty of boiling salted water until al dente, or firm to the bite, 2 minutes for fresh and 5 to 7 minutes for dried; drain.

5. Toss the fettuccine with the mushroom mixture, the parsley, and the almonds. Season with black pepper.

131 SPINACH FETTUCCINE WITH POPPY SEEDS

Prep: 5 minutes   Cook: 10 minutes   Serves: 4

4 tablespoons butter
1 cup packed, trimmed, chiffonade cut (¼-inch strips) fresh spinach leaves
1 garlic clove, crushed
1 tablespoon poppy seeds
12 ounces fresh or 8 ounces dried spinach fettuccine
Grated Parmesan cheese

1. Melt the butter in a medium skillet; stir in the spinach and the garlic. Cook, covered, 5 minutes, or until the spinach is wilted; add the poppy seeds and keep warm.

2. Meanwhile, cook the fettuccine in plenty of boiling salted water until al dente, or firm to the bite, 2 minutes for fresh and 5 to 7 minutes for dried. Drain.

3. Toss with the spinach mixture. Serve with grated cheese.

132 FETTUCCINE WITH SALMON CAVIAR AND ASPARAGUS

Prep: 10 minutes   Cook: 15 minutes   Serves: 4

12 ounces asparagus, trimmed and cut into ¼-inch diagonal slices
4 tablespoons butter
12 ounces fresh or 8 ounces dried fettuccine

½ cup shredded mozzarella cheese
1 tablespoon chopped fresh dill
2 tablespoons salmon caviar
Coarsely ground black pepper

1. Steam the asparagus, covered, on a rack set over 1 inch simmering water, until crisp-tender, about 5 minutes.

2. Melt the butter in a small saucepan; stir in the asparagus; set aside.

3. Meanwhile, cook the fettuccine in plenty of boiling salted water until al dente, or firm to the bite, 2 minutes for fresh and 5 to 7 minutes for dried; drain.

4. Toss the fettuccine with the asparagus, butter, mozzarella, and dill. Sprinkle with caviar and black pepper.

133 FETTUCCINE WITH CHICKEN LIVERS, TOMATO, AND BACON

Prep: 10 minutes   Cook: 20 minutes   Serves: 4

3 slices bacon
2 tablespoons butter
¼ cup chopped onion
4 ounces chicken livers, patted dry and cut into ¼-inch pieces
1 can (14 ounces) Italian-style plum tomatoes, cut up with scissors

½ teaspoon dried sage, or 1 teaspoon chopped fresh sage leaves
½ teaspoon salt, or to taste
Coarsely ground black pepper
12 ounces fresh or 8 ounces dried fettuccine

1. In a medium skillet, cook the bacon until barely crisp, about 5 minutes. Drain on paper towels. Discard all but 2 tablespoons of bacon fat from the skillet. Add the butter; heat until melted; add the onion; sauté over medium heat until golden. Stir in the chicken livers; sauté, stirring, just until cooked. Add the tomatoes and sage; cook, stirring occasionally, until sauce thickens slightly, about 10 minutes. Season with salt; add pepper to taste. Cut bacon into ¼-inch pieces and stir into sauce.

2. Meanwhile, cook the fettuccine in plenty of boiling salted water until al dente, or firm to the bite, 2 minutes for fresh and 5 to 7 minutes for dried; drain.

3. Toss with the sauce and serve at once.

134 FETTUCCINE WITH SHIITAKE AND GARLIC BUTTER

Prep: 10 minutes   Cook: 15 minutes   Serves: 4

If your market has shiitake, a newly popular cultivated mushroom, use them here, although the more common button mushroom can be used in a pinch. Discard the tough and inedible stems of the shiitake.

6 tablespoons butter
8 ounces shiitake, trimmed and sliced into ¼-inch strips
2 garlic cloves, minced
¼ cup finely chopped parsley
  Salt and coarsely ground black pepper

12 ounces fresh or 8 ounces dried fettuccine
1 tablespoon fresh lemon juice
1 tablespoon thinly sliced scallion tops

1. Melt 4 tablespoons of the butter in a medium skillet over medium heat. When foam subsides, stir in the mushrooms. Sauté, stirring, over medium heat until mushrooms are tender and lightly browned, about 10 minutes. Add the garlic; sauté 1 minute. Stir in parsley; season with salt and pepper. Keep warm.

2. Meanwhile, cook the fettuccine in plenty of boiling salted water until al dente, or firm to the bite, 2 minutes for fresh and 5 to 7 minutes for dried; drain.

3. Toss fettuccine with the mushroom mixture, 2 tablespoons remaining butter, and the lemon juice. Top with scallions.

135 FETTUCCINE WITH CAVIAR AND SOUR CREAM

Prep: 10 minutes   Cook: 15 minutes   Serves: 4

1 cup heavy cream
12 ounces fresh or 8 ounces dried fettuccine
¼ cup sour cream
2 tablespoons butter, softened

2 ounces salmon caviar
2 tablespoons chopped fresh chives
  Freshly ground black pepper

1. Boil heavy cream in a medium saucepan 3 minutes, or until slightly reduced and thickened, adjusting heat so cream does not boil over.

2. Meanwhile, cook the fettuccine in plenty of boiling salted water until al dente, or firm to the bite, 2 minutes for fresh and 5 to 7 for dried; drain.

3. In the fettuccine cooking pan, combine the cream and the cooked fettuccine; stir to blend. Add the sour cream and butter; stir until butter is melted. Add half of the salmon caviar and toss very gently.

4. Divide fettuccine among four plates. Sprinkle the remaining caviar and the chives over the fettuccine. Top with pepper.

136   FETTUCCINE WITH ZUCCHINI AND CARROT RIBBONS

Prep: 10 minutes   Cook: 10 minutes   Serves: 4

This extremely simple pasta dish is as pretty as a spring day. The carrot turns the butter a golden color, which then turns the fettuccine a rich yellow. Serve as a separate course or as a side dish; especially nice with chicken breasts or broiled fish steaks.

2 **small firm zucchini (about 4 ounces), washed and trimmed**
2 **medium carrots, pared and trimmed**
4 **tablespoons butter**

Salt and coarsely ground black pepper
12 **ounces fresh or 8 ounces dried fettuccine**
1 **tablespoon chopped parsley or chives**
Grated Parmesan cheese

1. Using a vegetable parer, slice wide paper-thin strips from the zucchini starting at end and slicing full length. Discard the first and last pieces. Do the same with the carrot.

2. Heat the butter in a medium skillet just until melted; stir in the zucchini and carrot "ribbons"; cover and cook over low heat 2 minutes. Season with salt and pepper.

3. Meanwhile, cook the fettuccine in plenty of boiling salted water until al dente, or firm to the bite, 2 minutes for fresh and 5 to 7 minutes for dried; drain.

4. Toss fettuccine with the carrot mixture and the herbs. Sprinkle generously with grated cheese before serving.

137   FETTUCCINE WITH FRESH CORN

Prep: 15 minutes   Cook: 15 minutes   Serves: 4

This recipe should be reserved for when corn is at its freshest and sweetest. Don't even be tempted to use frozen or canned corn; it just won't be the same.

1 **cup heavy cream**
1 **cup fresh corn kernels, cut from 2 ears of corn**
12 **ounces fresh or 8 ounces dried fettuccine**

½ **cup slivered, fully cooked ham, fat trimmed**
¼ **cup grated Parmesan cheese**
1 **tablespoon *each* minced red and green bell pepper**

1. Heat cream in a small saucepan until boiling. Stir in the corn; keep warm.

2. Cook the fettuccine in plenty of boiling salted water until al dente, or firm to the bite, about 2 minutes for fresh and 5 to 7 minutes for dried; drain.

3. Toss fettuccine with the cream and corn mixture, ham, and cheese. Sprinkle with red and green bell pepper. Pass additional cheese on the side.

138 FETTUCCINE WITH GORGONZOLA AND WALNUTS

Prep: 10 minutes   Cook: 20 minutes   Serves: 4

Gorgonzola, an Italian cow's milk cheese, is rich and creamy. Either sweet Gorgonzola, called dolci in Italian, or sharp, called piccante, can be used in this recipe.

½ cup broken walnuts
1 cup half-and-half or heavy cream
8 ounces Gorgonzola cheese, crumbled into small pieces
Pinch of nutmeg

Pinch of coarsely ground black pepper
12 ounces fresh or 8 ounces dried fettuccine
Grated Parmesan cheese (optional)

1. Heat a small skillet over low heat; stir in the walnuts. Toast, stirring, until fragrant and lightly browned, about 3 minutes. Set aside.

2. In a small saucepan, heat the half-and-half until hot but not boiling. Stir in the Gorgonzola until melted and sauce is creamy. Add the nutmeg and pepper.

3. Meanwhile, cook the fettuccine in plenty of boiling salted water until al dente, or firm to the bite, 2 minutes for fresh or 5 to 7 minutes for dried; drain.

4. Toss fettuccine with the sauce; sprinkle with walnuts and serve with grated Parmesan, if desired.

139 FETTUCCINE WITH SCALLION BUTTER AND RADISHES

Prep: 15 minutes   Cook: 10 minutes   Serves: 4

6 tablespoons butter
1 cup thinly sliced trimmed scallions (about 1 bunch)
12 ounces fresh or 8 ounces dried fettuccine

Freshly ground pepper
2 tablespoons minced trimmed radishes

1. Heat butter in a medium skillet; add scallions; sauté until tender, about 3 minutes.

2. Meanwhile, cook fettuccine in plenty of boiling salted water until al dente, or firm to the bite, 2 minutes for fresh and 5 to 7 minutes for dried; drain.

3. Toss fettuccine with scallion butter; sprinkle with pepper. Mound in a serving bowl and sprinkle with the minced radishes.

140 FETTUCCINE WITH VODKA AND TOMATO SAUCE

Prep: 10 minutes   Cook: 25 minutes   Serves: 4

2 tablespoons olive oil
½ cup chopped onion
1 garlic clove, finely chopped
1 can (28 ounces) plum
    tomatoes with juices
½ cup vodka
½ tablespoon crushed dried
    red pepper, or to taste

½ cup heavy cream, at room
    temperature
   Salt
12 ounces fresh or 8 ounces
    dried fettuccine
2 tablespoons chopped
    parsley

1. Heat oil in a medium skillet; add onion; sauté until tender but not browned, about 5 minutes; stir in garlic; sauté 1 minute. Add the tomatoes, vodka, and red pepper; simmer, stirring to break up tomatoes with the side of a spoon, until sauce is reduced and thickened, about 15 minutes. Stir in cream; simmer, stirring, until sauce is thickened slightly, about 5 minutes. Season with salt.

2. Meanwhile, cook fettuccine in plenty of boiling salted water until al dente, or firm to the bite, 2 minutes for fresh and 5 to 7 minutes for dried. Drain.

3. Toss fettuccine with sauce and parsley.

Variation:

141 FETTUCCINE WITH VODKA, TOMATO, AND CRAB MEAT

Omit cream. Add 6 ounces of fresh crab meat to the sauce after step 1.

142 FETTUCCINE WITH THREE CHEESES AND TOASTED ALMONDS

Prep: 10 minutes   Cook: 15 minutes   Serves: 4

3 tablespoons sliced
    unblanched almonds
1 cup heavy cream
6 ounces Fontina cheese,
    shredded
4 ounces Gorgonzola cheese,
    crumbled

¼ cup grated Parmesan cheese
12 ounces fresh or 8 ounces
    dried fettuccine
¼ cup torn Italian flat-leaf
    parsley leaves
   Coarsely ground black
    pepper

1. Heat a small skillet over low heat; add almonds; toast, stirring, untl lightly browned, about 2 minutes; set aside.

2. Boil heavy cream in a medium saucepan, adjusting heat to avoid boiling over, until slightly reduced, about 5 minutes. Stir in the cheeses until smooth.

3. Meanwhile, cook fettuccine in plenty of boiling salted water until al dente, or firm to the bite, about 2 minutes for fresh and 5 to 7 minutes for dried; drain.

4. Toss the fettuccine with the toasted almonds, sauce and parsley leaves. Sprinkle with pepper to taste.

143   FETTUCCINE WITH TOASTED BREAD CRUMBS

Prep: 10 minutes   Cook: 15 minutes   Serves: 4

2 tablespoons pignoli (pine nuts)
4 tablespoons butter
4 tablespoons olive oil
1 garlic clove, crushed
1 cup coarse bread crumbs made from day-old Italian bread

¼ cup chopped Italian flat-leaf parsley
12 ounces fresh or 8 ounces dried fettuccine
Coarsely ground black pepper

1. Toast the pignoli in a warm skillet over low heat, stirring, about 1 minute; set aside.

2. Heat the butter and oil in a medium skillet just until butter melts; stir in garlic; sauté over low heat 1 minute. Add bread crumbs; sauté, stirring, over low heat, until bread crumbs are toasted, about 5 minutes. Do not burn. Add the parsley.

3. Meanwhile, cook the fettuccine in plenty of boiling salted water until al dente, or firm to the bite, 2 minutes for fresh and 5 to 7 minutes for dried; drain.

4. Immediately toss fettuccine with crumbs and the reserved pignoli. Sprinkle with black pepper.

144   CAPELLI D'ANGELO WITH SOUR CREAM, CHIVES, AND CAVIAR

Prep: 5 minutes   Cook: 10 minutes   Serves: 4

12 ounces fresh or 8 ounces dried capelli d'angelo
2 tablespoons butter, softened
½ cup sour cream

2 tablespoons snipped chives
2 tablespoons black or golden caviar

1. Cook the pasta in plenty of boiling salted water until al dente, or firm to the bite, 2 minutes for fresh and 4 minutes for dried; drain. Toss with butter.

2. Heat the sour cream briefly in a small pan. Divide the pasta evenly among 4 small plates. Place 2 tablespoons of the sour cream on top of each serving. Sprinkle each with ½ tablespoon chives and place ½ teaspoon caviar in a small mound at the center of each plate.

145 FETTUCCINE WITH CHICKEN AND MUSHROOMS

Prep: 15 minutes   Cook: 20 minutes   Serves: 4

4 tablespoons butter
1 boneless and skinless chicken breast (about 8 ounces), cut into ¾-inch pieces
12 ounces mushrooms (use a mixture of white button, shiitake, and oyster mushrooms)
½ cup thinly sliced scallions
1 garlic clove, minced
½ cup heavy cream

1 can (14½ ounces) whole peeled tomatoes, drained and chopped
1 cup frozen tiny peas
½ teaspoon salt
Grinding of black pepper
12 ounces fresh or 8 ounces dried fettuccine
2 tablespoons finely chopped parsley
Grated Parmesan cheese

1. Heat butter in a large heavy skillet. Add the chicken; sauté until edges are golden, about 5 minutes. Cut the mushrooms into ⅛- to ¼-inch slices. Discard the tough stems from the shiitake. Add to the chicken; sauté until tender, about 5 minutes. Add the scallions and garlic; sauté 2 minutes.

2. Add the heavy cream and tomatoes; heat to boiling over medium-high heat; reduce heat to low and simmer until sauce is thickened. Add the peas, salt, and pepper. Heat, stirring, until peas are tender.

3. Meanwhile, cook the fettuccine in plenty of boiling salted water until al dente, or firm to the bite, 2 minutes for fresh and 5 to 7 minutes for dried; drain.

4. Place the fettuccine in a large serving bowl; top with chicken and mushroom mixture and toss. Sprinkle with parsley and grated Parmesan cheese.

146 FETTUCCINE WITH TUNA AND PEAS

Prep: 5 minutes   Cook: 10 minutes   Serves: 4

4 tablespoons butter
2 tablespoons olive oil
1 can (6½ ounces) tuna in olive oil, drained
1 cup tiny peas, thawed if frozen

12 ounces fresh or 8 ounces dried fettuccine
2 tablespoons chopped Italian flat-leaf parsley
Coarsely ground black pepper

1. Melt butter in a medium skillet; transfer 2 tablespoons to a large serving bowl; set aside. Add the oil to the butter left in the skillet. Stir in the tuna and peas; heat, stirring, over low heat.

2. Meanwhile, cook the fettuccine in plenty of boiling salted water until al dente, or firm to the bite, 2 minutes for fresh and 5 to 7 minutes for dried; drain.

3. Toss the fettuccine with the melted butter in the serving bowl. Add the tuna and the peas; toss. Sprinkle with parsley and black pepper.

147 CAPELLI D'ANGELO WITH HAZELNUT BUTTER AND CRISP ASPARAGUS

Prep: 20 minutes   Cook: 10 minutes   Serves: 4

¼ cup hazelnuts
6 tablespoons butter, at room temperature
1 tablespoon minced shallot

6 medium asparagus spears, trimmed, pared, and cut into ⅛-inch diagonals
12 ounces fresh or 8 ounces dried capelli d'angelo

1. Heat oven to 350°F. Toast hazelnuts in a baking pan until lightly browned and skins begin to crack, about 10 minutes. Transfer to a kitchen towel and rub briskly with the towel to loosen skins. Select 8 hazelnuts; coarsely chop and set aside for garnish. Grind the remaining nuts in a food processor or Mouli grater.

2. In a small bowl, stir 5 tablespoons of the butter and the ground hazelnuts to make a smooth paste; set aside.

3. Heat remaining 1 tablespoon butter in a medium skillet; add shallot; sauté until soft, about 3 minutes. Add asparagus; stir to coat with butter; cover and cook over low heat until asparagus is crisp-tender, about 4 minutes.

4. Cook the pasta in plenty of boiling salted water until al dente, or firm to the bite, 2 minutes for fresh and 4 minutes for dried; drain. Immediately add the hazelnut butter and the asparagus; toss lightly with a fork. Divide among four plates and sprinkle each serving with a few of the reserved coarsely chopped hazelnuts.

148 CAPELLI D'ANGELO WITH CREAM AND FRESH TOMATOES

Prep: 10 minutes   Cook: 20 minutes   Serves: 4

1 pound fresh ripe plum tomatoes, peeled, seeded, and chopped
1 tablespoon torn fresh basil leaves
½ cup heavy cream, at room temperature

Salt and pepper
12 ounces fresh or 8 ounces dried capelli d'angelo
2 tablespoons softened butter
Torn basil leaves, for garnish

1. In a medium skillet, simmer the tomatoes and basil until soft and juices have cooked out of tomatoes, about 10 minutes. Add the heavy cream; cook, stirring, over low heat until the sauce reduces and thickens slightly, about 10 minutes. Season to taste with salt and pepper.

2. Cook pasta in plenty of boiling salted water until al dente, or firm to the bite, 2 minutes for fresh and 4 minutes for dried; drain. Toss with butter. Divide among small plates and top each with a spoonful of sauce. Garnish with basil and serve additional sauce on the side.

149   FETTUCCINE WITH CUCUMBER AND DILL
Prep: 10 minutes   Cook: 10 minutes   Serves: 4

The capers add a nice salty touch to the cool taste of the cucumber. For an extra special addition, top each serving with a rounded teaspoonful of plump pink salmon caviar.

1 **small cucumber, pared**
4 **tablespoons butter**
2 **tablespoons capers, rinsed and blotted dry**
1 **tablespoon chopped fresh dill**

12 **ounces fresh or 8 ounces dried fettuccine**
  Coarsely ground black pepper
¼ **cup sour cream or crème fraîche (optional)**
4 **small sprigs of dill**

1. Halve the cucumber lengthwise; scoop out the seeds and cut crosswise into ⅛-inch slices; set aside.

2. Heat the butter in a medium skillet; add the capers and dill; heat just until dill is fragrant, about 1 minute.

3. Cook the fettuccine in plenty of boiling salted water until al dente, or firm to the bite, 2 minutes for fresh or 5 to 7 minutes for dried; drain.

4. Toss fettuccine with the cucumber, butter mixture, and black pepper. Top each serving with a spoonful of sour cream and a sprig of dill.

150   CAPELLI D'ANGELO WITH PORCINI CREAM
Prep: 5 minutes   Soak: 15 minutes   Cook: 15 minutes   Serves: 4

1 **ounce dried porcini**
½ **cup boiling water**
1 **cup heavy cream**

12 **ounces fresh or 8 ounces dried capelli d'angelo**
2 **tablespoons butter**
  Black pepper

1. Combine the porcini and water in a small saucepan. Heat to boiling; cover and let stand 15 minutes. Drain through a fine sieve lined with a dampened paper towel. Save the porcini liquid. Rinse any grit off the porcini; finely chop.

2. Heat the cream to boiling in a medium saucepan. Add the porcini liquid and boil gently until reduced by half. Add the finely chopped porcini.

3. Cook the pasta in plenty of boiling salted water until al dente, or firm to the bite, 2 minutes for fresh and 4 minutes for dried; drain. Add pasta and butter to the cream sauce and stir to coat pasta. Divide among four plates and sprinkle each with fresh pepper.

151 FETTUCCINE WITH MUSSELS AND PARSLEY CREAM SAUCE

Prep: 15 minutes   Cook: 20 minutes   Serves: 4

2 pounds mussels, rinsed, scrubbed, and debearded
½ cup chopped onion
½ cup chopped parsley

1 cup white wine or dry vermouth
1 cup heavy cream
12 ounces fresh or 8 ounces dried fettuccine

1. In a large heavy saucepan, combine the mussels, onion, ¼ cup of the parsley, and the white wine. Cook, covered, over high heat, shaking the pan to blend ingredients until all the mussels are opened, about 8 minutes. With a slotted spoon, carefully transfer mussels to a platter. Pour the juices into a bowl to allow any grit to settle to the bottom. Wipe out the saucepan; set aside.

2. When the mussels are cool enough to handle, pull them from their shells; reserve about 12 mussels in their shells for garnish. Ladle the reserved juices back into the saucepan, leaving any grit in the bottom of the bowl. Add the cream to the saucepan and boil mixture until reduced by half, about 5 minutes.

3. Cook the fettuccine in plenty of boiling salted water until al dente, or firm to the bite, 2 minutes for fresh and 5 to 7 minutes for dried; drain.

4. Toss fettuccine with the shelled mussels, cream mixture, and the remaining ¼ cup parsley. Garnish each serving with 3 mussels still in their shells.

Variation:

152 FETTUCCINE WITH MUSSELS IN TOMATO CREAM SAUCE

Add 1 cup drained and chopped canned or fresh tomatoes with the cream in step 2.

Cooking fresh pasta

Fresh pasta cooks more quickly than dried. Once the water comes to a hard rolling boil, add the salt; wait 10 seconds; then add the pasta. Stir with a long spoon from the bottom of the pot, and once the water rolls into a boil again, start testing the pasta for doneness. Fettuccine can be done in just 2 minutes; the finest angel hair pasta can be done as the water returns to boiling. Drain quickly and toss immediately with the sauce. *Remember, cooked pasta waits for no one.*

Chapter 9

Shapes, Shells, and a Few Rotelles

Experienced pasta cooks know their pasta shapes, although not all always agree on all things. The general rule is: match ribbed pasta or pasta with indentations (any of the rigati family, fusilli, or rotelle) that will "hold" the sauce with less thick sauces; match their tubular pasta with smooth surfaces (penne, ziti, or mezzani) with thick sauces that will "cling" to the smoothest exterior. To complete the lesson, the shapes of the other ingredients are also important. Vegetables should be cut to match the shape of the pasta. Cut vegetables in a fine julienne, for example, when the pasta is spaghetti or linguine; vegetables like broccoli and cauliflower should be cut in florets and matched with "boxy" shapes like shells or radiatore.

There are hundreds of pasta shapes and many more names. In Italy, for instance, the very same shapes are given different names in different regions. The following list describes just a few of these shapes, most of which are mentioned in this chapter.

Shapes are in

Bows: The American version of Italian *farfalle*, or "butterflies"; often egg noodle dough.

Cavatelli: A short curled noodle, available fresh, frozen, and dried; the dried are shell-shaped with a slightly ruffled outside.

Conchiglie: See Shells.

Farfalle: See Bows.

Fusilli: A long fat solid spiral spaghetti, or a short fat screwlike pasta similar to *rotelle*.

Gemelli: Means "twins," because it looks like two short fat pieces of spaghetti twisted together.

Mezzani: A tubular pasta 1 to 2 inches long with a smooth exterior; the same pasta with a ridged exterior is called *mezzani rigati*.

Mostaccioli: Means "small mustaches," but looks like penne.

Orecchiette: "Little ears," which are round fat little (about ½ inch) saucerlike disks.

Penne: A tubular pasta, about 1½ inches in length; the ends are cut diagonally to resemble a quill or a pen point. Smooth exterior or ridged (rigati).

Radiatore: A short fat pasta shape rippled and ringed like a radiator.

Rigatoni: Very large grooved tubular pasta.

Rotelle: A short (1½ to 2 inch) fat screwlike shape; sometimes called *fusilli*.

Shells: Available from tiny to jumbo; called *conchiglie* and *maruzze*.

Ziti: A large tubular macaroni, slightly curved, called "bridegrooms."

153 ROTELLE WITH BASIL AND PARSLEY RICOTTA

Prep: 15 minutes   Cook: 12 minutes   Serves: 4

This flavored ricotta can be varied with any combination of fresh herbs: all basil; a combination of parsley, basil, and dill; oregano and basil; or parsley with a leaf or two of mint thrown in.

1 cup ricotta cheese	¼ cup grated Parmesan cheese
1 egg	Pinch of nutmeg
¼ cup *each* packed Italian flat-leaf parsley and basil leaves, finely chopped	12 ounces rotelle

1. Whisk the ricotta, egg, parsley and basil, Parmesan, and nutmeg in a large bowl.

2. Cook the rotelle in a large pot of boiling salted water until al dente, or firm to the bite, about 12 minutes; drain. Add immediately to the bowl of ricotta. Toss to coat the hot pasta. Serve at once.

154 ROTELLE PRIMAVERA

Prep: 15 minutes   Cook: 15 minutes   Serves: 4

There are probably as many variations of pasta primavera as there are cooks *and* vegetables. This version uses almost all spring vegetables, so it is probably more true to its namesake than some others.

3 tablespoons butter	1 cup heavy cream
1 cup thinly sliced long thin carrots	¼ cup sliced (¼-inch diagonals) trimmed scallions
1 small leek, trimmed, soaked, and cut into thin slices (white part only)	1 tablespoon lemon juice
1 cup thinly sliced small tender zucchini	½ teaspoon salt, or to taste
1 cup sliced (½-inch diagonals) fresh asparagus	12 ounces rotelle
	4 ounces mozzarella cheese, cut into ¼-inch dice
	Grated Parmesan cheese

1. Heat the butter in a large skillet or sauté pan. Add the carrots and leek; sauté, stirring, over low heat 5 minutes. Add the zucchini and asparagus; sauté, stirring, 3 minutes. Add the cream; heat to boiling; boil until reduced and slightly thickened, about 8 minutes. Stir in the scallions, lemon juice, and salt.

2. Meanwhile, cook the rotelle in plenty of boiling salted water until al dente, or firm to the bite, about 12 minutes; drain. Add pasta and mozzarella to the sauce in the sauté pan; toss to blend. Sprinkle Parmesan cheese to taste on top of each serving.

155   WAGON WHEELS WITH SAUSAGE AND PEPPERS

Prep: 15 minutes   Cook: 20 minutes   Serves: 4

8 ounces Italian-style sausage
3 tablespoons olive oil
2 green bell peppers, seeded, cut into ½-inch strips
1 small onion, cut into ½-inch chunks

1 garlic clove, crushed
½ teaspoon salt
¼ teaspoon oregano
   Pinch of coarsely ground black pepper
12 ounces wagon wheels

1. Cut the sausage into ½-inch crosswise slices. Sauté in a medium skillet over low heat, stirring, until browned, about 10 minutes. Lift from pan with a slotted spoon; discard any sausage drippings and wipe out the pan.

2. Heat the oil in the skillet; sauté the peppers and onion over medium heat, stirring until edges begin to brown and vegetables are crisp-tender, about 5 minutes; add the garlic; sauté 1 minute. Return the sausage to the skillet; stir in the salt, oregano, and pepper; simmer, covered, 5 minutes.

3. Meanwhile, cook the pasta in plenty of boiling salted water until al dente, or firm to the bite, about 12 minutes; drain. Toss with the sausage and pepper mixture and serve at once.

Variation:

156   WAGON WHEELS WITH SAUSAGE, PEPPERS, AND TOMATOES

Add 1 can (14 ounces) chopped drained tomatoes with the sausage in step 2. Cook, stirring, uncovered, 5 minutes to concentrate the tomato juices before adding the seasonings and simmering for 5 minutes.

157   PENNE WITH ASPARAGUS AND PORCINI CREAM

Prep: 20 minutes   Cook: 20 minutes   Serves: 4

½ ounce dried porcini
½ cup water
8 ounces asparagus, washed, trimmed, and cut into 1-inch lengths (or same lengths as the penne)

1 cup heavy cream
2 teaspoons fresh lemon juice
   Salt
12 ounces penne
   Coarsely ground black pepper

1. Combine the porcini and water in a small saucepan; heat to boiling; simmer, covered, 5 minutes; let stand, off heat, 10 minutes. Strain the liquid through a fine sieve or a sieve lined with a piece of dampened cheesecloth; reserve the liquid. Rinse mushrooms, checking carefully for grit. Finely chop mushrooms and set aside.

2. Meanwhile, steam the asparagus on a steaming rack set over 1 inch boiling water, covered, until crisp-tender, about 5 minutes; remove rack from pan.

3. Combine the cream, porcini liquid, and the chopped porcini in a deep saucepan. Heat to boiling, stirring occasionally, until liquid is reduced to ⅔ cup, about 10 minutes. Add the lemon juice and a pinch of salt.

4. Meanwhile, cook the pasta in plenty of boiling salted water until al dente, or firm to the bite, about 10 minutes; drain. Toss with the cream mixture and the asparagus. Sprinkle with pepper.

---

158 RIGATONI WITH CAULIFLOWER AND ANCHOVY-GARLIC OIL

Prep: 15 minutes   Cook: 30 minutes   Serves: 4

This is a perfect quick fall supper—when cauliflower is at its best. The anchovies literally melt away, leaving a salty, tangy flavor.

1   small (1 pound) fresh
      cauliflower (or half a large
      head), trimmed, florets
      cut lengthwise into
      ¼-inch slices
3   tablespoons butter
3   tablespoons olive oil
1   tablespoon minced fresh
      garlic
1   tablespoon minced,
      drained, and blotted
      anchovy fillets

¼   red bell pepper, cut into
      slivers approximately
      ⅛ x 1 inch
12 ounces rigatoni
1   tablespoon julienned fresh
      basil leaves or chopped
      Italian flat-leaf parsley
¼   cup coarsely chopped
      Parmesan cheese, or
      2 tablespoons grated
      Parmesan
      Coarsely ground black
      pepper

1. Steam cauliflower on a steaming rack set over 1 inch of boiling water, covered, until very tender, about 12 minutes. Uncover saucepan; set aside.

2. Meanwhile, heat butter and oil in a medium skillet over low heat. Stir in garlic; sauté 1 minute. Add anchovies; stir until blended, about 1 minute. Add red pepper; stir over low heat 2 minutes.

3. Cook pasta in plenty of boiling salted water until al dente, or firm to the bite, about 15 minutes; drain. In a large bowl, toss the cauliflower, butter mixture, rigatoni, basil, and cheese. Sprinkle with black pepper.

Variation:

---

159 RIGATONI WITH BROCCOLI AND ANCHOVY-GARLIC OIL

Substitute 1 pound broccoli, trimmed and broken into florets, tender stems cut into 1-inch lengths for the cauliflower. Steam 10 minutes, or until very tender.

160 PENNE WITH ZUCCHINI AND BASIL
Prep: 15 minutes   Cook: 25 minutes   Serves: 4

Zucchini and onion are often sautéed in oil and flavored with either chopped fresh basil and/or fresh mint. With the addition of just a little extra olive oil, this popular first course is transformed into a very lovely pasta dish.

4 tablespoons olive oil
1 large sweet onion, quartered
   and cut crosswise into
   thin slices
2 garlic cloves, sliced thin
8 ounces zucchini, trimmed
   and sliced into rounds if
   small, or quartered if
   large and then sliced thin
  Salt
  Freshly ground black
   pepper

12 ounces penne, rotelle, or
   medium shells
1 tablespoon chopped fresh
   basil leaves
1 teaspoon chopped fresh
   mint leaves (optional)
1 tablespoon fresh lemon
   juice
2 tablespoons grated
   Parmesan cheese

1. Heat 2 tablespoons of the oil in a large skillet. Add the onion and garlic; sauté over low heat, stirring, until the onion is tender and just beginning to turn golden, about 10 minutes. Stir in the zucchini; sauté, stirring, until tender, about 10 minutes. Season with salt and pepper.

2. Meanwhile, cook the pasta in plenty of boiling salted water until al dente, or firm to the bite, about 12 minutes; drain. Stir the basil, mint, and lemon juice into the zucchini. Toss zucchini, pasta, and Parmesan together. Pass additional cheese on the side.

161 FARFALLE WITH LIMA BEANS AND SUN-DRIED TOMATOES
Prep: 10 minutes   Cook: 10 minutes   Serves: 4

Farfalle are often called bows, but the correct Italian translation is butterfly. A little version, called farfalline, is used in soups.

6 tablespoons olive oil
½ cup coarsely chopped onion
8 sun-dried tomato halves
   packed in olive oil,
   blotted and cut into thin
   slices

1 garlic clove, minced
8 ounces farfalle
1 package (10 ounces) frozen
   Fordhook lima beans
   Freshly ground black
   pepper

1. Heat oil in a medium skillet; add the onion and sauté until golden; stir in the tomatoes and garlic; set aside.

2. Meanwhile, cook the farfalle in plenty of boiling salted water 3 minutes; add the lima beans and cook until the pasta is al dente, or firm to the bite, and the lima beans are tender, about 8 minutes; drain.

3. Toss the oil mixture and the pasta mixture together until blended. Sprinkle with black pepper.

---

162   SHELLS WITH COOKED GREENS AND GARLIC OIL

Prep: 15 minutes   Cook: 20 minutes   Serves: 4

4   cups packed rinsed, trimmed, torn escarole, or half escarole and half outside romaine leaves
1   cup seasoned chicken broth
3   tablespoons olive oil

1   garlic clove, sliced thin
¼   teaspoon crushed dried red pepper, or to taste
12   ounces large shells
Grated Parmesan cheese

1. Combine the greens and the broth in a large saucepan. Cook, covered, over low heat until greens are very tender, about 20 minutes. Stir and check the amount of moisture in the pan once or twice during cooking; add small amounts of broth as needed. The greens will be quite soupy if cooked at a low enough temperature.

2. Heat the oil in a small skillet over low heat; stir in the garlic; sauté, stirring, until golden, about 3 minutes. Add the red pepper; let stand off heat.

3. Meanwhile, cook the pasta in plenty of boiling salted water until al dente, or firm to the bite, about 12 minutes; drain. In a large bowl, toss the cooked greens and pasta together. Drizzle the hot oil on top and toss again. Sprinkle with cheese to taste.

---

163   RADIATORE WITH POTATOES, BROCCOLI, AND RED PEPPER

Prep: 10 minutes   Cook: 12 minutes   Serves: 4

6   tablespoons olive oil
1   small red bell pepper, seeded, cut into thin strips
½   teaspoon crushed dried red pepper
1   small garlic clove, cut into thin slivers

2   cups radiatore
3   cups cubed (½ inch) unpared new potatoes
3   cups broccoli florets and stems, cut into approximate ½-inch pieces
Grated Parmesan cheese

1. Heat oil in a medium skillet; add bell pepper; sauté 3 minutes, or until crisp-tender. Add the red pepper and garlic; sauté 1 minute.

2. Meanwhile, cook the pasta in plenty of boiling salted water 6 minutes; stir in the potatoes and broccoli. Cook until the pasta is al dente, or firm to the bite, and the potatoes and broccoli are tender, about 8 minutes; drain.

3. Toss with the red pepper oil and plenty of grated cheese. Serve at once with additional cheese on the side.

164 GREEN BEANS AND PENNE CARBONARA

Prep: 10 minutes   Cook: 12 minutes   Serves: 4

4 slices bacon
2 large eggs, at room
  temperature
½ cup grated Parmesan cheese
2 tablespoons softened butter
½ pound fresh green beans,
  trimmed and cut into
  2-inch lengths

½ pound penne or other 1½- to
  2-inch tubular pasta
  shape
½ cup chopped walnuts,
  briefly toasted in a warm
  skillet

1. Sauté bacon in a skillet until crisp; drain; crumble; set aside.

2. Beat the eggs, cheese, and butter in a large bowl.

3. Cook the green beans and penne in plenty of boiling salted water until penne is al dente, or firm to the bite, about 12 minutes. Drain. Immediately transfer to the bowl and toss to blend. Sprinkle with bacon and walnuts. Sprinkle with additional cheese to taste.

165 CAVATELLI WITH FENNEL, TOMATO, AND SUN-DRIED TOMATO SAUCE

Prep: 15 minutes   Cook: 20 minutes   Serves: 4

Dried cavatelli bear absolutely no resemblance to the fresh or frozen variety. The dried are simply another pasta shape that "catch" the sauce nicely. The fresh or frozen cook up to wonderful little oval-shaped "pillows," or as the children in our family call them, "lumps." Use either variety in this recipe. Another popular way to sauce cavatelli is to use a robust tomato and meat sauce or Bolognese sauce (see Chapter 14).

¼ cup olive oil
1 cup finely chopped fresh
  fennel bulb (well
  trimmed; save tops)
2 tablespoons minced onion
1 can (14 ounces) Italian-style
  plum tomatoes with
  juices, cut up with
  scissors

¼ cup minced, drained, and
  blotted sun-dried
  tomatoes, packed in oil
2 tablespoons finely chopped
  fernlike tops from fennel
Salt and pepper
12 ounces dried cavatelli, or
  1 pound fresh or frozen

1. Heat the oil in a medium skillet; add the fennel and onion. Sauté, stirring, over low heat until the fennel is very soft but not browned, about 15 minutes. Add the plum tomatoes; cook, stirring and crushing tomatoes with the side of a spoon, until juices are slightly reduced and the sauce is thickened, about 15 minutes. Add the sun-dried tomatoes and fennel tops; simmer over low heat 5 minutes. Season with salt and pepper to taste.

2. Cook the cavatelli in plenty of boiling salted water, 12 to 15 minutes for the dried and 20 to 25 minutes for the fresh or frozen (time can vary considerably); drain. Sauce immediately and serve.

166 ROTELLE WITH BACON, MUSHROOMS, AND PIGNOLI

Prep: 15 minutes   Cook: 20 minutes   Serves: 4

4 ounces thick-sliced bacon, cut into 2-inch lengths
2 tablespoons pignoli (pine nuts)
2 tablespoons butter
2 tablespoons olive oil

6 ounces small mushrooms, trimmed and quartered
Salt and pepper
12 ounces rotelle
1 scallion, trimmed and sliced thin

1. Sauté bacon in a medium skillet until crisp; transfer to a double thickness of paper towels to drain. Spoon off and discard all but 1 tablespoon of the bacon fat. Add the pignoli; sauté, stirring, until golden; transfer to the paper towels with the bacon.

2. Heat the butter and oil in the same skillet; add the mushrooms and sauté over moderately high heat, stirring, until the mushroom liquid cooks off and the mushrooms begin to brown. Stir in the reserved bacon and pignoli; sprinkle with salt and pepper.

3. Cook the pasta in plenty of boiling salted water until al dente, or firm to the bite, about 12 minutes; drain. Toss with the bacon and mushroom mixture and the scallion.

167 PENNE WITH GRILLED SALMON, ASPARAGUS, AND LEMON BUTTER

Prep: 10 minutes   Cook: 20 minutes   Serves: 4

2 salmon steaks, each about 8 ounces and ½ inch thick
1 teaspoon soy sauce
8 ounces asparagus, trimmed, stems peeled, cut into diagonals the same length as the penne
8 ounces penne

6 tablespoons butter
1 small garlic clove
½ teaspoon grated fresh ginger
1 tablespoon fresh lemon juice
1 tablespoon grated lemon zest

1. Brush the salmon steak lightly on both sides with the soy. Grill or broil until almost cooked through, about 3 minutes a side for a steak ½ inch thick. Cool slightly; remove and discard outside skin and center bone. Pull salmon into large flakes.

2. Steam the asparagus, covered, on a steaming rack set over 1 inch of simmering water until crisp-tender, about 4 minutes. Transfer to a plate; cover to keep warm.

3. Meanwhile, cook the pasta in plenty of boiling salted water until al dente, or firm to the bite, about 12 minutes; drain.

4. Melt the butter in the pasta cooking pot; add the garlic and ginger; sauté 30 seconds. Add the lemon juice and zest. Toss the pasta, asparagus, and melted butter until pasta is coated. Add the salmon and gently toss.

168   RIGATONI WITH TOMATO AND ANCHOVY SAUCE WITH RAISINS

Prep: 15 minutes   Cook: 20 minutes   Serves: 4

3   tablespoons olive oil
1   tablespoon minced garlic
1   tablespoon minced anchovies
1   can (14 ounces) Italian-style plum tomatoes, with juices, cut up with scissors
1   tablespoon raisins or dried currants

1   tablespoon chopped Italian flat-leaf parsley
¼   teaspoon black pepper
12 ounces rigatoni
1   tablespoon pignoli (pine nuts), stirred in a hot skillet until lightly toasted, 1 to 2 minutes

1. Heat oil in a medium skillet; stir in garlic and anchovies; sauté, stirring, over low heat until anchovies dissolve. Stir in the tomatoes and raisins; heat to boiling, stirring and mashing tomatoes. Simmer, uncovered, 10 minutes, or until slightly thickened. Stir in parsley and season with pepper.

2. Meanwhile, cook pasta in plenty of boiling salted water until al dente, or firm to the bite, about 15 minutes; drain. Toss with sauce; sprinkle with pignoli.

169   ROTELLE WITH FRESH ARTICHOKE SAUCE

Prep: 15 minutes   Cook: 25 minutes   Serves: 4–6

Tiny artichokes, usually less than 2 inches in length, are available several times a year in our markets. They are perfectly delectable, and although frozen artichokes can be used in this recipe, we suggest you hold out for the fresh ones, usually available in September and then again in April.

8   tiny fresh artichokes
    Juice of 1 lemon
⅓   cup olive oil
½   cup coarsely chopped sweet (Spanish) onion
3   garlic cloves, peeled and bruised with the side of a knife
1   medium carrot, pared and sliced thin

1   stalk celery, trimmed and sliced thin
½   teaspoon salt, or to taste
½   teaspoon dried oregano
    Freshly ground black pepper
1   can (14 ounces) Italian plum tomatoes with juices
1   pound rotelle

1. Trim the stems and pull all the outside leaves off the artichokes. Cut the artichokes in half; scoop out the choke with the tip of a small spoon or knife. Halve lengthwise. Add the lemon juice to a bowl of water; add the artichokes to prevent darkening.

2. In a sauté pan, combine the oil, onion, garlic, carrot, and celery; cover and cook over low heat, stirring occasionally, 5 minutes. Drain the artichokes and add to the pan; stir to coat. Cover and cook over low heat, stirring occasionally, until artichokes are tender, about 25 minutes. Mash the garlic with the back of a spoon; season with salt, oregano, and pepper. Stir in the tomatoes and cook, uncovered, until the liquid is slightly reduced, about 10 minutes.

3. Meanwhile, cook the pasta in plenty of boiling salted water until al dente, or firm to the bite, about 12 minutes; drain. Toss the pasta with a spoonful of the sauce to coat. Spoon into a large shallow bowl and spoon the remaining sauce over the top. Toss completely just before serving.

---

170 RIGATONI WITH ROASTED PEPPERS AND OLIVES

Prep: 1 hour   Marinate: 1–24 hours   Cook: 15 minutes   Serves: 6

There is a little bonus in this recipe. The roasted and marinated peppers make a wonderful first course. Double the recipe and serve half as a first course for dinner one day and then toss the remaining half of the recipe with some fresh cooked pasta for a main course the following day.

4 large sweet red bell peppers	1/8 teaspoon freshly ground black pepper
1/2 cup flavorful olive oil	12 ounces rigatoni
2 tablespoons tiny imported black olives, pitted	2 tablespoons pignoli (pine nuts), toasted in a skillet 1 to 2 minutes
1 garlic clove, bruised	Large shavings of Parmesan cheese
1 tablespoon whole fresh oregano leaves, or 1/2 teaspoon dried	Sprigs of fresh oregano, if available
1/2 teaspoon salt	

1. Heat the broiler. Place the peppers in a baking pan lined with foil; broil about 3 inches from the heat until well charred on all sides. Cover with a towel and let stand until cool enough to handle. Carefully peel off the charred skin, working over the foil to reserve all of the pepper juices. Split the peppers in half and remove the seeds and stem. Rinse any clinging seeds and skins from the pepper under running water. Cut the peppers in 1/2-inch strips and place in a shallow bowl. Drain the skins and seeds in the foil through a sieve and reserve the pepper juices; pour juices over the peeled peppers. Add the oil, olives, garlic, oregano, salt, and pepper. Cover and marinate at room temperature 1 to 2 hours, or refrigerate overnight.

2. Bring marinated peppers to room temperature before serving, if refrigerated. Remove the garlic clove. Cook the pasta in plenty of boiling salted water until al dente, or firm to the bite, 15 to 18 minutes; drain.

3. Toss rigatoni with the marinated peppers. Sprinkle with the pignoli, Parmesan shavings, and oregano sprigs.

171   BAKED SHELLS WITH RICOTTA PESTO

Prep: 20 minutes   Cook: 8 minutes   Bake: 30 minutes   Serves: 4

We offer yet another version of Pesto Genovese in this adaptation of baked ziti. It is a great way to use up that excess pesto that I always make with abandon in mid-August.

½ cup packed fresh basil
    leaves
¼ cup chopped unblanched
    almonds
1 garlic clove, chopped
½ teaspoon salt
¼ cup olive oil
4 tablespoons grated
    Parmesan cheese

12 ounces medium or large
    shells
3 cups ricotta cheese
8 ounces mozzarella cheese,
    shredded
    Freshly ground black
    pepper

1. In a blender or food processor, purée the basil leaves, almonds, garlic, and salt. With the motor running, gradually add the oil through the feed tube. Stir in 2 tablespoons Parmesan cheese; set aside. There will be about ½ cup.

2. Cook pasta in plenty of boiling salted water until still quite firm, about 8 minutes; drain.

3. In a large bowl, stir together the pesto, ricotta, half the mozzarella, and the black pepper; add the pasta; stir to blend.

4. Pour into a 10-inch square or any 1½-quart shallow baking dish; sprinkle the top with the remaining 2 tablespoons Parmesan and the remaining mozzarella.

5. Bake in a 350°F oven 30 minutes, or until cheese is melted and bubbly.

172   SHELLS WITH CHUNKY TOMATO SAUCE, CHÈVRE, AND FRESH THYME

Prep: 15 minutes   Cook: 15 minutes   Serves: 4

Quick Chunky Tomato
    Sauce (page 142)
1 teaspoon finely shredded
    orange zest
8 ounces shells

3 ounces fresh goat cheese, cut
    into small pieces
1 teaspoon fresh thyme leaves
    Sprigs of fresh thyme

1. Prepare the Quick Chunky Tomato Sauce according to the recipe. Stir in the orange zest; keep warm.

2. Meanwhile, cook the shells in plenty of boiling salted water until al dente, or firm to the bite, about 12 minutes; drain.

3. Toss the shells with half the sauce. Sprinkle with goat cheese and thyme leaves; top with remaining sauce. Lightly toss. Garnish with a few graceful sprigs of fresh thyme.

Chapter 10

Tiny Pasta Shapes

I have fallen in love with tiny pastas. Partly I love the names—all those wonderful *ina* and *ette* words. And the imagery! Who but an Italian would name a pasta after a melon seed? A tiny thimble? A little butterfly? But romance aside, these tiny pastas are wonderful to eat, especially in soups, and they are particularly appealing to the American palate as a side dish.

173　ORZO WITH TOASTED ALMONDS AND CURRANTS

Prep: 4 minutes　Cook: 12 minutes　Serves: 4

This side dish is especially nice with curry or other Indian-inspired dishes. It is also good with Middle Eastern flavors like a yogurt and cumin marinade for broiled boned leg of lamb. For a pretty and flavorful variation, add 1 to 2 teaspoons curry powder to the melted butter before stirring in the orzo and broth.

2　tablespoons butter	Pinch of ground cardamom
1　cup orzo	¼　cup coarsely chopped
2　cups seasoned chicken broth	unblanched almonds
2　tablespoons dried currants	

1. Melt butter in a medium saucepan; stir in orzo; sauté over low heat 1 minute. Add the broth, currants, and cardamom; heat to boiling. Cover and simmer until all the broth is absorbed, about 12 minutes.

2. Meanwhile, sprinkle almonds in a small skillet; stir over low heat until almonds are lightly browned and fragrant, about 1 minute.

3. Spoon orzo into a serving dish and sprinkle with almonds.

Variations:

174　ORZO WITH CINNAMON, ORANGE, AND DATES

Omit the currants, cardamom, and almonds and add ½ cinnamon stick, 1 strip (2 x ½ inch) orange zest, and 2 tablespoons chopped dried dates to the orzo and broth mixture. Cook, covered, until broth is absorbed, about 12 minutes.

175　ORZO WITH PISTACHIO BUTTER

Finely grind ¼ cup shelled natural pistachios in a food processor or Mouli grater. Combine nuts and ¼ cup softened butter in a small bowl until blended. Stir into the cooked orzo just before serving.

176　ORZO WITH TOASTED HAZELNUT BUTTER

Toast ¼ cup hazelnuts in a 350°F oven 10 minutes, or until skins begin to brown and crack. Wrap in a towel and rub briskly to remove most of skins. Grind nuts in a food processor or Mouli grater. Combine nuts and ¼ cup softened butter in a small bowl until blended. Stir into the cooked orzo just before serving.

177 TUBETTINI WITH FRESH TOMATOES AND BASIL

Prep: 10 minutes   Cook: 15 minutes   Serves: 4

Prepare this dish when tomatoes and basil are at the height of their season. It is a nice side dish with grilled fish or meats, especially beef.

1 **cup tubettini**	**Coarsely ground black**
1 **cup heavy cream**	**pepper**
1 **cup chopped fresh tomatoes**	
2 **tablespoons chopped fresh basil**	

1. Cook pasta in plenty of boiling salted water until al dente, or firm to the bite, 8 to 10 minutes; drain.

2. In a saucepan, combine the pasta, heavy cream, tomatoes, and basil; heat to boiling, stirring constantly. Cook mixture, stirring until most of cream is absorbed and mixture is creamy. Add pepper to taste.

178 PASTINA WITH PARMESAN, BUTTER, AND CREAM

Prep: 5 minutes   Cook: 6 minutes   Serves: 4

Think of this rich, creamy side dish as a substitute for mashed potatoes. It is wonderful with pot roast, roasted chicken, or grilled Italian sausages.

2 **tablespoons unsalted butter**	¼ **cup heavy cream, or more as**
1 **cup pastina**	**needed**
2 **cups water**	2 **tablespoons grated**
½ **teaspoon salt**	**Parmesan cheese, or to taste**

1. Melt butter in a medium saucepan; stir in pastina to coat with butter; add water and salt. Heat to boiling, stirring; cook over low heat, uncovered, stirring occasionally, 6 minutes, or until pastina is tender and mixture is thickened.

2. Stir in heavy cream and cheese. Serve while piping hot. Sprinkle with additional grated cheese, if desired.

Variation:

179 PASTINA WITH BUTTER AND PARMESAN

Substitute 4 tablespoons butter for the heavy cream.

180   FARFALLINE WITH PEAS AND CREAM
Prep: 5 minutes   Cook: 10 minutes   Serves: 4

Served with broiled tomato halves sprinkled with Garlic Bread Crumbs (page 67), this side dish becomes a satisfying main dish for a light supper. The pasta will continue to absorb the cream as it stands, so add more, if needed.

1 cup farfalline (tiny butterfly pasta)	Pinch of salt
1 cup frozen peas	Grated Parmesan cheese
⅔ cup heavy cream, or more as needed	

1. Cook the pasta in plenty of boiling salted water until al dente, or firm to the bite, 8 to 10 minutes; drain.

2. Combine the peas and heavy cream in a saucepan; heat to boiling. Stir in the pasta and a pinch of salt. Cook, stirring, over medium heat until pasta absorbs most of the cream, about 2 minutes. Pass the grated cheese to be sprinkled on each serving.

181   CURRIED MEAT LOAF WITH ACINI DI PEPE
Prep: 20 minutes   Bake: 1 hour 30 minutes   Serves: 6–8

This succulent meat loaf is guaranteed to transform the most reluctant meat loaf eater. The recipe is fairly large; but leftovers are great eaten cold. If you add a row of hard-cooked eggs down the center before shaping the loaf, each slice of meat loaf will have a cross section of the egg, making it pretty enough for party fare.

2 tablespoons butter	1 teaspoon ground ginger
1 cup chopped onion	1 to 2 teaspoons salt, to taste
1 cup chopped mushrooms	½ teaspoon ground black pepper
1 cup shredded carrot	2 pounds ground meat loaf mixture (½ beef; ¼ each pork and veal)
2 garlic cloves, crushed	
1½ cups cold water	
½ cup fine dry bread crumbs	4 hard-cooked eggs, shells removed (optional)
1 egg, beaten	
1 cup cooked acini di pepe (⅓ cup dried before cooking)	2 to 3 tablespoons Dijon mustard
⅓ cup finely chopped parsley	
2 teaspoons curry powder	

1. Heat butter in a medium skillet; add the onion and mushrooms and sauté, over low heat, until very tender, about 10 minutes. Stir in the carrot and garlic; cover and cook until tender, about 5 minutes.

2. In a large bowl, combine the water, bread crumbs, egg, acini di pepe, parsley, curry powder, ginger, salt, and pepper.

3. Add the ground meats and the sautéed vegetables; mix very well with hands. Transfer to a shallow 9 x 13-inch baking dish. If using the hard-cooked eggs, smooth surface of meat and line the eggs, end to end length-wise down the center. Rinse hands with cold water and shape the meat in a long oval completely covering the row of eggs. If not using eggs, simply shape meat into an oval mound. Spread the entire surface of the meat loaf with a thin layer of mustard.

4. Bake in a preheated 350°F oven 1 hour. Increase oven temperature to 400°F and bake until surface of meat loaf is browned and crusty, about 30 minutes. Let stand at least 20 minutes before serving. Also good served at room temperature or cold.

---

182 TUBETTINI WITH PORCINI AND CREAM
Prep: 5 minutes   Soak: 15 minutes   Cook: 15 minutes   Serves: 4

Serve this simple side dish, enhanced with the woodsy flavor and aroma of dried wild mushrooms, with roasted squab, pheasant, or medallions of venison.

1 ounce dried porcini	**½ teaspoon salt**
1 cup water	**Coarsely ground black**
1 cup tubettini	**pepper**
½ to ¾ cup heavy cream	

1. Combine the porcini and water in a small saucepan; heat to boiling, over low heat. Let stand, off heat, covered, 15 minutes. Drain through a fine sieve lined with a piece of dampened paper towel or double thickness of dampened cheesecloth; reserve the liquid (about ½ cup, depending on dryness of mushrooms; use more heavy cream if mushroom liquid is less than ½ cup). Rinse any grit from mushrooms; coarsely chop; set aside.

2. Cook the pasta in plenty of boiling salted water until al dente, or firm to the bite, 8 to 10 minutes; drain.

3. Combine the pasta, mushrooms, mushroom liquid, heavy cream, and salt in a saucepan. Heat, stirring constantly, to boiling. Cook, stirring, over low heat until most of the liquid has been absorbed and the mixture is creamy, about 3 minutes. Season with pepper.

---

183 STELLINE WITH LEMON AND CREAM
Prep: 10 minutes   Cook: 10 minutes   Serves: 4

2 cups seasoned chicken broth	**½ cup heavy cream**
1 cup stelline	**½ teaspoon grated lemon zest**
2 tablespoons fresh lemon	
** juice**	

1. Heat chicken broth to boiling; stir in stelline and lemon zest. Cover and cook over low heat until liquid is absorbed, about 10 minutes.

2. Stir in heavy cream and lemon zest. Serve at once.

184   ORZO WITH ASIAGO AND PARSLEY
Prep: 10 minutes   Cook: 10 minutes   Serves: 4

Asiago is a dry, salty cow's milk cheese, both imported and domestic. This highly flavored side dish is especially good with breaded sautéed chicken cutlets with a chunky tomato sauce or with beef pizzaiola.

1 **cup orzo**	2 **tablespoons unsalted butter**
½ **cup crumbled or chopped Asiago cheese**	2 **tablespoons chopped Italian flat-leaf parsley**

1. Cook orzo in plenty of boiling salted water until al dente, or firm to the bite, about 10 minutes; drain.

2. Return to saucepan with cheese, butter, and parsley. Stir just to blend and serve immediately.

185   FARFALLINE WITH PARSLEY AND GARLIC BUTTER
Prep: 5 minutes   Cook: 10 minutes   Serves: 4

1 **cup farfalline**	2 **tablespoons very finely chopped parsley**
4 **tablespoons unsalted butter**	
2 **garlic cloves, crushed**	

1. Cook farfalline in plenty of boiling salted water until al dente, or firm to the bite, 8 to 10 minutes; drain.

2. Melt butter in a small skillet. Add garlic; sauté, stirring, over low heat 1 minute; stir in parsley. Toss pasta and sauce together until blended. Serve at once.

186   ORZO WITH BROWNED GARLIC
Prep: 10 minutes   Cook: 15 minutes   Serves: 4

1 **cup orzo**	1 **tablespoon minced chives**
¼ **cup olive oil**	**Freshly ground black pepper**
1 **tablespoon thinly sliced peeled garlic cloves**	

1. Cook orzo in plenty of boiling salted water until al dente, or firm to the bite, about 10 minutes; drain.

2. While pasta is cooking, heat oil in a small skillet over low heat; stir in garlic. Sauté, stirring, until garlic turns a pale golden color; remove from heat. Pour over orzo; fluff with a fork. Sprinkle with chives and black pepper.

187 ORZO COOKED IN SAFFRON BROTH
Prep: 5 minutes   Cook: 10 minutes   Serves: 4

This side dish is inspired by the popular Risotto alla Milanese, which is arborio rice cooked in a saffron broth. Saffron, the stamens of the crocus flower, turns the orzo a brilliant yellow and lends a pervasive aroma. For a richer dish, add ¼ cup grated Parmesan cheese before serving.

2 cups chicken broth	1 cup orzo
⅛ teaspoon saffron threads, or	2 tablespoons unsalted butter
a pinch of powdered	1 tablespoon thinly sliced
saffron	green scallion tops

1. In a medium saucepan, heat the broth to boiling; stir in the orzo and butter. Cook, covered, over low heat until liquid is absorbed, about 10 minutes.

2. Sprinkle with scallions; serve at once.

Variation:

188 ORZO COOKED IN SAFFRON BROTH WITH SHRIMP AND PEAS

Cook 8 ounces shelled and deveined shrimp until tender; drain; cool; coarsely chop. Add 1 cup frozen tiny peas to the orzo before cooking. When the orzo is tender, add the shrimp; toss just to blend.

189 COUSCOUS WITH DRIED FRUITS AND ALMONDS
Prep: 10 minutes   Cook: 5 minutes   Serves: 4

Couscous is a popular African "noodle." It is available boxed or loose in health food stores, and frequently in supermarkets. It is a tiny granular pasta and cooks very quickly. Traditionally it is steamed in a special utensil called a *couscoussier* and served with a stew.

1 cup couscous	1 tablespoon dried currants or
1½ cups *boiling* homemade	chopped raisins
light chicken broth, or	1 tablespoon sliced
equal parts canned broth	unblanched almonds,
and water	toasted 1 to 2 minutes in a
2 tablespoons butter	warm skillet
1 tablespoon minced dried	
apricots	

1. Place couscous in a medium bowl; stir in the boiling broth. Cover and let stand until broth is absorbed, about 5 minutes.

2. Melt the butter in a small skillet; add the dried fruits and almonds. Add to couscous and toss.

190   ACINI DI PEPE WITH LEMON AND BUTTER
Prep: 5 minutes   Cook: 6 minutes   Serves: 4

1 cup acini di pepe
3 tablespoons fresh lemon
      juice

2 tablespoons butter, cut into
      small pieces
1 teaspoon finely shredded or
      grated lemon zest

1. Cook the pasta in plenty of boiling salted water until al dente, or firm to the bite, about 5 minutes; drain.

2. Add the lemon juice, butter, and zest to the pasta; stir gently. Serve while still hot.

Variations:

191   ACINI DI PEPE WITH LEMON, BUTTER, AND ZUCCHINI

Trim and finely shred 1 small (about 3 ounces) zucchini (about ½ cup). Add to the hot acini di pepe with the lemon, butter, and lemon zest.

192   ACINI DI PEPE WITH LEMON, BUTTER, AND CARROTS

Trim, pare, and shred 1 medium carrot (about ½ cup). Add to the hot acini di pepe with the lemon, butter, and lemon zest.

193   ORZO WITH PEAS AND MINT
Prep: 10 minutes   Cook: 10 minutes   Serves: 4

1 cup orzo
1 cup fresh or frozen peas
2 tablespoons butter
1 tablespoon very finely
      chopped fresh mint

1 tablespoon very finely
      chopped Italian flat-leaf
      parsley

1. Cook orzo in plenty of boiling salted water 5 minutes; stir in peas. Cook until pasta is al dente, or firm to the bite, and the peas are tender, about 5 minutes longer; drain.

2. Melt the butter in the saucepan; stir in the mint and parsley; add the orzo and peas. Toss to blend. Serve at once.

194 TUBETTINI WITH PEAS AND PROSCIUTTO
Prep: 10 minutes   Cook: 10 minutes   Serves: 4

1 cup tubettini
1 cup fresh or frozen peas
¼ cup heavy cream
1 egg

2 tablespoons grated
    Parmesan cheese
¼ cup slivered prosciutto or
    other cured ham (about 3
    very thin slices)

1. Cook tubettini in plenty of boiling salted water 5 minutes; stir in peas. Cook until pasta is al dente, or firm to the bite, and the peas are tender, about 5 minutes longer; drain.

2. Beat cream, egg, and cheese together in a serving bowl; add the hot pasta and the prosciutto; toss until blended. Serve at once.

195 PASTINA WITH SCRAMBLED EGGS AND PARMESAN
Prep: 10 minutes   Cook: 15 minutes   Serves: 4

Served with steamed fresh asparagus spears, this makes a lovely brunch or light supper dish.

2 cups homemade chicken
    broth, or half canned
    broth and half water
1 cup pastina
2 eggs

2 tablespoons milk or heavy
    cream
2 tablespoons unsalted butter
1 small garlic clove, crushed
2 tablespoons grated
    Parmesan cheese

1. Heat broth in a small saucepan to boiling; stir in pastina; cover and cook over low heat until liquid is absorbed, about 10 minutes.

2. In a small bowl, beat eggs and milk together. Heat butter in a small skillet until foam subsides; stir in the garlic. Add the beaten egg mixture. Scramble eggs until soft cooked, about 3 minutes. Stir cooked eggs and cheese into the pastina. Serve at once.

Tiny pasta shapes

Acini di pepe: "peppercorns"; tiny little solid beads
Anellini: "little rings"
Capellini: "fine hairs"
Conchigliette: "tiny shells"
Coralli: tiny tubes; similar to *tubettini*
Ditalini: "little thimbles"
Elbows: tiny shapes suitable for soups
Farfalline: "tiny butterflies"

Orzo: rice shape; also called *riso* or *rosamarina*
Pastina: very tiny grains of dough; for soup
Quadrettini: small flat squares
Riso: *orzo; rosamarina*
Semi di mela: "apple seeds"
Semi di melone: "melon seeds"
Stellini: "little stars"
Tubettini: "tiny tubes"

Chapter 11

Emergency Dinners

In a rush? Is dinner often a last-minute hassle? Be prepared! Stock your kitchen with the following sixteen ingredients and you'll be ready to create any of the following simply scrumptious emergency dinners.

Staples for the Pantry

1. 1 pound linguine or spaghetti
2. 1 can (10½ ounces) chopped clams
3. 1 can (14½ to 16 ounces) whole peeled tomatoes
4. 1 ounce dried porcini or cepe mushrooms
5. 1 jar (7 ounces) roasted peppers
6. Crushed dried red pepper
7. Good-quality olive oil
8. 1 can (6½ ounces) tuna packed in olive oil
9. 1 can (2 ounces) flat anchovy fillets
10. 1 jar imported black olives, such as niçoise, Kalamata, or Gaeta
11. 1 garlic bulb
12. 1 large onion

Staples for the Refrigerator

13. Grated Parmesan cheese
14. 1 lemon
15. ¼ pound butter

And in Your Freezer

16. 6 strips thick-sliced bacon

Something a Little Extra

Any of these dishes will be greatly enhanced by a small handful of chopped fresh parsley, perhaps even a snip of a fresh herb, if you are lucky enough to have a small pot on your windowsill or sitting in the garden.

196 LINGUINE WITH RED CLAM SAUCE AND BACON

Prep: 10 minutes   Cook: 25 minutes   Serves: 4–5

2 strips bacon, cut into ¼-inch
  pieces
2 tablespoons olive oil
½ cup chopped onion
1 garlic clove, minced
1 can (14½ ounces) whole
  peeled tomatoes with
  juices

1 can (10½ ounces) chopped
  clams
  Salt and freshly ground
  pepper
2 tablespoons chopped fresh
  parsley, or other fresh
  herbs to taste (optional)
1 pound linguine

1. Sauté the bacon in a medium skillet until lightly browned, about 5 minutes; spoon off most of the bacon fat. Add the olive oil; sauté the onion over low heat until very tender and golden, about 8 minutes. Add the garlic; sauté 1 minute. Stir in the tomatoes and clams. Simmer over medium heat, uncovered, stirring to break up tomatoes with side of a spoon, until slightly reduced and sauce has thickened, about 10 minutes. Season with salt, pepper, and parsley.

2. Meanwhile, cook the linguine in plenty of boiling salted water until al dente, or firm to the bite, about 6 minutes; drain. Toss with the sauce and serve at once.

197 SPAGHETTI WITH TOMATO AND PORCINI SAUCE

Prep: 5 minutes   Soak: 15 minutes   Cook: 20 minutes   Serves: 4–5

½ ounce dried porcini
½ cup water
2 tablespoons olive oil
½ cup chopped onion
1 garlic clove, minced
1 can (14½ ounces) whole
  peeled tomatoes with
  juices

  Salt and freshly ground
  pepper
2 tablespoons chopped fresh
  parsley, or other fresh
  herbs to taste (optional)
1 pound spaghetti
  Grated Parmesan cheese

1. In a small saucepan, combine the mushrooms and water; heat to simmering; let stand, covered, 15 minutes. Drain mushrooms through a sieve lined with a dampened paper towel. Reserve liquid. Rinse any grit from mushrooms; drain and chop.

2. Heat oil in a medium skillet; sauté onion until tender, about 8 minutes; stir in garlic; sauté 1 minute. Add the tomatoes, porcini liquid, and porcini; heat to boiling. Simmer, uncovered, over medium heat, stirring to break up tomatoes with the side of a spoon, until slightly reduced and sauce is thickened, about 10 minutes. Add salt, pepper, and parsley.

3. Meanwhile, cook spaghetti in plenty of boiling salted water until al dente, or firm to the bite, about 6 minutes; drain. Toss with the sauce and serve with cheese, if desired.

198 SPAGHETTI WITH TUNA AND OLIVE SAUCE

Prep: 15 minutes   Cook: 10 minutes   Serves: 4–5

4 tablespoons oil
½ cup chopped onion
1 garlic clove, crushed
1 can (6½ ounces) tuna packed
   in olive oil, drained
¼ cup pitted and coarsely cut
   up imported black olives

2 tablespoons chopped fresh
   parsley, or other fresh
   herbs to taste (optional)
1 pound spaghetti
2 tablespoons fresh lemon
   juice
Salt and coarsely ground
   black pepper

1. Heat oil in a medium skillet; add onion; sauté until tender, about 5 minutes. Add garlic; sauté 1 minute. Add the tuna; sauté 1 minute. Add the olives and parsley or herbs, if available.

2. Meanwhile, cook the spaghetti in plenty of boiling salted water until al dente, or firm to the bite, about 6 minutes. Ladle out ¼ cup of pasta cooking liquid and reserve; drain pasta. Toss pasta with tuna sauce, pasta cooking liquid, and lemon juice. Season with salt and plenty of black pepper.

199 LINGUINE WITH CARAMELIZED ONION, BACON, AND OLIVES

Prep: 10 minutes   Cook: 15 minutes   Serves: 4–5

For tuna lovers, this recipe can be varied by adding 1 can (6½ ounces) tuna in olive oil, drained, after the onion is sautéed. Omit cheese if using tuna.

6 strips bacon, cut into ½-inch
   pieces
4 tablespoons olive oil
1 onion, quartered, and cut
   into thin lengthwise
   strips
1 garlic clove, minced
¼ cup pitted and chopped
   imported black olives

1 pound linguine
2 tablespoons chopped fresh
   parsley, or other fresh
   herbs to taste (optional)
Coarsely ground black
   pepper
Grated Parmesan cheese

1. Cook the bacon in a medium skillet until partially browned; drain off most of the fat. Add the olive oil; heat over low heat; add the onion; sauté until soft and edges begin to turn golden, about 8 minutes. Add the garlic; sauté 1 minute. Stir in the olives.

2. Meanwhile, cook the linguine in plenty of boiling salted water until al dente, or firm to the bite, about 6 minutes; drain. Toss with the onion and bacon sauce and the parsley, if using. Sprinkle with pepper and grated cheese.

200 SPAGHETTI WITH RED PEPPER AND PORCINI SAUCE

Prep: 10 minutes   Soak: 15 minutes   Cook: 20 minutes   Serves: 4–5

1 ounce dried porcini
1 cup water
1 jar (7 ounces) roasted red peppers, rinsed and drained
4 tablespoons olive oil
½ cup chopped onion
1 garlic clove, minced

Salt and coarsely ground black pepper
1 pound spaghetti
2 tablespoons chopped fresh parsley, or other fresh herbs to taste (optional)
Grated Parmesan cheese

1. Combine the porcini and water in a small saucepan; heat, covered, to simmering over low heat. Let stand, covered, 15 minutes. Drain through a sieve lined with a dampened paper towel; reserve liquid. Rinse porcini of any grit; blot dry and coarsely chop.

2. Purée the red peppers in a food processor with half the reserved porcini soaking liquid. Heat the oil in a medium skillet over low heat. Add the onion; sauté until tender but not browned, about 5 minutes; stir in the garlic; sauté 1 minute. Add the red pepper purée, the remaining porcini liquid, and the chopped porcini. Cook, stirring, over low heat, until sauce is slightly reduced, about 10 minutes. Season with salt and pepper.

3. Meanwhile, cook spaghetti in plenty of boiling salted water until al dente, or firm to the bite, about 6 minutes. Drain. Toss with the sauce and parsley, if using. Serve with cheese on the side.

201 SPAGHETTI WITH TOMATOES, BACON, AND ONIONS

Prep: 10 minutes   Cook: 20 minutes   Serves: 4–5

4 slices bacon, cut into ¼-inch pieces
4 tablespoons olive oil
1 cup chopped onion
1 garlic clove, minced
1 can (14½ ounces) whole peeled tomatoes with juices

Salt and coarsely ground black pepper
1 pound spaghetti
2 tablespoons chopped fresh parsley, or other fresh herbs to taste (optional)
Grated Parmesan cheese

1. Sauté the bacon in a skillet until partially browned; drain off most of the fat. Add the olive oil; heat over low heat. Add the onion; sauté, stirring, until tender but not browned, about 5 minutes. Add garlic; sauté 1 minute. Add tomatoes; cook, stirring to break up the tomatoes with the side of a spoon, until sauce is slightly thickened, about 10 minutes. Season with salt and pepper.

2. Meanwhile, cook the spaghetti in plenty of boiling salted water until al dente, or firm to the bite, about 6 minutes; drain. Toss with the sauce and parsley, if using. Sprinkle with grated cheese.

202 SPAGHETTI WITH ROASTED RED PEPPER AND TUNA

Prep: 15 minutes   Cook: 10 minutes   Serves: 4–5

4 tablespoons olive oil
1 onion, quartered lengthwise and cut into thin lengthwise strips
1 garlic clove, crushed
1 jar (7 ounces) roasted red peppers, rinsed, drained, and cut into thin strips
1 can (6½ ounces) tuna packed in olive oil, drained

2 tablespoons pitted and chopped imported black olives
1 pound spaghetti
2 tablespoons chopped fresh parsley, or other fresh herbs if available (optional)

1. Heat oil in a medium skillet; add onion; sauté over low heat, stirring, until tender and edges just begin to turn golden, about 8 minutes. Stir in the garlic; sauté 1 minute. Add the red peppers, tuna, and olives; sauté just to heat through.

2. Meanwhile, cook the spaghetti in plenty of boiling salted water until al dente, or firm to the bite, about 6 minutes; drain. Toss with the sauce and parsley, if using; serve at once.

203 SPAGHETTI WITH BACON, ONION, AND RED PEPPER

Prep: 10 minutes   Cook: 20 minutes   Serves: 4–5

4 slices bacon, cut into ¼-inch pieces
2 tablespoons olive oil
1 onion, quartered and cut into thin lengthwise slices
1 garlic clove, crushed
1 jar (7 ounces) roasted peppers, rinsed, drained, and cut into thin strips

2 tablespoons pitted and coarsely chopped imported black olives
2 tablespoons chopped fresh parsley, or other fresh herbs to taste (optional)
1 pound spaghetti
Coarsely ground black pepper
Grated Parmesan cheese

1. Cook bacon in a medium skillet over low heat until lightly browned; drain off most of the fat. Add olive oil. Sauté onion over low heat until golden, about 8 minutes. Stir in garlic; sauté 1 minute. Add the red peppers, olives, and parsley or herbs, if using. Stir over medium heat 2 minutes.

2. Meanwhile, cook the spaghetti in plenty of boiling salted water until al dente, or firm to the bite, about 6 minutes. Drain. Toss with the red pepper mixture. Sprinkle with black pepper. Serve with plenty of grated Parmesan cheese.

204 SPAGHETTI WITH BUTTER, PARMESAN, AND BROWNED BACON

Prep: 10 minutes   Cook: 20 minutes   Serves: 4–5

4 strips bacon, cut into ½-inch
   pieces
1 pound spaghetti
4 tablespoons butter

½ cup grated Parmesan cheese
2 tablespoons chopped fresh
   parsley, or other fresh
   herbs to taste (optional)

1. Sauté the bacon until browned; drain on paper toweling; discard fat.

2. Cook the spaghetti in plenty of boiling salted water until al dente, or firm to the bite, about 6 minutes; ladle out ¼ cup of the pasta cooking liquid; reserve. Drain pasta.

3. Melt the butter in the pasta cooking pan until just creamy; add the pasta, reserved cooking liquid, and cheese; toss. Sprinkle with the bacon and the parsley, if using. Toss once and serve.

205 LINGUINE WITH TOMATOES AND BUTTER

Prep: 10 minutes   Cook: 15 minutes   Serves: 4–5

If available, add a few fresh basil leaves, torn into ragged pieces and tossed with the pasta at the last minute.

1 can (14½ ounces) whole
   peeled tomatoes, drained
1 pound linguine
4 tablespoons butter
1 small garlic clove, crushed
2 tablespoons grated
   Parmesan cheese

2 tablespoons chopped fresh
   parsley, or other fresh
   herbs to taste (optional)
Salt and coarsely ground
   black pepper

1. Carefully squeeze the seeds from the tomatoes; discard or reserve with the drained juices for another use. Cut the tomatoes into strips.

2. Cook the linguine in plenty of boiling salted water until al dente, or firm to the bite, about 6 minutes; drain. Melt the butter just until creamy in the pasta cooking pot; add the garlic and sauté over low heat 1 minute. Add the pasta, tomatoes, cheese, parsley, if using, and salt and pepper to taste. Toss gently; serve at once with grated cheese on the side.

Dried herbs in your pantry

Use restraint when using dried herbs. They are much more potent than fresh herbs and a little too much can render a dish bitter. Always start with about a pinch, but not more than ¼ teaspoon, of dried oregano, marjoram, basil, thyme, sage, or tarragon.

Dried herbs can be successfully reconstituted by chopping along with a sprig or two of fresh parsley. The natural moisture from the parsley dampens the dried herbs just enough to give the flavorful oils a little nudge in the right direction.

206 LINGUINE WITH TOMATO, LEMON, AND BUTTER SAUCE

Prep: 10 minutes   Cook: 10 minutes   Serves: 4–5

4 tablespoons butter
1 can (14½ ounces) whole tomatoes, drained and cut up
2 teaspoons finely shredded fresh lemon zest
2 tablespoons fresh lemon juice

2 tablespoons chopped fresh parsley, or other fresh herbs to taste (optional)
Salt and coarsely ground black pepper
1 pound linguine
Grated Parmesan cheese

1. Melt the butter in a small skillet over low heat just until creamy. Stir in tomatoes; sauté over low heat; stir in lemon zest, lemon juice, parsley, if using, and salt and pepper.

2. Meanwhile, cook the linguine in plenty of boiling salted water until al dente, or firm to the bite, about 6 minutes; drain. Add to sauce and toss. Serve with cheese on the side.

207 SPAGHETTI WITH TOMATO, ANCHOVY, AND BLACK OLIVE SAUCE

Prep: 10 minutes   Cook: 15 minutes   Serves: 4–5

2 tablespoons olive oil
1 garlic clove, minced
4 anchovy fillets, blotted with paper towels, chopped
1 can (14½ ounces) whole peeled tomatoes with juices
Pinch of crushed dried red pepper

1 pound spaghetti
2 tablespoons pitted and chopped imported black olives
2 tablespoons chopped fresh parsley, or other fresh herbs to taste (optional)
Coarsely ground black pepper

1. Heat oil in a medium skillet over low heat; add the garlic and anchovies; cook, stirring, until anchovies are dissolved, about 3 minutes. Add the tomatoes and red pepper. Heat to simmering; cook over medium heat, breaking up tomatoes with the side of a spoon, until sauce is slightly reduced, about 10 minutes.

2. Meanwhile, cook the spaghetti in plenty of boiling salted water until al dente, or firm to the bite, about 6 minutes. Drain. Toss with the sauce, olives, and parsley, if available. Sprinkle with black pepper.

208 SPAGHETTI WITH GARLIC AND HOT RED PEPPER OIL

Prep: 5 minutes   Cook: 15 minutes   Serves: 4–5

6 tablespoons olive oil
1 tablespoon thin slices of garlic (4 or 5 cloves)
½ teaspoon crushed dried red pepper
1 pound spaghetti

2 tablespoons coarsely chopped parsley, if available
Salt
Coarsely ground black pepper

1. Heat oil in a small skillet over low heat just until warm. Stir in the garlic; cook, stirring, over very low heat until garlic is soft and a light golden color, about 8 minutes. Stir in the red pepper; sauté, stirring, just until oil takes on a yellow color, about 1 minute.

2. Cook the spaghetti in plenty of boiling salted water until al dente, or firm to the bite, about 6 minutes. Ladle out ½ cup of the pasta cooking liquid; reserve. Drain pasta. Toss with the garlic oil, pasta cooking liquid, and parsley, if using. Season with salt and generously add black pepper.

209 LINGUINE WITH TUNA, BLACK OLIVES, AND TOMATOES

Prep: 15 minutes   Cook: 15 minutes   Serves: 4–5

1 can (14½ ounces) whole peeled tomatoes, drained
4 tablespoons olive oil
1 garlic clove, minced
1 can (6½ ounces) tuna packed in olive oil
3 tablespoons pitted and chopped imported black olives

Salt
1 pound linguine
2 tablespoons chopped fresh parsley, or other fresh herbs to taste (optional)
Coarsely ground black pepper

1. Coarsely chop the tomatoes; reserve the juice for another use.

2. Heat oil in a skillet until warm; add garlic; sauté 1 minute. Add tomatoes, tuna, and black olives; sauté, stirring occasionally, 5 minutes. Add salt to taste.

3. Meanwhile, cook linguine in plenty of boiling salted water until al dente, or firm to the bite, about 6 minutes; drain. Toss with the tuna sauce and sprinkle with freshly ground pepper.

210 LINGUINE WITH PEPPERY WHITE CLAM SAUCE

Prep: 10 minutes   Cook: 15 minutes   Serves: 4–5

¼ cup olive oil
2 garlic cloves, minced or crushed
¼ teaspoon crushed dried red pepper
1 can (10½ ounces) chopped clams with juice
1 pound linguine

¼ cup pasta cooking liquid
Juice of 1 lemon
2 tablespoons chopped fresh parsley, or other fresh herbs to taste (optional)
Coarsely ground black pepper (optional)

1. Heat the oil in a medium skillet over low heat; stir in garlic. Sauté over low heat 2 minutes (do not brown); add the red pepper; sauté 1 minute. Add the clams with their juice; simmer, uncovered, 10 minutes.

2. Meanwhile, cook the linguine in plenty of boiling salted water until al dente, or firm to the bite, about 6 minutes. Drain pasta, reserving ¼ cup cooking liquid. Toss the linguine with the clam sauce, pasta cooking liquid, lemon juice, and parsley. Sprinkle with pepper, if desired.

211 SPAGHETTI WITH ANCHOVY SAUCE

Prep: 10 minutes   Cook: 10 minutes   Serves: 4

This recipe was inspired by a batch of leftover *bagna cauda*, a rich raw vegetable dip.

6 tablespoons olive oil
2 tablespoons butter
1 teaspoon finely minced garlic
1 can (2 ounces) anchovy fillets, drained, blotted dry, and finely chopped

1 pound spaghetti
2 tablespoons chopped fresh parsley, or other fresh herbs to taste (optional)
Coarsely ground black pepper

1. Heat oil and butter in a skillet over low heat until butter is creamy; add garlic; sauté, stirring over very low heat just until fragrant. Add the anchovies; sauté, stirring, over low heat, until anchovies dissolve into a paste.

2. Cook spaghetti in plenty of boiling salted water until al dente, or firm to the bite, about 6 minutes. Toss with the anchovy oil and parsley, if using. Sprinkle with plenty of black pepper.

Chapter 12

No-Cook Sauces for Hot Pasta

The concept of tossing a hot pasta with a room-temperature sauce of chopped raw ingredients, olive oil, and other seasonings is fairly new to Americans. Uncooked tomato sauces, called *salsa di pomodoro crudo,* are delicious and popular summer fare in Italy. What could be more appealing than chopped fresh ripe tomatoes seasoned with chopped fresh basil and tossed with a tiny pasta on a hot summer day? What follows are surprisingly simple and delectable variations on this theme.

212   FRESH TOMATO, BASIL, AND RICOTTA SAUCE

Prep: 10 minutes   Yield: 3 cups, or enough for 1 pound pasta, such as rotelle, fusilli, ziti, penne, or tubetti

3 cups chopped ripe tomatoes
½ cup chopped fresh basil
2 tablespoons minced red onion
1 garlic clove, crushed

1 cup ricotta cheese
¼ cup olive oil
Salt
Freshly ground black pepper

Combine the tomatoes, basil, onion, and garlic. Stir in the ricotta, oil, and salt and pepper to taste. Toss hot pasta with the sauce and serve at once.

213   BASIL, WALNUT, AND GARLIC SAUCE

Prep: 15 minutes   Yield: 1 cup, or enough for 1 pound fettuccine, penne, ziti, or spaghetti

1 cup chopped fresh basil
¼ cup chopped Italian flat-leaf parsley
½ cup finely chopped walnuts
2 tablespoons grated Parmesan cheese

2 tablespoons pitted and chopped imported black olives
½ cup olive oil
2 garlic cloves, crushed

Combine the basil, parsley, walnuts, cheese, olives, olive oil, and garlic in a small bowl. Stir to blend. Toss hot pasta with the sauce and serve at once.

214   ARTICHOKE, ROASTED RED PEPPER, AND SUN-DRIED TOMATO SAUCE

Prep: 15 minutes   Yield: 2 cups, or enough for 16 ounces penne, medium shells, or twists

1 jar (6 ounces) marinated artichokes, rinsed, well drained, and chopped
1 jar (7 ounces) roasted red peppers, rinsed, well drained, and chopped
¼ cup chopped Italian flat-leaf parsley
2 tablespoons minced sun-dried tomatoes in oil, well drained

1 tablespoon pitted and slivered brine-cured black olives
½ cup olive oil
1 tablespoon red wine vinegar
1 garlic clove, crushed
⅛ teaspoon freshly ground black pepper

Combine all ingredients in a small bowl. Stir well to blend. Toss hot pasta with sauce and serve at once.

215 PARSLEY PESTO SAUCE
Prep: 5 minutes   Yield: 1 cup, or enough for 1 pound pasta

A delightful variation on the classic pesto; perfect for when basil is out of season. Use flavorful Italian flat-leaf parsley.

2 cups packed Italian flat-leaf parsley	⅓ cup pignoli (pine nuts)
2 garlic cloves, chopped	½ cup olive oil
½ teaspoon salt	3 tablespoons grated Parmesan cheese

1. Finely chop the parsley and garlic in a food processor or blender. Add the salt and pine nuts; process until finely chopped. With motor running, slowly add the oil through the feed tube.

2. Stir in the Parmesan cheese. If not using immediately, scrape into a container. Refrigerate for up to 3 days.

3. Bring the sauce to room temperature and toss with hot pasta. Serve at once, with extra cheese to taste.

Variation:

216 TUNA AND PARSLEY PESTO SAUCE
Yield: enough sauce for 12 ounces spaghetti or 8 ounces small tubular pasta

Drain 1 can (6½ ounces) imported Italian tuna packed in olive oil; stir in ¼ cup Parsley Pesto Sauce and ¼ cup pasta cooking liquid. Toss with hot pasta and serve at once.

217 WALNUT PESTO SAUCE
Prep: 5 minutes   Yield: 1½ cups, or enough for 1½ pounds pasta

Pesto freezes very well if the cheese is left out and added to the sauce once it is thawed and ready to use.

½ cup broken walnuts	1 cup packed Italian flat-leaf parsley
1 large garlic clove, chopped	
2 cups packed fresh basil leaves	¾ cup olive oil
¼ teaspoon salt	⅓ cup grated Parmesan cheese

1. Finely chop the walnuts and the garlic in a food processor; add half the basil and the salt; coarsely chop. Add the remaining basil and the parsley. With the food processor running, add the oil in a slow steady stream through the feed tube until mixture is thoroughly blended. Transfer to a bowl; fold in the cheese.

2. Remove ½ cup of the pasta cooking liquid before draining the pasta. Toss hot pasta with the sauce and the reserved cooking liquid. Serve at once with additional cheese, if desired.

218 TUNA, ARTICHOKE, AND OLIVE SAUCE

Prep: 15 minutes   Yield: 1½ cups, or enough for 8 ounces medium shells or tubetti

½ cup chopped marinated artichoke hearts
1 can (6½ ounces) imported Italian tuna in olive oil, rinsed and drained
⅓ cup olive oil

2 tablespoons chopped Italian flat-leaf parsley
1 tablespoon pitted and chopped imported black olives
1 garlic clove, crushed

Combine all the ingredients in a bowl; stir to blend. Toss hot pasta with the sauce and serve at once.

219 ANCHOVY, RED PEPPER, AND CAPER SAUCE

Prep: 10 minutes   Yield: 1 cup, or enough for 16 ounces linguine or spaghetti

1 jar (7 ounces) roasted red peppers, rinsed, well drained, and cut into thin strips
½ cup olive oil
4 flat anchovy fillets, finely chopped

2 tablespoons chopped Italian flat-leaf parsley
2 teaspoons small capers, rinsed and drained
1 garlic clove, chopped

Combine all the ingredients in a bowl. Toss the hot pasta with the sauce and serve at once.

220 GREEN OLIVE AND CELERY SAUCE

Prep: 10 minutes   Yield: 1 cup, or enough for 8 ounces small pasta like ditalini, tubetti, or small shells

½ cup pitted and crushed green olives with red pepper (often called salad olives)
½ cup diced (¼ inch) celery
2 tablespoons chopped celery leaves

6 tablespoons olive oil
¼ cup diced (¼ inch) red onion
¼ cup finely chopped parsley
1 garlic clove, crushed
⅛ teaspoon freshly ground black pepper

1. Rinse the olives in a sieve; drain; wrap in paper towels and squeeze out excess moisture.

2. Combine the olives, celery and leaves, oil, red onion, parsley, garlic, and pepper in a bowl; stir to blend. Toss hot pasta with the sauce and serve warm.

Variation:

221 GREEN OLIVE, CELERY, AND SALMON SAUCE

Add 1 can (7½ ounces) sockeye (red) salmon, drained and flaked, and 2 tablespoons fresh lemon juice to the olive sauce.

222 ROASTED RED PEPPER AND RICOTTA SAUCE

Prep: 15 minutes
Yield: 2½ cups, or enough for 1 pound spaghetti or medium-size grooved pasta, such as radiatore, fusilli, or shells

1 container (15 ounces) whole milk ricotta cheese
1 jar (7 ounces) roasted red peppers, rinsed and well drained
¼ cup olive oil
1 tablespoon grated Parmesan cheese

1 small garlic clove, crushed
2 tablespoons chopped Italian flat-leaf parsley
1 teaspoon fresh oregano leaves, or ¼ teaspoon dried oregano

Purée ricotta, roasted red peppers, oil, Parmesan, and garlic in the bowl of a food processor. Stir in parsley and oregano. Toss sauce with hot pasta and serve at once.

223 CREAMY TUNA SAUCE WITH CAPERS AND LEMON

Prep: 15 minutes   Yield: 2 cups, or enough for 12 ounces plain or spinach linguine

½ cup heavy cream, at room temperature
2 tablespoons lemon juice
1 teaspoon grated lemon zest
1 small garlic clove, crushed

1 can (6½ ounces) imported tuna in olive oil, well drained
2 tablespoons chopped Italian flat-leaf parsley
2 teaspoons small capers, rinsed and drained

1. Combine the cream, lemon juice, lemon zest, and garlic in the bowl of a food processor. Process just to blend and thicken cream slightly. Do not overprocess.

2. Fold the tuna, parsley, and capers into the cream. Toss hot pasta with the sauce and serve at once.

224   RICOTTA AND FRESH HERB SAUCE

Prep: 15 minutes   Yield: 2 cups, or enough for 12 ounces medium-size tubular pasta like penne, shells, or rotelle

1 container (15 ounces) whole milk ricotta cheese
¼ cup grated Parmesan cheese
2 tablespoons chopped fresh Italian flat-leaf parsley
2 tablespoons chopped fresh basil

2 tablespoons chopped fresh dill
2 tablespoons chopped fresh oregano
⅛ teaspoon black pepper

Combine all the ingredients and stir to blend. Fold sauce into hot pasta and serve at once.

225   THREE-HERB PESTO WITH WALNUTS

Prep: 15 minutes   Yield: 1 cup, or enough for 1 pound spaghetti

1 cup packed basil leaves
½ cup packed Italian flat-leaf parsley
½ cup packed dill sprigs
½ cup chopped walnuts

2 garlic cloves, minced
½ cup olive oil
2 tablespoons grated Romano cheese
½ cup pasta cooking liquid

1. Finely chop the basil, parsley, dill, walnuts, and garlic in the bowl of a food processor. With motor running, gradually add the oil through the feed tube. Add the cheese.

2. Remove ½ cup of the pasta cooking liquid before draining the pasta. Toss the hot pasta with the sauce and reserved pasta cooking liquid; serve at once.

226   ROASTED RED PEPPER, OLIVE, AND ROSEMARY SAUCE

Prep: 10 minutes   Yield: 1 cup, or enough for 8 ounces linguine

1 jar (7 ounces) roasted red peppers, rinsed, well drained, and finely chopped
¼ cup olive oil

¼ cup pitted and chopped imported black olives
1 tablespoon chopped fresh rosemary leaves, or ½ teaspoon dried
1 garlic clove, crushed

Combine the peppers, oil, olives, rosemary, and garlic; stir to blend. Toss hot pasta with sauce and serve at once.

227   FRESH TOMATO AND TUNA SAUCE

Prep: 15 minutes   Yield: 3 cups, or enough for 1 pound ridged pasta shape

2 pounds firm ripe small
   tomatoes or plum
   tomatoes, diced (¼-inch
   pieces, about 3 cups)
1 can (6½ ounces) chunk light
   tuna, well drained
¼ cup minced red onion

¼ cup minced Italian flat-leaf
   parsley
6 tablespoons olive oil
2 garlic cloves, crushed
½ teaspoon salt
¼ teaspoon freshly ground
   black pepper

Combine the tomatoes, tuna, red onion, parsley, oil, garlic, salt, and pepper in a large bowl; stir to blend. Toss hot pasta with tomato and tuna mixture; serve at once.

228   TOMATO, ONION, AND SARDINE SAUCE

Prep: 15 minutes   Yield: 3 cups, or enough for 12 ounces penne, ziti, or medium shells

2 cups finely chopped fresh
   tomatoes
¼ cup finely chopped red
   onion
¼ cup finely chopped scallions
¼ cup finely chopped Italian
   flat-leaf parsley
¼ cup olive oil

1 tablespoon fresh lemon
   juice
1 garlic clove, crushed
½ teaspoon salt
⅛ teaspoon freshly ground
   black pepper
1 can (3¾ ounces) imported
   sardines packed in water,
   drained

Combine the tomatoes, red onion, scallions, parsley, olive oil, lemon juice, garlic, salt, and pepper in a bowl. Gently stir in the sardines. Toss hot pasta with sauce and serve at once.

229   FRESH AND SUN-DRIED TOMATO SAUCE I

Prep: 15 minutes   Yield: 3 cups, or enough for 12 ounces small pasta like tubetti, small shells, or elbows

2 cups chopped ripe tomatoes
½ cup thinly sliced scallions
¼ cup drained and chopped
   sun-dried tomatoes in
   olive oil
¼ cup chopped fresh basil

¼ cup chopped Italian flat-leaf
   parsley
2 garlic cloves, crushed
½ teaspoon salt
⅛ teaspoon black pepper
½ cup olive oil

Combine the fresh tomatoes, scallions, sun-dried tomatoes, basil, parsley, garlic, salt, and pepper. Stir in the oil. Toss sauce with hot pasta and serve at once.

230   FRESH AND SUN-DRIED TOMATO SAUCE II

Prep: 10 minutes   Yield: 2 cups, or enough for 8 ounces small pasta such as tubetti, ditalini, or small shells

2 cups diced (¼ inch) tomatoes (use half yellow tomatoes, if available)
2 tablespoons drained and minced sun-dried tomatoes in olive oil
2 tablespoons chopped fresh basil

2 tablespoons chopped Italian (flat leaf) parsley
2 tablespoons olive oil
1 garlic clove, crushed
⅛ teaspoon freshly ground black pepper

Combine the fresh tomatoes, sun-dried tomatoes, basil, parsley, olive oil, garlic, and black pepper; stir to blend. Toss sauce with hot pasta and serve at once.

Variation:

231   FRESH AND SUN-DRIED TOMATO SAUCE WITH ANCHOVIES AND BLACK OLIVES

Add 3 anchovies, finely chopped, and 2 tablespoons pitted and chopped imported black olives to Fresh and Sun-Dried Tomato Sauce I or II; omit salt in recipes.

232   TRICOLOR TOMATO SAUCE WITH MINT

Prep: 15 minutes   Yield: 2 cups, or enough for 12 ounces fusilli, small shells, or tubetti

This is an especially pretty sauce if yellow tomatoes are available. The green tomato adds a pleasant astringency that is nicely balanced by the mint flavor.

1 cup chopped ripe red tomatoes
1 cup chopped yellow tomatoes
¼ cup minced green tomato
¼ cup olive oil

2 tablespoons finely chopped parsley
2 tablespoons finely chopped fresh mint
1 garlic clove, crushed
⅛ teaspoon coarsely ground black pepper

Stir all the ingredients together in a bowl. Toss hot pasta with the sauce and serve at once.

233   MARINATED MUSHROOM SAUCE

Prep: 15 minutes   Marinate: 1–2 hours
Yield: 2 cups, or enough for 8 ounces large pasta like rigatoni, shells, or fusilli

8 ounces small white mushrooms, wiped and coarsely chopped
¼ cup finely chopped red onion
¼ cup finely chopped red bell pepper
¼ cup chopped Italian flat-leaf parsley
1 tablespoon fresh oregano leaves, or ½ teaspoon dried

1 teaspoon fresh thyme leaves, or ¼ teaspoon dried
⅓ cup olive oil
2 tablespoons fresh lemon juice
½ teaspoon salt
⅛ teaspoon freshly ground black pepper

Combine the mushrooms, onion, red pepper, parsley, oregano, and thyme in a small bowl. Whisk the oil, lemon juice, salt, and pepper in a separate bowl; fold together. Cover and marinate, refrigerated, 1 to 2 hours. Toss sauce with hot pasta and serve at once.

234   FRESH FROM THE GARDEN SAUCE

Prep: 15 minutes   Yield: 2½ cups, or enough for 12 ounces small pasta, such as small shells, tubetti, or elbows

1½ cups chopped ripe tomatoes
¼ cup diced pared cucumber
¼ cup seeded green bell pepper
¼ cup trimmed zucchini
¼ cup chopped scallions
1 ear corn, husked, kernels cut from the cob (uncooked), about ½ cup
1 medium carrot, pared and coarsely shredded

¼ cup finely chopped parsley
¼ cup finely chopped basil
2 tablespoons diced radishes
6 tablespoons olive oil
1 tablespoon red wine vinegar
1 garlic clove, crushed
½ teaspoon salt, or to taste
Coarsely ground black pepper

Combine the tomatoes, cucumber, green pepper, zucchini, scallions, corn, carrot, parsley, basil, and radishes. Add the oil, vinegar, garlic, salt, and pepper; toss to blend. Let stand, covered, 20 minutes before using. (Can be made ahead and refrigerated, but best when eaten the same day as assembled.) Toss sauce with hot pasta and serve at once.

235 YELLOW TOMATO, CUCUMBER, AND CORIANDER SAUCE

Prep: 10 minutes   Yield: 2 cups, or enough for 12 ounces pasta

1½ cups chopped yellow
   tomato
½ cup coarsely shredded pared
   and seeded cucumber
2 tablespoons minced red bell
   pepper
1 tablespoon chopped fresh
   basil
1 tablespoon chopped fresh
   coriander (cilantro)

1 teaspoon minced, seeded
   hot chili pepper, or to
   taste
1 scallion, trimmed and sliced
   very thin
6 tablespoons olive oil
3 tablespoons fresh lime juice
½ teaspoon salt, or to taste
1 garlic clove, crushed

Combine the yellow tomato, cucumber, red bell pepper, basil, coriander, chili pepper, and scallion. Add the oil, lime juice, salt, and garlic; toss to blend. Toss hot pasta with the sauce and serve at once.

236 TRICOLOR BELL PEPPER SAUCE WITH BLACK OLIVES AND ANCHOVIES

Prep: 15 minutes   Yield: 2 cups, or enough for 12 ounces pasta, such as wagon wheels, fusilli, or shells

½ cup *each* finely chopped red,
   yellow, and green bell
   pepper
¼ cup finely chopped light
   green frying pepper
½ cup chopped tomato
3 tablespoons pitted and
   chopped imported black
   olives
2 tablespoons finely chopped
   Spanish or other sweet
   onion

1 tablespoon chopped fresh
   basil
1 tablespoon chopped parsley
6 tablespoons olive oil
4 flat anchovy fillets, blotted
   dry and finely chopped
2 garlic cloves, crushed
¼ teaspoon salt, or to taste
⅛ teaspoon coarsely ground
   black pepper

Combine the peppers, tomato, olives, onion, basil, and parsley. Add the oil, anchovies, garlic, salt, and pepper; mix very well with a wooden spoon so that the anchovies dissolve. Toss the hot pasta with the sauce. Serve at once.

Chapter 13

Quick-Cook Sauces

These sauces, many based on fresh, seasonal ingredients, cook in less than 30 minutes to keep the flavors fresh and clean. Unlike the richer, slow simmering, classic tomato sauces, these are prepared almost exclusively in a skillet or wide shallow sauté pan. With such a broad cooking surface, the liquids cook down quickly, which allows the sauces to thicken and the other ingredients to cook just until done. Prepare these sauces and serve them immediately with the appropriate pasta.

237 QUICK CHUNKY TOMATO SAUCE

*Prep: 5 minutes   Cook: 20 minutes   Yield: 2½ cups, or enough for
1 pound pasta*

This chunky sauce is best on large pasta shapes, preferably ridged to catch some of the sauce. Try medium shells, rigatoni, mostaccioli, or rotelle. A classic marinara sauce can be created by doubling this recipe and pressing the tomatoes through a sieve or food mill. Simmer sauce about 25 minutes. Makes about 1 quart sauce.

2 tablespoons olive oil	1 tablespoon thin julienne
¼ cup chopped onion	strips of fresh basil, or
1 garlic clove, crushed	1 teaspoon dried basil
1 can (1 pound 12 ounces)	1 tablespoon torn fresh basil
whole Italian-style plum	leaves
tomatoes, with juices	Salt and coarsely ground
	black pepper, to taste

Heat olive oil in a medium skillet; stir in onion. Sauté over low heat until tender, about 5 minutes. Stir in garlic; sauté 1 minute. Add tomatoes; cook over medium heat, stirring and breaking up tomatoes with the side of a spoon, until boiling. Simmer sauce, uncovered, until slightly thickened, about 15 minutes. Stir in basil, salt, and pepper. Toss with hot pasta.

Variations:

238 CREAMY TOMATO SAUCE

Add ½ cup heavy cream to the slightly thickened sauce. Simmer, uncovered, stirring until sauce is slightly thickened, about 5 minutes.

239 ANCHOVY TOMATO SAUCE

Add 6 rinsed, blotted, and chopped anchovy fillets to the reduced tomatoes; simmer 2 minutes.

240 GREEN OLIVE AND TOMATO SAUCE

Add 3 tablespoons pitted and chopped brine-cured green olives to the slightly thickened tomato sauce. Simmer 2 minutes.

241 RICOTTA TOMATO SAUCE

Add ½ cup ricotta cheese to the thickened tomato sauce; heat through.

242 PORCINI TOMATO SAUCE

Soak ½ ounce dried porcini in ½ cup boiling water for 15 minutes. Strain through a coffee filter or a sieve lined with a dampened paper towel; reserve liquid. Rinse the mushrooms so they are free of grit; chop fine. Add mushrooms, reserved liquid, and canned tomatoes to the sautéed onion and garlic. Heat to boiling; simmer, uncovered, until slightly thickened, about 20 minutes.

243 QUICK CHUNKY TOMATO MEAT SAUCE

Heat 1 tablespoon olive oil and sauté 8 ounces Italian sausage meat (casings removed), lean ground beef, ground veal, or ground turkey until browned; transfer to a sieve set over a small bowl to drain off fat; discard fat; wipe out skillet. Sauté onion and garlic in 2 tablespoons oil as directed; add browned meat to skillet with the tomatoes and simmer until thickened.

244 THREE-MUSHROOM SAUCE

Prep: 10 minutes   Soak: 10 minutes   Cook: 20 minutes
Yield: 2½ cups, or enough for 1 pound pasta

½ ounce dried porcini	1 garlic clove, crushed
½ cup water	¼ teaspoon dried thyme
¼ cup olive oil	Salt and freshly ground
½ cup chopped onion	black pepper
¼ cup chopped carrot	1 can (14 ounces) Italian plum
4 ounces white cultivated	tomatoes with juices,
mushrooms, trimmed	coarsely chopped
and chopped (about	1 tablespoon chopped Italian
1 cup)	flat-leaf parsley
4 ounces shiitake mushrooms,	
stems discarded, chopped	
(about 1 cup)	

1. In a small saucepan, bring the porcini and water to a boil; let stand off heat 10 minutes. Drain through a fine sieve; reserve the juices. If mushrooms feel gritty, return to sieve and rinse under running water. Finely chop mushrooms; set aside.

2. Meanwhile, heat the oil in a wide skillet; add the onion and carrot and sauté 5 minutes. Stir in the cultivated and shiitake mushrooms; sauté over high heat until tender and lightly browned, about 5 minutes; stir in garlic; sauté 1 minute. Add the reserved chopped porcini, the porcini liquid, and thyme. Sprinkle with salt and pepper. Add the tomatoes; heat to boiling. Simmer, uncovered, until sauce is slightly thickened, about 10 minutes. Stir in parsley. Toss hot pasta with the sauce and serve at once.

245 ITALIAN SAUSAGE AND MUSHROOM SAUCE

Prep: 10 minutes   Cook: 25 minutes   Yield: 2½ cups, or enough for
1 pound pasta

This chunky sauce is good with rigatoni, wagon wheels or mostaccioli.

6 ounces Italian sausage,
   casings removed
2 tablespoons olive oil
½ cup chopped onion
2 cups chopped trimmed and
   wiped mushrooms (about
   8 ounces)
1 garlic clove, crushed

Salt and freshly ground
   black pepper
¼ teaspoon dried oregano
1 can (8 ounces) tomato sauce
2 tablespoons chopped Italian
   flat-leaf parsley
Grated Parmesan cheese

1. Cook sausage in a large heavy skillet over medium heat, breaking up pieces with a fork until lightly browned; transfer to a side dish. Drain off fat and wipe out pan.

2. Heat oil in skillet over low heat; add onion; sauté until tender, about 5 minutes. Add mushrooms; sauté, stirring, until moisture has evaporated and mushrooms are golden, about 10 minutes. Add garlic; sauté 1 minute. Add salt, pepper, and oregano. Stir in tomato sauce, sausage meat, and parsley. Simmer 5 minutes.

3. Toss hot pasta with the sauce and serve at once. Sprinkle with cheese, if desired.

246 TRICOLOR PEPPER SAUCE

Prep: 10 minutes   Cook: 20 minutes   Yield: 1½ cups, or enough for
8 ounces pasta

Try this pretty sauce with spinach and plain fettuccine, a fat spaghetti called perciatelli, or a narrow lasagne-type noodle.

¼ cup olive oil
1 medium Spanish onion, cut
   into thin lengthwise
   slices (about 1 cup)
1 *each* red, yellow, and green
   bell pepper, cut into ¼-
   inch lengthwise strips

4 flat anchovy fillets, well
   drained and finely
   chopped
1 garlic clove, crushed
¼ cup chopped Italian flat-leaf
   parsley
Freshly ground black
   pepper

Heat oil in a large wide skillet over medium heat; add the onion and sauté until tender, about 10 minutes. Add the peppers; sauté over low heat, stirring until wilted and tender, about 5 minutes. Stir in anchovies and garlic; sauté, over low heat, 5 minutes. Stir in parsley and pepper. Toss hot pasta with the sauce and serve at once.

247 EGGPLANT AND OLIVE SAUCE

Prep: 15 minutes   Cook: 20 minutes   Yield: 3 cups, or enough for 1 pound pasta

This sauce was inspired by a Sicilian eggplant appetizer called caponata. It is especially good with penne or ziti.

6 tablespoons olive oil	1 tablespoon rinsed and drained small capers
1 small (about 1 pound) eggplant, trimmed, pared, and cut into ½-inch chunks	1 tablespoon chopped fresh basil
1 cup chopped onion	1 tablespoon chopped Italian flat-leaf parsley
½ cup chopped green pepper	2 teaspoons red wine vinegar
½ cup chopped celery	½ teaspoon salt
1 cup chopped fresh tomatoes	Freshly ground black pepper
¼ cup chopped crushed green olives (often called salad olives)	Pinch of sugar

1. Heat 4 tablespoons of the oil in a large nonstick skillet over high heat; add the eggplant. Sauté, stirring constantly, until eggplant is tender and browned, about 10 minutes. Transfer to a plate lined with paper towels to drain.

2. Add remaining 2 tablespoons oil to skillet. Add onion, green pepper, and celery; sauté, stirring, until tender, about 5 minutes. Stir in the eggplant, tomatoes, olives, capers, basil, parsley, vinegar, salt, pepper, and sugar. Cover and simmer 5 minutes. Toss hot pasta with the sauce and serve at once.

248 EASY PRIMAVERA SAUCE

Prep: 10 minutes   Cook: 5 minutes   Yield: 2 cups, or enough for 12 ounces pasta

Serve with the traditional fettuccine.

2 tablespoons butter	⅓ cup heavy cream
1 bag (16 ounces) frozen Italian-style vegetables (contains zucchini, cauliflower, lima beans, carrots, and green beans)	½ cup grated Parmesan cheese
	½ basket cherry tomatoes, rinsed
1 egg	1 tablespoon chopped Italian flat-leaf parsley

1. Melt butter in a wide skillet; stir in vegetables. Cook, stirring, over low heat until tender, about 5 minutes.

2. Beat egg, cream, and Parmesan cheese in a serving bowl.

3. Add hot pasta to the bowl with the cream mixture; toss to coat. Add the vegetables, cherry tomatoes, and parsley; toss and serve.

249 ARUGULA AND GARLIC SAUCE

Prep: 10 minutes   Cook: 10 minutes   Yield: 1 cup, or enough for
8 ounces pasta

2 tablespoons olive oil
2 tablespoons butter
½ red onion, cut into thin
    lengthwise slices
2 garlic cloves, minced

1 bunch arugula, rinsed and
    trimmed, about 1 cup
    packed
Salt and freshly ground
    black pepper

Heat oil and butter in a medium skillet over low heat; stir in red onion; sauté until crisp-tender, about 3 minutes. Stir in garlic; sauté 1 minute. Add the arugula; sauté, stirring, about 2 minutes. Season with salt and pepper. Toss hot pasta with the sauce and serve.

250 CHICKEN LIVER, TOMATO, AND SAGE SAUCE

Prep: 10 minutes   Cook: 25 minutes   Yield: 2 cups, or enough for
12 ounces pasta

Serve this chunky sauce over large tubular pasta like rigatoni, penne, or ziti.

3 tablespoons olive oil
8 ounces chicken livers,
    trimmed and patted dry
    with paper towels
Salt and freshly ground
    black pepper
½ cup chopped onion
2 garlic cloves, crushed

½ cup red wine
1 can (28 ounces) Italian plum
    tomatoes with juices
½ teaspoon crumbled dried
    sage
1 tablespoon chopped Italian
    flat-leaf parsley
Grated Parmesan cheese

1. Heat oil in a large heavy skillet; sprinkle chicken livers with salt and pepper. Sauté in hot oil, turning often until the outsides are browned but they are still pink in the center, about 3 minutes. Transfer livers to a side dish.

2. Add the onion to the skillet; simmer in the juices until tender, about 5 minutes. Add the garlic; cook 1 minute. Add wine; over high heat, boil wine until reduced by half, about 5 minutes.

3. Using kitchen shears, coarsely cut up the tomatoes while still in the can. Add tomatoes and sage to the skillet; heat to boiling. Cook sauce, stirring, over medium heat 10 minutes, or until slightly thickened.

4. Coarsely chop the chicken livers; transfer livers and their juices to the sauce. Simmer briefly; stir in parsley. Toss with hot pasta and serve at once. Sprinkle with cheese, if desired.

251   LATE SUMMER GARDEN SAUCE

Prep: 15 minutes   Cook: 15 minutes   Yield: 2½ cups, or enough for
1 pound pasta

This sauce, perfect for a late August supper, is especially good on penne, ziti, or fusilli.

5 tablespoons olive oil	1 pound fresh ripe tomatoes,
1 cup chopped Spanish onion	cored and diced
1 medium red bell pepper,	1 garlic clove, crushed
stems and seeds removed,	1 teaspoon salt
diced	¼ teaspoon black pepper
1 medium green bell pepper,	2 tablespoons chopped fresh
stems and seeds removed,	basil
diced	Grated Parmesan cheese
1 small eggplant (about 1	
pound), trimmed, peeled,	
and cut into ½-inch cubes	

1. Heat olive oil in a large heavy skillet, preferably nonstick. Add onion and red and green peppers; sauté until tender, about 10 minutes. Add eggplant; cook over high heat, stirring frequently, until eggplant begins to brown, about 5 minutes. Stir in tomatoes, garlic, salt, and pepper. Cook, stirring, 5 minutes. Stir in basil.

2. Toss hot pasta with the sauce and serve at once. Serve with cheese, if desired.

252   MUSHROOM AND ASPARAGUS SAUCE WITH TOASTED PIGNOLI

Prep: 10 minutes   Cook: 15 minutes   Yield: 2 cups, or enough for
12 ounces pasta

This sauce is especially nice with fettuccine or any broad noodle.

1 pound asparagus, trimmed,	¾ cup heavy cream
rinsed, and cut into 1-inch	2 teaspoons pignoli (pine
diagonals	nuts), stirred in a hot
4 tablespoons butter	skillet until toasted,
2 cups chopped, trimmed	about 1 minute
mushrooms	2 tablespoons grated
¼ cup chopped onion	Parmesan cheese
1 garlic clove, crushed	

1. Cook asparagus in a steaming rack set over simmering water, covered, until crisp-tender, about 5 minutes; set aside.

2. In large wide skillet, melt butter; add mushrooms and onion; sauté, stirring until tender and moisture has cooked off, about 5 minutes. Add garlic; sauté 1 minute.

3. Stir in heavy cream; heat to boiling; add asparagus. Toss hot pasta with sauce, pignoli, and Parmesan cheese.

253 ZUCCHINI, MUSHROOM, AND FRESH TOMATO SAUCE

Prep: 10 minutes   Cook: 20 minutes   Yield: 2½ cups, or enough for 1 pound pasta

2 tablespoons olive oil	1 cup chopped fresh tomatoes
½ cup chopped onion	½ teaspoon salt
1 cup diced (½ inch) trimmed zucchini	¼ cup chopped Italian flat-leaf parsley
1 cup diced trimmed mushrooms	2 tablespoons chopped fresh basil
1 garlic clove, crushed	Grated Parmesan cheese

1. Heat oil in a wide saucepan; add onion; sauté 5 minutes. Stir in zucchini and mushrooms; sauté over high heat, stirring, until tender, about 10 minutes. Stir in garlic; sauté 1 minute. Add tomatoes; cook, stirring, 5 minutes. Add salt, parsley, and basil.

2. Toss hot pasta with the sauce and serve at once. Serve with Parmesan cheese, if desired.

254 FRESH TOMATO, SARDINE, AND GREEN BEAN SAUCE

Prep: 10 minutes   Cook: 15 minutes   Yield: 2 cups, or enough for 12 ounces medium shells

¼ cup olive oil	1 can (3¾ ounces) sardines in olive oil, drained
½ cup chopped onion	2 tablespoons chopped Italian flat-leaf parsley
1 cup trimmed and cut-up (½ inch) green beans	2 tablespoons chopped fresh basil
1 garlic clove, crushed	Salt
1 cup chopped fresh tomatoes	
1 teaspoon grated orange zest	

Heat oil in a large skillet; add onion and sauté 5 minutes. Stir in green beans; sauté over low heat until crisp-tender, about 5 minutes. Stir in garlic; sauté 1 minute. Add tomatoes and orange zest; simmer 10 minutes, or until sauce is slightly thickened. Add sardines, parsley, and basil; stir gently. Add salt to taste. Toss hot pasta with the sauce and serve at once.

255   FRESH TOMATO SAUCE WITH GARDEN HERBS

Prep: 10 minutes   Cook: 15 minutes   Yield: 2½ cups, or enough for 1 pound pasta

This sauce is good with spaghetti, linguine, or penne.

¼ cup olive oil
2 garlic cloves, crushed
3 cups chopped fresh ripe tomatoes (about 2 pounds)
¼ cup chopped fresh basil
¼ cup chopped Italian flat-leaf parsley

1 teaspoon fresh oregano leaves (optional)
½ teaspoon fresh thyme leaves (optional)
½ teaspoon salt, or to taste
Freshly ground black pepper

1. Heat oil in large deep skillet over low heat; stir in garlic; sauté 1 minute; do not brown. Add tomatoes. Simmer, uncovered, until mixture boils and sauce begins to thicken, about 15 minutes.

2. Stir in fresh herbs and salt and pepper. Toss hot pasta with the sauce and serve.

256   FRESH TOMATO SAUCE WITH RICOTTA

Prep: 10 minutes   Cook: 10 minutes   Yield: 2 cups, or enough for 12 ounces pasta

Try this rich sauce with rigatoni, penne, or ridged ziti.

2 tablespoons olive oil
1 garlic clove, crushed
1½ cups chopped fresh ripe tomatoes (about 1 pound)
2 tablespoons chopped fresh basil
1 tablespoon chopped Italian flat-leaf parsley

½ teaspoon fresh oregano leaves (optional)
¼ teaspoon fresh thyme leaves (optional)
1 cup whole milk ricotta cheese
Salt and freshly ground black pepper
Grated Parmesan cheese

Heat oil in a medium skillet over low heat; stir in garlic; sauté 1 minute. Add tomatoes. Simmer, uncovered, until mixture boils and begins to thicken, about 10 minutes. Add basil, parsley, oregano, and thyme; whisk in ricotta until blended. Heat, stirring, about 1 minute. Add salt and pepper. Toss hot pasta with the sauce; serve with Parmesan.

257 FRESH TOMATO SAUCE WITH SAFFRON AND GREEN PEPPER

Prep: 10 minutes   Cook: 15 minutes   Yield: 2 cups, or enough for 12 ounces pasta

This sauce is particularly good when served tossed with tricolored shells or twists.

⅛ teaspoon saffron threads, or
    a pinch of powdered
    saffron
2 tablespoons boiling water
2 tablespoons olive oil
¼ cup chopped green pepper

¼ cup chopped onion
1 garlic clove, crushed
1½ cups chopped fresh ripe
    tomatoes (about 1 pound)
    Salt and freshly ground
    black pepper

1. Stir saffron and water in a small bowl; set aside.

2. Heat oil in a medium skillet over low heat; add green pepper and onion; sauté 5 minutes; stir in garlic; sauté 1 minute. Add tomatoes and saffron mixture. Heat to boiling over low heat; cook, stirring, until sauce begins to thicken, about 10 minutes. Season with salt and pepper. Toss hot pasta with the sauce and serve.

258 FRESH TOMATO SAUCE WITH CREAM AND SUN-DRIED TOMATOES

Prep: 10 minutes   Cook: 10 minutes   Yield: 2 cups, or enough for 12 ounces pasta

2 tablespoons olive oil
1 garlic clove, crushed
1½ cups chopped fresh ripe
    tomatoes (about 1 pound)
½ cup heavy cream

1 tablespoon minced sun-
    dried tomatoes
1 tablespoon chopped Italian
    flat-leaf parsley
    Salt and freshly ground
    black pepper

Heat oil in a medium skillet; stir in garlic; sauté 1 minute. Add tomatoes; heat to boiling; simmer, stirring, until sauce begins to thicken, about 10 minutes. Stir in cream and sun-dried tomatoes; simmer gently until sauce cooks down slightly, about 5 minutes. Add salt and pepper to taste. Toss hot pasta with the sauce and serve.

259   RED PEPPER AND CARAMELIZED ONION SAUCE

Prep: 15 minutes   Cook: 15 minutes   Yield: 1½ cups, or enough for 8 ounces pasta

This sauce goes well with spinach-flavored pasta; try thin lasagne noodles or fettuccine.

¼ cup olive oil
1 large Spanish onion, halved, sliced thin
2 red bell peppers, cut into ¼-inch lengthwise strips

1 garlic clove, crushed
¼ cup chopped Italian flat-leaf parsley
Salt and freshly ground black pepper

Heat oil in a large heavy skillet over low heat; stir in onion. Sauté onion over very low heat, stirring often, until very soft and golden, about 7 minutes. Stir in peppers; turn heat to medium and sauté until peppers wilt and edges begin to brown, about 5 minutes. Stir in garlic; sauté 1 minute. Add parsley and sprinkle with salt and pepper. Toss hot pasta with the sauce and serve at once.

260   ZUCCHINI, CARROT, AND PARMESAN SAUCE

Prep: 10 minutes   Cook: 5 minutes   Yield: 1½ cups, or enough for 8 ounces pasta

This brightly colored sauce is good on twists, rotelle, or any pasta that will "catch" the sauce. Shred the vegetables in a food processor or on the widest side of a hand grater.

¼ cup olive oil
1 cup shredded pared carrot (1 medium)
1 cup shredded trimmed zucchini (2 small)

1 garlic clove, crushed
2 tablespoons grated Parmesan cheese

Heat the oil over low heat in a medium skillet. Stir in the carrot, zucchini, and garlic; sauté, stirring, 3 minutes. Toss hot pasta with the sauce. Serve with cheese.

261   ARUGULA AND PLUM TOMATO SAUCE

Prep: 10 minutes   Cook: 10 minutes   Yield: 1½ cups, or enough for
8 ounces pasta

This sauce is nice on a wide flat pasta such as fresh fettuccine or tagliatelle, although dried linguine or fettuccine can be used as well.

2 tablespoons olive oil
2 tablespoons butter
1 garlic clove, crushed
1 cup chopped plum tomatoes
    (about 3 medium)

1 bunch arugula, rinsed and
    trimmed, about 1 cup
    packed
Salt and freshly ground
    black pepper
Grated Parmesan cheese

Heat oil and butter in a medium skillet over low heat; stir in the garlic; sauté 1 minute. Add the plum tomatoes and heat to boiling, about 5 minutes. Stir in arugula and simmer, stirring, until wilted and sauce is slightly reduced, about 3 minutes. Season with salt and pepper. Toss hot pasta with the sauce. Sprinkle with cheese, if desired.

Chapter 14

Meat Sauces

Because of the wonderful wealth of flavor combinations and the comfort and culinary romance of that "pot of sauce simmering on the stove," these meat sauces are all Italian inspired, which means, in part, that they are tomato based. They are robust sauces, all flavored with the rich juices of the meats that have been slowly simmering in a cocoon of tomatoes and herbs. Pasta sauced with any of these recipes is sure to create a delicious meal. From the simple but wonderful Tomato Sauce with Meatballs to toss with spaghetti, to the delicate Rabbit Sauce traditionally served over homemade pappardelle, there is sure to be a meat sauce in this chapter for every taste. Generally 2 cups is enough sauce for 1 pound pasta.

262 BOLOGNESE SAUCE WITH GROUND MEATS AND CREAM

Prep: 20 minutes   Cook: 2 hours 30 minutes   Yield: 4 cups

4 tablespoons butter	1 cup white wine
½ cup finely chopped onion	1 cup milk
⅓ cup finely chopped carrot	Salt and pepper
⅓ cup finely chopped celery	2 cans (28 ounces each) Italian-
½ pound ground veal	style plum tomatoes with
¼ pound lean ground beef	juices
¼ pound lean ground pork	½ cup heavy cream

1. Melt the butter in a large wide saucepan; when the foam subsides, stir in the vegetables; sauté, stirring, until very tender, about 10 minutes. Crumble the meats while gradually adding to the sauce. Cook over low heat, stirring, just until the meat is barely cooked through (do not brown).

2. Add the wine to the saucepan; cook, stirring, until wine is absorbed and reduced by half. Add the milk; cook, stirring, over low heat 10 minutes. Season with salt and pepper to taste.

3. Purée the tomatoes through a food mill set directly over the saucepan. Cook sauce over very low heat, stirring occasionally, for 2 hours. Maintain a very gentle simmer; sauce should not be allowed to boil hard. Add salt and pepper to taste. Just before serving, stir the cream into the sauce; heat through and serve with pasta.

263 TOMATO SAUCE WITH GROUND BEEF

Prep: 5 minutes   Cook: 1 hour 30 minutes   Yield: 6 cups

This is a basic tomato sauce, popularly used with spaghetti or any macaroni shape. For convenience, freeze in 2-cup portions.

2 tablespoons olive oil	2 tablespoons coarsely
1 cup chopped onion	chopped Italian flat-leaf
1 garlic clove, minced	parsley
1 pound lean ground beef	Salt
1 can (28 ounces) Italian-style	1 teaspoon dried basil
peeled plum tomatoes	½ teaspoon dried oregano
with juices, cut up with	¼ teaspoon coarsely ground
scissors	black pepper, or to taste
1 can (15 ounces) tomato sauce	1 whole bay leaf
1 can (6 ounces) tomato paste	

1. Heat oil in a large heavy saucepan; add onion; sauté over low heat, stirring, until tender and golden, about 5 minutes. Add the garlic; sauté 1 minute.

2. Meanwhile, brown the ground beef in a skillet, stirring to crumble meat; drain off fat; add to the onion mixture. Add the tomatoes, tomato sauce, 1 tomato sauce can filled with water, the tomato paste, parsley, 1 teaspoon salt, the basil, oregano, pepper, and bay leaf. Heat over medium-low heat to simmering. Simmer, uncovered, over low heat, stirring occasionally until sauce is thickened and flavorful, about 1 hour 15 minutes.

Variations:

264   TOMATO, GROUND BEEF, AND MUSHROOM SAUCE

Add 2 cups coarsely cut up mushrooms to the sautéed onion; sauté over high heat until liquid is evaporated and mushrooms begin to brown on edges, about 5 minutes; stir in garlic and proceed with recipe.

265   TOMATO, GROUND BEEF, AND VEGETABLE SAUCE

Sauté ½ cup *each* diced carrot, celery, and green pepper with the onion until tender; stir in the garlic and proceed with recipe.

266   TOMATO SAUCE WITH GROUND BEEF AND RED WINE

To the ground beef and onion, mushroom, or vegetable mixture, add ½ cup red wine. Cook over high heat until wine is reduced by half. Add the tomatoes and seasonings and proceed with recipe.

267   PROSCIUTTO AND TOMATO SAUCE
Prep: 10 minutes   Cook: 40 minutes   Yield: 3 cups

¼ cup olive oil
½ cup chopped onion
¼ cup diced carrot
2 ounces prosciutto, diced
1 can (28 ounces) Italian-style
   peeled plum tomatoes
   with juices

Salt
Coarsely ground black
   pepper

1. Heat oil in a medium skillet; add onion and carrot; sauté until tender, about 5 minutes. Add prosciutto; sauté 5 minutes.

2. Add tomatoes; heat to boiling, stirring and breaking up tomatoes with the side of a spoon. Simmer until sauce is slightly reduced and thickened, about 25 minutes. Season to taste with salt; add plenty of black pepper.

268   VEAL, TOMATO, AND ANCHOVY SAUCE

Prep: 15 minutes   Cook: 2 hours 15 minutes   Yield: 3 cups

This is an adaptation of a classic dish from the Italian province called Friuli. In the city of Trieste, which is tucked in at the easternmost corner of Italy, on the Adriatic sea and very close to Yugoslavia, the veal shank is carved whole at the table and served with the flavorful sauce. Here the shank is cooked until it falls from the bone and is shredded into the sauce. Especially delicious served on spinach tagliatelle or fettuccine.

3 tablespoons olive oil	1 can (28 ounces) Italian-style
½ cup chopped onion	peeled plum tomatoes
¼ cup very finely chopped	with juices, puréed
carrot	through a food mill
¼ cup very finely chopped	1 cup chicken or beef broth
celery	(unseasoned)
2 garlic cloves, minced	1 can (2 ounces) flat anchovy
½ cup red wine	fillets, drained and
1 veal shank, about 2 pounds	blotted dry
	Black pepper

1. Heat oil in a large flameproof casserole. Add onion, carrot, and celery; sauté over low heat until golden, about 10 minutes. Stir in garlic; sauté over medium heat 2 minutes. Stir in wine; heat to boiling; simmer, stirring, over high heat, 1 minute. Add the veal shank, tomatoes, broth, and anchovies; cover and heat to boiling. Stir well.

2. Heat oven to 350°F. Bake casserole, covered, 2 hours, or until shank meat is falling from the bone. Remove from oven and let stand until shank is cool enough to handle. Remove shank from sauce and pull the meat from the bone in shreds. Return meat to the sauce and simmer to heat through. Blot surface with a folded paper towel to remove excess fat. Add pepper to taste.

269   PORCINI, PROSCIUTTO, AND TOMATO SAUCE

Prep: 25 minutes   Soak: 15 minutes   Cook: 40 minutes
Yield: 3 cups

1 ounce dried porcini	1 tablespoon tomato paste
1 cup water	½ cup heavy cream
2 tablespoons olive oil	Salt
2 ounces prosciutto, diced	Freshly ground black
1 can (28 ounces) Italian-style	pepper
peeled plum tomatoes	
with juices	

1. Combine the porcini and water in a small saucepan. Heat to simmering. Cover and let stand 15 minutes. Drain through a sieve lined with a piece of dampened paper towel; reserve liquid. Rinse porcini to remove any grit; finely chop; set aside.

2. Heat oil in a medium skillet; add the prosciutto; sauté 5 minutes. Add the tomatoes, the tomato paste, the reserved porcini liquid, and the chopped porcini. Simmer, uncovered, until sauce is thickened and slightly reduced, about 30 minutes. Stir in the cream; simmer 5 minutes. Season to taste with salt and pepper.

---

270   RABBIT SAUCE

Prep: 20 minutes   Marinate: 3 hours or overnight   Cook: 2 hours
Yield: 4 cups

The rabbit is cooked in a very light tomato sauce laced with just a suggestion of lemon. The juices from the rabbit give the sauce its distinctive flavor. There are two or three ways to serve this dish. Cook the rabbit in its rich sauce and serve the rabbit for one meal. Save the sauce and any leftover pieces of rabbit; pull the meat from the bones; add to the sauce. Serve this especially elegant sauce on spinach fettuccine or tagliatelle. Or nontraditionally but very delicious, serve the rabbit in the sauce over pasta. Especially delicious with egg bows (farfalle). Rabbit Sauce is traditionally made with hare, which produces a darker and richer sauce and is served on a wide ribbon noodle, called pappardelle, not yet available commercially in this country.

1 fresh or frozen (thawed) rabbit, 3 to 4 pounds, cut into serving pieces	¼ teaspoon black pepper All-purpose flour Olive oil
3 tablespoons olive oil Juice of 1 lemon	½ cup finely chopped onion ½ cup finely chopped carrot
2 strips lemon zest, each ½ x 2 inches	1 cup dry white or red wine 2 cups chicken broth
2 garlic cloves, bruised	1 can (14 ounces) Italian-style
1 teaspoon fresh or dried rosemary leaves	peeled plum tomatoes with juices
1 bay leaf	Chopped parsley
1 teaspoon salt	

1. In a large bowl, combine the rabbit, oil, lemon juice and zest, garlic, rosemary, bay leaf, salt, and pepper; toss to coat. Cover and marinate, refrigerated, 3 hours or overnight.

2. Scrape marinade ingredients off pieces of rabbit; reserve. Pat rabbit dry with paper toweling. Dust very lightly with flour. Heat a thin layer of olive oil in a Dutch oven or large heavy wide saucepan; lightly brown the rabbit on all sides; set aside on a platter. Scrape the reserved marinating mixture into the skillet; add the onion and carrot; sauté, stirring, until vegetables are tender and golden. Add the wine; boil, stirring to scrape up any browned bits from bottom of pan.

3. Add the chicken broth to pan; set a food mill on the rim of the pan and purée the tomatoes into the pan. Heat to a slow simmer. Add the pieces of rabbit and cook, tightly covered, over very low heat 1½ hours. Remove rabbit from sauce. Cook sauce, uncovered, until slightly reduced. Season with salt and pepper. Add parsley. See headnote for serving suggestions.

271   TOMATO SAUCE WITH SPARERIBS
Prep: 30 minutes   Cook: 2–3 hours   Yield: 6 cups

Serve this rich tomato sauce, as a first course over a large shaped pasta like rigatoni, shells, or rotelle. Serve the spareribs as a second course accompanied by blanched escarole or broccoli rabe sautéed in oil with garlic.

3 pounds meaty spareribs (or use country-style ribs)	2 tablespoons coarsely chopped Italian flat-leaf parsley
Olive oil	
1 cup chopped onion	1 teaspoon dried basil
1 garlic clove	½ teaspoon dried oregano
2 cans (28 ounces each) Italian-style peeled plum tomatoes with juices	1 whole bay leaf
	¼ teaspoon coarsely ground black pepper
1 can (8 ounces) tomato sauce	Salt and pepper
1 can (6 ounces) tomato paste	

1. Cut the spareribs into individual ribs. Heat a thin film of oil in a large heavy skillet. Add ribs and brown on all sides; remove to a side dish. Drain the fat from the skillet; add 1 cup water and simmer, scraping the browned bits with a spatula; set aside off heat.

2. In a large wide saucepan, heat 2 tablespoons olive oil; add the onion and sauté until golden, about 10 minutes. Add the garlic; sauté 1 minute.

3. Purée the tomatoes through a food mill into the saucepan. Add the tomato sauce, tomato paste, and the water in the skillet. Add the parsley, basil, oregano, bay leaf, and the browned ribs. Heat to simmring; cook, stirring occasionally, over low heat until sauce is thickened, 1½ to 2 hours. Add salt and pepper to taste.

272   TOMATO SAUCE WITH MEATBALLS
Prep: 30 minutes   Cook: 2 hours   Yield: 4 cups sauce; 16 meatballs

Sauce

2 tablespoons olive oil	2 cans (28 ounces each) Italian-style peeled plum tomatoes with juices
1 strip thick-cut bacon, minced	
1 cup chopped onion	1 can (6 ounces) tomato paste
1 cup chopped mushrooms	1 teaspoon dried basil
½ cup minced carrot	1 bay leaf
½ cup minced green pepper	½ teaspoon dried oregano
1 garlic clove, crushed	Salt and pepper

Meatballs

½ cup cold water	2 tablespoons chopped Italian flat-leaf parsley
⅓ cup fine dry bread crumbs	
2 eggs, beaten	1 teaspoon salt
1½ pounds meat loaf mixture (beef, veal, and pork)	¼ teaspoon pepper
	Pinch of dried oregano
⅓ cup grated Parmesan cheese	Olive oil

1. For the sauce, heat the oil in a large wide saucepan; add the onion, mushrooms, carrot, and green pepper. Sauté, stirring, until golden, about 10 minutes. Add the garlic; sauté 1 minute.

2. Purée the canned tomatoes through a food mill directly into the saucepan. Add the tomato paste. Heat, stirring, to simmering. Add the basil, bay leaf, and oregano. Simmer, covered, over low heat while preparing the meatballs.

3. In a large bowl, combine the water, bread crumbs, and eggs; stir to blend; let stand 5 minutes. Add the ground meats, cheese, parsley, salt, pepper, and oregano. Stir with a wooden spoon until blended.

4. Shape meat into balls; rinse hands repeatedly with cold water to discourage sticking. Heat ½ inch olive oil in a large skillet. Brown the meatballs a few at a time in the hot oil. Transfer directly to the simmering tomato sauce as they are browned. Cook meatballs in the sauce, uncovered, until the sauce is thickened and slightly reduced, about 1½ hours. Add salt and pepper to taste. Serve with spaghetti.

---

273 CHICKEN LIVER AND TOMATO SAUCE
Prep: 10 minutes   Cook: 30 minutes   Yield: 2 cups

The chicken livers should be crisp on the outside and cooked just to juicy tenderness in the center. It is best to prepare this sauce just before serving; add the chicken livers at the last minute. Sage and chicken livers are a classic herb and meat combination, but here thyme is used for a change of pace. For a pleasant variation, sauté a few chopped mushrooms along with the onion in step 1. You might also like to add ½ cup red wine; reduce by half over medium heat before adding the tomatoes.

5 tablespoons olive oil	1 teaspoon fresh thyme
¼ cup finely chopped onion	leaves, or ½ teaspoon
1 small garlic clove, minced	dried
1 can (28 ounces) Italian-style	Salt and pepper
peeled plum tomatoes	8 ounces fresh chicken livers,
with juices	trimmed and halved
1 tablespoon tomato paste	All-purpose flour
	2 tablespoons butter

1. Heat 3 tablespoons oil in a medium skillet; add onion and sauté until tender, about 5 minutes. Stir in garlic; sauté 2 minutes. Add the tomatoes, tomato paste, and half the thyme; cook, stirring to break up tomatoes with the side of a spoon, until boiling. Simmer sauce until reduced and thickened, about 30 minutes. Season to taste with salt and pepper.

2. Pat chicken livers dry; sprinkle with salt, pepper, and remaining thyme. Lightly dust with flour. Heat the remaining 2 tablespoons oil and the butter in a large heavy skillet until the butter melts and the foam subsides. Sauté the chicken livers, adding a few at a time and carefully turning until lightly browned and crisp, about 5 minutes. Transfer to the simmering tomato sauce; turn heat off under sauce. Toss with hot spinach or plain fettuccine and serve at once.

Tomato paste

Tomato paste is now frequently available in a handy tube: just squeeze out a table-spoon or two, then screw the cap back on and refrigerate the remainder for future use.

Tomato paste is more commonly available in a small 6-ounce can. To reserve the remainder after a recipe calls for just 1 tablespoon of tomato paste: Use a measur-ing tablespoon to measure out portions of the tomato paste onto a sheet of alumi-num foil. Place the foil in the freezer until the paste is frozen firm. Carefully pull the little blobs of tomato paste off the foil, place in a plastic container with a tight-fitting lid, and put in the freezer. All ready to pop into a sauce or a pot of soup the next time a recipe calls for just 1 tablespoon of tomato paste!

---

274   TOMATO SAUCE, BOLOGNESE STYLE
Prep: 20 minutes   Cook: 2 hours   Yield: 4 cups

Bolognese Sauce is basically a tomato sauce flavored with vegetables and meat. According to some experts, the meat is first simmered in milk, never browned; others brown the vegetables in bacon fat, butter, and/or olive oil. Often white wine is added; occasionally dried porcini; sometimes chicken livers. What follows is a simple but delicious version.

2 **tablespoons olive oil**	½ **teaspoon dried oregano**
½ **cup chopped onion**	1 **bay leaf**
½ **cup chopped carrot**	8 **ounces pork with bone in**
½ **cup chopped green bell**	**(thick end pork chop or**
pepper	**piece off the small end of**
2 **garlic cloves, minced**	**rack of spareribs)**
½ **cup white wine**	1 **pound beef chuck or round**
1 **can (2 pounds 3 ounces)**	**in one piece**
Italian-style peeled	1 **teaspoon salt, or to taste**
tomatoes with juices	¼ **teaspoon coarsely ground**
1 **can (15 ounces) tomato sauce**	**black pepper**
1 **tablespoon chopped fresh**	
basil leaves, or 1 teaspoon	
dried	

1. Heat oil in a large heavy saucepan. Add onion, carrot, and green pepper; sauté over low heat, stirring often, until vegetables are tender but not browned, about 10 minutes. Stir in the garlic; sauté 2 minutes.

2. Place a food mill over the saucepan. Purée the whole tomatoes directly into the sautéed vegetables. Add the tomato sauce; fill the sauce can half-way with water and rinse can, emptying water into saucepan. Add the basil, oregano, and bay leaf. Simmer, uncovered, 15 minutes.

3. Meanwhile, lightly brown the pork and beef on both sides in a large heavy skillet over medium-low heat, just until the outside is golden and the meat is still juicy, about 8 minutes a side. Add the meat to the tomato sauce along with any drippings in the pan. (If there is excess fat, spoon off and dis-card first.) Simmer sauce and meat over low heat, stirring occasionally, 1½ hours. Season with salt and pepper. Serve the meat separately. Spoon the sauce over cooked pasta.

Chapter 15

Seafood and Pasta Combinations

In this chapter we offer a mixed bag of pasta and seafood recipes. The Spaghetti with White Wine Clam Sauce, Pasta with Mussels and Saffron Cream Sauce, and the Orecchiette with Cauliflower, Shrimp, and Red Pepper Oil are all simple, yet elegant enough for your next dinner party. The Spinach Linguine with Salmon, Lemon, and Dill or the Penne with Fresh Tomato and Sardine Sauce are quick and easy enough for a family meal at the end of a very busy day. The seemingly endless variety of delicious seafood and pasta combinations is proof, once again, of the enormous versatility of pasta.

275　SHELLS WITH SHRIMP AND GREEN BEANS IN GARLIC OIL

Prep: 20 minutes　Cook: 15 minutes　Serves: 4

¼ cup olive oil
2 garlic cloves, crushed
¼ teaspoon crushed dried red pepper
8 ounces shrimp, shelled, deveined, and coarsely chopped
2 tablespoons thinly slivered sun-dried tomatoes packed in oil

2 tablespoons coarsely chopped Italian flat-leaf parsley
8 ounces medium shells
8 ounces fresh green beans, trimmed and cut into 1-inch lengths

1. Heat the olive oil in a medium skillet; stir in garlic and red pepper; sauté over low heat 1 minute. Raise heat to high; immediately add the shrimp all at once. Sauté, stirring constantly, until they become pink, about 3 minutes (do not overcook). Stir in sun-dried tomatoes and parsley. Remove from heat.

2. Cook the shells and beans together in plenty of boiling salted water until they are tender, about 12 minutes; drain.

3. Toss shrimp mixture, shells, and beans together. Serve at once.

Variation:

276　SHELLS WITH SHRIMP, GREEN BEANS, AND TOMATO IN GARLIC OIL

Add 1 cup chopped fresh tomato and 2 tablespoons chopped fresh basil leaves to pasta in step 3.

277　LINGUINE WITH TUNA, LEMON, AND ARUGULA

Prep: 10 minutes　Cook: 15 minutes　Serves: 4

¼ cup olive oil
¼ cup chopped onion
¼ cup chopped green pepper
1 garlic clove, crushed
1 can (6 ounces) imported Italian tuna in olive oil, drained and blotted dry with paper towels

3 tablespoons fresh lemon juice
12 ounces linguine
1 cup lightly packed washed and trimmed arugula leaves

1. Heat oil in a medium skillet; add onion and green pepper; sauté 5 minutes. Add garlic; sauté 1 minute. Stir in tuna and lemon juice.

2. Meanwhile, cook linguine in plenty of boiling salted water until al dente, or firm to the bite, about 12 minutes; drain. Toss the tuna sauce and the arugula with the pasta and serve.

278 SPINACH LINGUINE WITH SALMON, LEMON, AND DILL

Prep: 10 minutes   Cook: 15 minutes   Serves: 4

6 tablespoons unsalted butter
1 garlic clove, crushed
1 can (7¾ ounces) red salmon, drained
3 tablespoons fresh lemon juice

1 teaspoon finely shredded or grated lemon zest
2 tablespoons chopped fresh dill
12 ounces spinach linguine

1. Heat butter in a skillet; stir in garlic; sauté 1 minute. Add salmon, lemon juice, lemon zest, and dill; do not stir.

2. Meanwhile, cook the linguine in plenty of boiling salted water until al dente, or firm to the bite, about 12 minutes; drain. Place linguine in a large shallow bowl; add the salmon sauce; toss just once, being careful not to break up the pieces of salmon.

279 SHELLS WITH TUNA, BROCCOLI, AND RED ONION

Prep: 10 minutes   Cook: 15 minutes   Serves: 4

¼ cup olive oil
½ medium red onion, cut into thin vertical slices (about ½ cup)
2 garlic cloves, crushed
1 can (6 ounces) imported Italian tuna in olive oil, well drained and blotted with paper towels
3 tablespoons fresh lemon juice

1 tablespoon chopped Italian flat-leaf parsley
1 teaspoon grated or finely shredded lemon zest
¼ teaspoon dried oregano
¼ teaspoon coarsely ground black pepper
8 ounces medium shells
2 cups broccoli florets and stems cut into 1-inch pieces

1. Heat olive oil in a medium skillet over low heat; stir in onion and garlic; sauté 2 minutes (garlic shouldn't brown and onion should still be crunchy). Off heat add the tuna, lemon juice, parsley, lemon zest, oregano, and black pepper.

2. Cook the shells in plenty of boiling salted water 5 minutes; add the broccoli; cook until pasta is al dente, or firm to the bite, and broccoli is tender, 5 to 7 minutes longer. Remove ¼ cup of the pasta cooking water and add to the tuna sauce. Drain pasta; toss with tuna mixture and serve at once.

280 FETTUCCINE WITH TOMATO AND SQUID SAUCE

Prep: 15 minutes   Cook: 40 minutes   Serves: 4

¼ cup olive oil
½ cup chopped onion
1 garlic clove, minced
1 can (1 pound 12 ounces) Italian-style peeled tomatoes with juices
1 teaspoon dried basil
½ teaspoon dried oregano
½ teaspoon crushed dried red pepper

1 bay leaf
½ teaspoon salt
¼ teaspoon coarsely ground black pepper
1 pound cleaned squid (preferably small), cut into ¼-inch rings, tentacles left intact
12 ounces fettuccine

1. Heat oil in a large skillet with a tight-fitting cover. Add onion; sauté over low heat, stirring often, until a rich golden color but not browned on the edges, about 15 minutes. Stir in the garlic; sauté 1 minute. Add the tomatoes, basil, oregano, red pepper, and bay leaf; simmer over medium heat, stirring and breaking up tomatoes with the side of a spoon, until sauce is thickened, about 15 minutes. Season with salt and black pepper.

2. Add the squid; cook, covered, over medium-low heat (do not boil or the squid will be tough) 5 minutes, or until squid is tender.

3. Meanwhile, cook the fettuccine in plenty of boiling salted water until al dente, or firm to the bite, about 5 minutes. Drain and place on a large platter. Spoon sauce and squid over top and toss lightly.

281 LINGUINE WITH BACON, SCALLOPS, AND GREEN PEPPER

Prep: 10 minutes   Cook: 15 minutes   Serves: 4

4 strips bacon
6 tablespoons olive oil
½ cup chopped onion
1 cup chopped green bell pepper
2 garlic cloves, crushed
¼ teaspoon crushed dried red pepper

12 ounces bay scallops (or sea scallops, halved or quartered)
12 ounces linguine
3 tablespoons pignoli (pine nuts), stirred in a hot skillet 1 minute until toasted

1. Cook bacon in a medium skillet until browned; drain on paper towels; cut into thin crosswise pieces. Discard fat; wipe out skillet.

2. Heat oil in skillet; add onion; sauté until tender, about 5 minutes. Stir in green pepper, garlic, and red pepper; sauté 2 minutes. Add scallops; sauté over high heat until cooked through, about 3 minutes. Add reserved bacon.

3. Meanwhile, cook the linguine in plenty of boiling salted water until al dente, or firm to the bite, about 12 minutes; drain. Toss with the scallop mixture. Sprinkle with pignoli before serving.

282   SPAGHETTI WITH WHITE WINE CLAM SAUCE

Prep: 10 minutes   Cook: 25 minutes   Serves: 4

For this recipe buy the smallest littlenecks you can find so that you can serve them arranged on top of the pasta still in their shells.

- 4 tablespoons butter
- 4 tablespoons olive oil
- 1 cup chopped sweet white onion
- 1 tablespoon thinly sliced garlic
- 1 cup dry white wine
- 3 to 4 dozen littleneck clams, scrubbed
- 1 pound linguine
- ¼ cup chopped Italian flat-leaf parsley

1. Melt butter and oil in a large heavy saucepan over low heat. Add onion and garlic; sauté until tender but not browned, about 10 minutes. Stir in wine; heat to boiling; boil 5 minutes. Add clams; cover and cook over high heat until clams are steamed open, 5 to 10 minutes.

2. Meanwhile, cook linguine in plenty of boiling salted water until al dente, or firm to the bite, about 8 minutes; drain.

3. With tongs, transfer the clams to a large platter. Toss the cooked linguine with the broth in the saucepan; add the parsley. Heap on a large platter. Arrange the clams on top of the linguine. Serve with plenty of crusty bread to soak up the broth.

283   FETTUCCINE WITH SCALLOPS, RED PEPPER, AND ANCHOVY SAUCE

Prep: 10 minutes   Cook: 15 minutes   Serves: 4

This pretty dish could serve 6 as a first course or 4 as a main course. Cut the red pepper strips about the same width as the pasta.

- 6 tablespoons olive oil
- 2 medium red bell peppers (about 12 ounces), seeded and cut into ¼-inch strips
- 2 garlic cloves, crushed
- 4 anchovy fillets, finely chopped
- 12 ounces bay scallops (or sea scallops, halved or quartered)
- 1 pound fettuccine
- ¼ cup thinly sliced scallions, white and green parts

1. Heat oil in a medium skillet; add red peppers. Sauté over medium-high heat 5 minutes, or until peppers begin to blister and brown on the edges. Stir in the garlic and anchovy fillets; sauté 2 minutes, stirring, to dissolve the anchovies. Add the scallops; sauté over high heat until just cooked through, about 3 minutes; adjust heat so that the other ingredients don't brown.

2. Meanwhile, cook the fettuccine in plenty of boiling salted water until al dente, or firm to the bite, about 10 minutes; drain. Toss with the scallop mixture and sprinkle with sliced scallions before serving.

284 LINGUINE WITH SALMON AND LEMON SAUCE

Prep: 10 minutes   Cook: 15 minutes   Serves: 4

¼ **cup olive oil**	2 **tablespoons coarsely**
½ **cup vertically sliced onion**	**chopped Italian flat-leaf**
2 **garlic cloves, crushed**	**parsley**
1 **teaspoon finely shredded**	1 **can (7¾ ounces) red salmon,**
lemon zest	**drained**
2 **tablespoons lemon juice**	12 **ounces linguine**
	Grated Parmesan cheese

1. Heat oil in a skillet over low heat; stir in onion slices. Sauté, stirring, until tender but not browned, about 10 minutes. Add garlic; sauté 2 minutes. Stir in lemon zest, juice, and parsley. Add salmon; carefully break up with a fork. Do not stir.

2. Meanwhile, cook pasta in plenty of boiling salted water until al dente, or firm to the bite, 8 to 10 minutes; drain.

3. Reheat sauce over high heat; do not stir. Toss linguine and sauce together. Serve at once sprinkled with Parmesan.

285 PASTA WITH MUSSELS AND SAFFRON CREAM SAUCE

Prep: 10 minutes   Cook: 25 minutes   Serves: 4

This dish would make an excellent first course for 6 or a main course for 4. There are usually 18 medium-sized mussels to a pound so there will be plenty to go around. Fresh pasta, if available, would be especially appropriate for this dish. Remember, cut the cooking time by half when using fresh pasta.

1 **cup dry white wine**	2 **pounds mussels, scrubbed**
1 **thickly sliced onion**	**and debearded**
1 **strip orange zest (2 x ½ inch)**	1 **cup heavy cream**
2 **garlic cloves, bruised with**	1 **teaspoon fresh lemon juice**
side of a knife	12 **ounces fettuccine,**
8 **saffron threads**	**tagliatelle, or linguine**

1. Combine the wine, onion, orange zest, garlic, and 4 of the saffron threads in a large wide saucepan; cover and heat to boiling. Add the mussels; cover and cook over high heat until mussels have opened, about 5 minutes.

2. With tongs, transfer mussels to a bowl; cool slightly. Meanwhile, boil the wine and mussel juice mixture left in the saucepan until reduced by about half, 5 minutes. Pour through a very fine mesh sieve or a sieve lined with a double thickness of dampened cheesecloth to remove any grit. Wipe out saucepan and return reduced wine mixture to saucepan. Stir in heavy cream and the remaining 4 saffron threads and boil gently until reduced by half and slightly thickened. Stir in the lemon juice.

3. Carefully remove cooked mussels from their shells. If there is any liquid in the bottom of the bowl, strain and add to the boiling cream mixture. Reserve the mussels in a small bowl.

4. Cook the fettuccine in plenty of boiling salted water until just barely cooked, about 5 minutes; drain.

5. Add the fettuccine and the mussels to the cream mixture. Heat, stirring, over medium heat until the cream coats the mussels and the pasta, about 2 minutes. When serving, distribute the mussels evenly.

---

286 SPINACH LINGUINE WITH ROASTED RED PEPPER SAUCE AND ROSEMARY-MARINATED SHRIMP

Prep: 30 minutes   Marinate: 1 hour   Cook: 15 minutes   Serves: 4

- 8 ounces medium shrimp, shelled and deveined
- 3 tablespoons olive oil
- 1 garlic clove, crushed
- 1 teaspoon minced fresh rosemary leaves pulled from stem, or 2 teaspoons dried

- 3 large red bell peppers
- ½ cup chopped onion
- 12 ounces spinach linguine
- ½ cup heavy cream or low-fat milk

1. Combine shrimp, 1 tablespoon of the olive oil, garlic, and rosemary; cover and marinate in refrigerator 1 hour.

2. Meanwhile, broil peppers in a shallow pan, 4 inches from heat source, until evenly charred on all sides, about 15 minutes. Transfer to a bowl, cover with plastic wrap, and let stand 20 minutes. Working over bowl to save pepper juices, cut peppers in half and carefully lift out seeds and stems; discard. Scrape charred skins from the pepper halves; rinse peppers under running water to remove any seeds or charred skin remaining. Cut two pepper halves into ⅛-inch strips; reserve separately. Place the remaining pepper halves in a small bowl. Strain the reserved pepper juices through a sieve into the bowl with pepper halves.

3. Heat the remaining 2 tablespoons oil in a medium skillet; add onion; sauté 5 minutes. Stir in the pepper halves and the reserved juice; stir to blend. Purée in a food processor until very smooth. (Can be prepared ahead up to this point.)

4. At serving time, cook pasta in plenty of boiling salted water until al dente, or firm to the bite, about 12 minutes; drain.

5. While pasta is cooking, heat a medium skillet over high heat until a drop of water sizzles and evaporates immediately upon touching. Add the shrimp with their marinade. Stir-fry until shrimp are pink on both sides and cooked through, about 3 minutes. Add the red pepper purée, the reserved pepper strips, and the cream to the skillet. Heat, stirring, until blended and simmering. Toss with the pasta and serve at once.

287 SPINACH LINGUINE WITH TOMATO AND SHELLFISH SAUCE

Prep: 15 minutes   Cook: 45 minutes   Serves: 4

4 tablespoons olive oil	1 dozen clams, scrubbed
½ cup chopped onion	1 dozen mussels, scrubbed
2 garlic cloves, crushed	and debearded
1 can (1 pound 12 ounces) Italian-style peeled plum tomatoes with juices	2 lobster tails, split lengthwise (thaw if frozen)
1 strip orange zest (2 x ½ inch)	½ pound large shrimp, shelled and deveined
½ teaspoon salt, or to taste	1 pound spinach linguine or fettuccine
¼ teaspoon coarsely ground pepper	¼ cup chopped fresh basil and/or Italian flat-leaf parsley
¼ teaspoon crushed dried red pepper	

1. Heat oil in a large saucepan over medium heat. Add onion; sauté over low heat until onion is tender, about 5 minutes; stir in garlic; sauté 1 minute. Add the tomatoes, orange zest, salt, and black and red pepper; heat to boiling. Simmer, uncovered, over medium-low heat 15 minutes, or until tomatoes are slightly reduced.

2. Add the clams in a single layer in the sauce. Cover and cook over medium heat 5 minutes. Add the mussels and lobster tails; cover and cook 5 minutes. Add the shrimp; cover and cook until shrimp are opaque, about 5 minutes, and the clams have all opened. Total cooking time should be under 15 minutes, but if the broth is not hot enough it might take a few minutes longer. The trick is not to overcook the lobster and the shrimp.

3. Meanwhile, cook the linguine in plenty of boiling salted water until al dente, or firm to the bite, about 8 minutes; drain. Toss in a large bowl with half the basil and half the shellfish sauce. Spoon the remaining sauce over the top and sprinkle with the remaining basil.

288 SPINACH SHELLS WITH SALMON, PARMESAN, TOMATO, AND BASIL

Prep: 10 minutes   Cook: 15 minutes   Serves: 4

6 tablespoons unsalted butter	2 tablespoons coarsely chopped fresh basil
½ cup chopped onion	Freshly ground black pepper
1 garlic clove, crushed	
1 cup chopped fresh or canned tomatoes	2 cups medium spinach shells
1 can (7¾ ounces) red salmon, drained	2 tablespoons grated Parmesan cheese

1. Heat butter in a medium skillet; add onion; sauté 5 minutes. Add garlic; sauté 1 minute. Stir in tomatoes; simmer 5 minutes. Add salmon, basil, and black pepper; do not stir.

2. Meanwhile, cook pasta in plenty of boiling salted water until al dente, or firm to the bite, about 12 minutes; drain. Spoon into a shallow bowl; pour salmon sauce over top. Sprinkle with cheese and toss just once, being careful not to break up the pieces of salmon. Serve at once.

289 ORECCHIETTE WITH CAULIFLOWER, SHRIMP, AND RED PEPPER OIL

Prep: 15 minutes   Marinate: 1–24 hours   Cook: 20 minutes
Serves: 8

Shrimp and Marinade
1½ pounds medium shrimp, shelled and deveined
¼ cup olive oil
2 tablespoons lemon juice
1 garlic clove, crushed

½ teaspoon dried rosemary
Grinding of black pepper
Pinch of crushed dried red pepper

1 pound orecchiette or other thick pasta shape like radiatore or large shells

1 medium head cauliflower, broken into florets and cut into ½- to ¾-inch pieces

Oil
½ cup olive oil
2 garlic cloves, sliced thin
½ teaspoon crushed dried red pepper, or to taste

¼ cup chopped Italian flat-leaf parsley

1. Combine the shrimp, oil, lemon juice, garlic, rosemary, black and red pepper; toss to blend. Cover and marinate 1 to 24 hours.

2. Cook the pasta in plenty of boiling salted water until half cooked, about 10 minutes; add the cauliflower and cook with the pasta until both are tender, about 10 minutes longer. Ladle out ½ cup of the pasta cooking liquid; reserve. Drain the pasta.

3. Meanwhile, heat the ½ cup oil in a medium skillet over low heat; stir in the garlic; sauté until golden, about 2 minutes. Add the red pepper; sauté 30 seconds. Remove from heat.

4. Heat another skillet over medium heat; add the shrimp and marinade and stir-fry until shrimp are pink and cooked through, about 5 minutes.

5. In a large bowl, toss the cooked pasta and the cauliflower with the reserved pasta cooking liquid, red pepper oil, the cooked shrimp, and the parsley. Serve at once.

290 SPAGHETTI WITH RED CLAM SAUCE

Prep: 10 minutes   Cook: 25 minutes   Serves: 4

2 tablespoons olive oil
½ cup chopped onion
1 garlic clove, crushed
1 can (14 ounces) Italian-style plum tomatoes with juices, pressed through a food mill or sieve
1 tablespoon tomato paste
¼ teaspoon dried oregano

¼ teaspoon crushed dried red pepper, or less to taste
1 dozen medium-size cherrystone clams, shucked and cut into bite-size pieces, liquid reserved
12 ounces spaghetti
2 tablespoons chopped Italian flat-leaf parsley leaves

1. Heat olive oil in a medium skillet; stir in onion; sauté until translucent, about 5 minutes. Stir in garlic; sauté 1 minute.

2. Add tomatoes, tomato paste, oregano, and red pepper to onion; heat to boiling. Simmer over low heat 10 minutes, or until sauce is reduced and slightly thickened.

3. Add clams and their juices; simmer over low heat 5 minutes.

4. Meanwhile, cook spaghetti in plenty of boiling salted water until al dente, or firm to the bite, about 7 minutes; drain. Toss with half the sauce; transfer to a platter; spoon remaining sauce over top. Sprinkle with parsley.

291 PENNE WITH FRESH TOMATO AND SARDINE SAUCE

Prep: 10 minutes   Cook: 20 minutes   Serves: 4

This dish can be served hot as a main dish or at room temperature as a salad or side dish.

¼ cup olive oil
½ medium Spanish onion, cut into thin vertical slices (about ¾ cup)
½ cup diced green bell pepper
2 garlic cloves, minced
2 cups diced fresh ripe tomatoes (about 12 ounces) or chopped canned tomatoes, drained
¼ teaspoon crushed dried red pepper

1 can (3¾ ounces) imported sardines packed in olive oil, well drained and blotted with paper towels
¼ cup chopped Italian flat-leaf parsley
Salt and coarsely ground black pepper
12 ounces penne or other tubular pasta shape

1. Heat olive oil in a medium skillet; add onion and sauté until translucent, about 7 minutes. Stir in bell pepper and garlic; sauté 2 minutes. Add tomatoes and red pepper; heat to boiling; simmer, stirring, until tomatoes are cooked down, about 10 minutes. Add the sardines, parsley, and a generous pinch of salt and pepper; do not stir so that the sardines will remain in large pieces.

2. Meanwhile, cook the pasta in plenty of boiling salted water until al dente, or firm to the bite, about 10 minutes; drain. Toss gently with the sauce. Serve at once.

---

292 SPINACH FETTUCCINE WITH SMOKED MUSSELS AND BASIL CREAM

Prep: 10 minutes   Cook: 10 minutes   Serves: 4

Prepare this dish with fresh fettuccine, if available. It is rich and exotic and will serve 6 as a first course or 4 as a main course.

3 tablespoons butter
2 garlic cloves, crushed
1 cup heavy cream
3 tablespoons thinly sliced fresh basil leaves
4 ounces smoked mussels

1 pound fresh or 8 ounces dried spinach fettuccine
2 tablespoons sliced unblanched almonds, stirred in a hot skillet 2 minutes, or until toasted
Basil sprigs for garnish

1. Heat butter in a large skillet; when foam subsides, stir in garlic; sauté over low heat 2 minutes. Add cream; heat to boiling; boil until slightly thickened, about 3 minutes. Stir in basil and mussels.

2. Meanwhile, cook pasta in plenty of boiling salted water until al dente, or firm to the bite, about 2 minutes for fresh and 8 to 10 minutes for dried; drain.

3. Toss pasta with cream sauce and toasted almonds. Garnish with basil sprigs.

Variation:

---

293 SPINACH FETTUCCINE WITH SMOKED MUSSELS, TOMATO, AND BASIL CREAM

Add 1 cup chopped fresh tomatoes to the butter; sauté until tender, about 5 minutes. Proceed with recipe, substituting toasted pignoli (pine nuts) for the almonds.

Chapter 16

Light and Easy

Experts call it the perfect food. Pasta is low in calories—only 210 calories for each 2-ounce (dry weight) portion—an excellent source of complex carbohydrates and fiber, and a good source of B-vitamins. It is low in sodium, cholesterol, and fat. So why have we heard that pasta is a fattening food? Well, the blame must fall on the sauces. Smothering pasta in butter, oil, cream, and cheese is not the way to go if we are trying to watch our waistlines.

The recipes in this chapter use a minimum of olive oil (no cholesterol) and, rather than caloric and high-fat ingredients like butter, cream, or mayonnaise to keep the pasta dishes moist, substitute the flavorful pasta cooking liquid or broths. Saving a ladleful of the pasta cooking liquid before draining the pasta is one of those "best kept cooking secrets" that often are forgotten from generation to generation. Lots of fresh vegetables, simply steamed or quickly sautéed in a minimum of olive oil, lend endless variety and texture to the light and easy pasta dish. Low-fat meats like chicken and turkey are used and nutritious fish, including high Omega-3 sardines and salmon, packed in water, not oil. Tuna packed in water is another great product when trying to lower fat consumption. So keep in shape the light and easy way with dishes like Pasta with Fresh Tomato and Vegetable Sauce, Rotelle with Shrimp, Peas, and Tomatoes, and Linguine with Light Red Sauce and Asparagus.

294 PASTA WITH FRESH TOMATO AND VEGETABLE SAUCE

Prep: 10 minutes   Cook: 15 minutes   Serves: 4

The flavor of this dish can become more or less robust by the amount of olive oil used. If you are very seriously cutting fat from your diet, then use just 1 tablespoon of a fruity, flavorful extra-virgin olive oil; if you are only moderately serious about cutting fat, feel free to use an extra tablespoon of oil. A nice touch is to stir a spoonful of olive oil into the dish at the very end of the cooking time. If using fresh herbs, stir them in at the very end also. They tend to turn a drab olive color and lose some of their fresh flavor if they are subjected to prolonged cooking.

3 cups diced (¼ to ½ inch) fresh tomatoes (about 2 pounds)
1 tablespoon olive oil, or more to taste
1 garlic clove, crushed
4 cups prepared vegetables (use a variety from the following suggestions: broccoli and/or cauliflower florets; trimmed green beans, cut into 1-inch lengths; sliced carrots; cubed zucchini; diced (½ inch) red bell pepper)

1 tablespoon chopped fresh basil, or ½ teaspoon dried
1 teaspoon fresh thyme leaves, or ¼ teaspoon dried
1 teaspoon fresh oregano leaves, or a pinch of dried
Salt and freshly ground black pepper
8 ounces tubular pasta such as penne or ziti
Grated Parmesan cheese

1. Combine the tomatoes, oil, and garlic in a medium skillet; cook, covered, over low heat until the tomatoes are softened and their juices are cooked out, about 5 minutes. Add the vegetables of choice, dried herbs, if using, and salt and pepper to taste; stir to blend. Cook, covered, until vegetables are tender, about 10 minutes. Stir in fresh herbs, if using.

2. Meanwhile, cook the pasta in plenty of boiling salted water until al dente, or firm to the bite, about 10 minutes; spoon out ½ cup of the pasta cooking liquid and add to the sauce. Drain the pasta. Toss pasta and sauce together. Serve at once with grated cheese, if desired.

Variation:

295 PASTA WITH FRESH TOMATO, VEGETABLES, AND TUNA

Add 1 can (6½ ounces) tuna packed in water and 1 tablespoon lemon juice to the cooked sauce just before tossing with the hot pasta. Omit the cheese.

296 ROTELLE WITH SHRIMP, PEAS, AND TOMATOES

Prep: 15 minutes   Cook: 10 minutes   Serves: 4

1 tablespoon olive oil
8 ounces large shrimp, peeled and deveined
1 scallion, cut into thin diagonal slices
1 garlic clove, crushed
1 medium tomato, cut into ½-inch dice (about 1 cup)

1 tablespoon chopped fresh oregano leaves, or ¼ teaspoon dried
8 ounces rotelle
1 cup frozen tiny peas, rinsed with hot water until thawed, drained
Salt and freshly ground black pepper

1. Heat oil in a medium skillet; add shrimp and sauté over high heat, stirring, until pink and tender, about 3 minutes. Stir in scallion and garlic; add tomato and sprinkle with oregano; set aside, covered.

2. Meanwhile, cook pasta in plenty of boiling salted water until al dente, or firm to the bite, about 10 minutes. Ladle out ¼ cup of pasta liquid; add to shrimp mixture.

3. Toss pasta, shrimp mixture, and peas. Season with salt and pepper.

297 *SPINACH LINGUINE WITH LIGHT RED SAUCE*

Prep: 10 minutes   Cook: 20 minutes   Serves: 4

The brightly colored spinach noodle makes a striking contrast with the pink sauce, but plain egg noodles can also be used. Fettuccine also works well with this recipe.

1 tablespoon olive oil
½ cup chopped sweet yellow onion
1 garlic clove, crushed
2 cans (14½ ounces each) whole tomatoes with juices
1 parsley sprig
1 bay leaf

¼ cup chopped fresh basil, or 1 teaspoon dried
1 teaspoon fresh oregano leaves, or ¼ teaspoon dried
Salt and freshly ground black pepper
12 ounces fresh or 8 ounces dried spinach linguine

1. Heat oil in a medium skillet; add onion; sauté over low heat until very tender, but not browned, about 5 minutes. Add garlic; sauté 1 minute.

2. Select 1 whole tomato from the can; squeeze the juices and seeds back into the can; coarsely chop the flesh and add to the skillet. Press remaining tomatoes and pulp through a sieve or food mill; add to skillet; add parsley and bay leaf. Heat to simmering; cook until sauce is thickened and reduced to 2 cups, about 10 minutes. Stir in herbs and salt and pepper to taste.

3. Meanwhile, cook linguine until al dente, or firm to the bite, about 5 minutes for dried and 2 minutes for fresh; drain.

4. Coil a portion of linguine on each plate and top with a spoonful of sauce. Pass remaining sauce on the side.

Variations:

298   LINGUINE WITH LIGHT RED SAUCE AND ASPARAGUS

Steam 8 ounces trimmed and diagonally sliced (½-inch lengths) asparagus on a rack set over 1 inch simmering water, covered, 3 minutes. Toss with linguine and ½ cup of the sauce. Coil a portion of linguine on each plate and top with a spoonful of sauce. Pass remaining sauce on the side.

299   LINGUINE WITH LIGHT RED SAUCE AND TUNA

Stir 1 can (6½ ounces) tuna packed in water into the sauce with the herbs. Add plenty of black pepper.

300   LINGUINE WITH LIGHT RED SAUCE AND SARDINES

Add 1 can (3¾ ounces) imported sardines packed in water, drained, ½ teaspoon grated orange zest, and herbs to the sauce. Add plenty of black pepper.

301   LINGUINE WITH LIGHT RED SAUCE AND TWO CHEESES

Toss the cooked linguine with ½ cup low-fat ricotta cheese and ½ cup of the sauce. Coil a portion of pasta on each plate. Top with a spoonful of sauce and a tablespoon of shredded low-fat mozzarella cheese. Pass the remaining sauce on the side.

302   LINGUINE WITH SAFFRON-SCENTED LIGHT RED SAUCE

Soak a generous pinch of saffron threads in ¼ cup boiling water. Add to sauce with the sieved tomatoes.

303   SPAGHETTI WITH YOGURT AND RAW VEGETABLE SAUCE

Prep: 15 minutes   Cook: 10 minutes   Serves: 4

2 cups chopped fresh
   tomatoes
½ cup chopped pared and
   seeded cucumber
½ cup chopped raw broccoli
¼ cup chopped red onion
¼ cup finely chopped Italian
   flat-leaf parsley

1 small garlic clove, crushed
½ teaspoon salt, or to taste
   Ground black pepper
2 tablespoons olive oil
12 ounces spaghetti
½ cup plain low-fat yogurt, or
   more to taste, at room
   temperature

1. Stir the tomatoes, cucumber, broccoli, red onion, parsley, garlic, salt, pepper, and oil in a large bowl; let stand at room temperature.

2. Cook the spaghetti in plenty of boiling salted water until al dente, or firm to the bite, 8 to 10 minutes. Ladle out ¼ cup of the pasta cooking liquid; add to the tomatoes. Drain the pasta; add to the tomatoes. Toss with the yogurt; add more to taste, if desired.

304   ROTELLE WITH ASPARAGUS AND MUSHROOM SAUCE

Prep: 10 minutes   Cook: 15 minutes   Serves: 4

The best cheese to use in this dish is a hard, preferably imported, Parmesan, the best choice being Parmigiano Reggiano. Use a vegetable parer to shave off paper-thin curls of cheese; a little goes a long way.

8 ounces fresh mushrooms,
   trimmed, halved, if large,
   and sliced
1 tablespoon olive oil
1 garlic clove, crushed
12 ounces fresh asparagus,
   trimmed and cut into
   ½-inch diagonals

Salt and freshly ground
   black pepper
2 tablespoons fresh lemon
   juice
8 ounces rotelle
2 tablespoons minced red bell
   pepper
   Shavings of Parmesan
   cheese

1. Combine the mushrooms, oil, and garlic in a medium skillet. Cook, covered, over low heat until the mushrooms exude their juices, 5 to 7 minutes. Add the asparagus; cook, covered, 3 minutes. Uncover and cook over medium-high heat, stirring until most of the liquid is evaporated, about 3 minutes. Add salt, pepper, and lemon juice.

2. Meanwhile, cook the pasta in plenty of boiling salted water until al dente, or firm to the bite, about 10 minutes; spoon out ½ cup of the pasta cooking liquid and add to the mushroom mixture. Drain the pasta. Toss the pasta with the mushroom mixture and the red pepper. Serve with shavings of Parmesan cheese.

Variation:

305 ROTELLE WITH ASPARAGUS, CHICKEN OR TURKEY, AND MUSHROOM SAUCE

Heat ½ cup water, a slice of onion, a pinch of salt, and bay leaf to simmering in a skillet; add 8 ounces boneless and skinless chicken or turkey cutlet; cover and cook until tender, about 7 minutes. Cool in broth. Shred meat and toss with pasta. Strain the broth and use instead of the pasta cooking liquid.

306 ROTELLE WITH SCALLOPS, PEPPERS, AND CORN

Prep: 10 minutes Cook: 10 minutes Serves: 4

This dish has all the elements of the cooking of the American Southwest. Add fresh coriander (cilantro), if you like the flavor. Otherwise keep the flavors fairly neutral by using parsley. Tiny, tender bay scallops are wonderful in this dish, but large sea scallops, quartered, can be used.

1 tablespoon olive oil
1 scallion, trimmed and sliced thin
1 medium green bell pepper, cut into ¼-inch dice
½ medium red bell pepper, cut into ¼-inch dice
8 ounces bay scallops
½ cup fresh corn kernels, cut from 1 medium ear
1 garlic clove, crushed
2 tablespoons fresh lime juice
2 tablespoons chopped fresh coriander (cilantro) or Italian flat-leaf parsley
Salt and freshly ground black pepper
8 ounces rotelle or penne

1. Heat oil in a medium skillet; add scallion and peppers; sauté over medium heat until tender, about 5 minutes. Turn heat to high; add scallops and corn. Stir-fry until just tender, about 3 minutes. Off heat, stir in the garlic, lime juice, coriander or parsley, and salt and pepper to taste.

2. Meanwhile, cook the pasta in plenty of boiling salted water until al dente, or firm to the bite, 10 to 12 minutes; drain.

3. Toss the scallop mixture with the hot pasta and serve at once.

Variation:

307 PASTA WITH SCALLOPS AND SUMMER SAUCE

Add 1 medium tomato, chopped, and 1 small seeded and chopped cucumber to the sautéed scallops.

308 SPAGHETTI WITH SAUCE OF THE SEA
Prep: 10 minutes   Cook: 25 minutes   Serves: 4

1 tablespoon olive oil
2 tablespoons finely chopped
   onion
1 small garlic clove, crushed
1 can (14 ounces) Italian-style
   plum tomatoes with
   juices, puréed
1 tablespoon tomato paste
1 tablespoon chopped fresh
   herbs (parsley, oregano,
   basil, or thyme), or equal
   parts fresh and dried

1 strip (2 x ½ inch) orange zest
1 bay leaf
12 ounces boneless and
   skinless flounder fillets,
   cut into 1-inch pieces
   Salt and freshly ground
   black pepper
12 ounces spaghetti

1. Heat oil in a skillet or wide saucepan; add onion and sauté until tender, about 5 minutes. Add garlic; sauté 1 minute. Add tomatoes and paste, herbs, orange zest, and bay leaf; simmer, stirring, until sauce is reduced and slightly thickened, about 10 minutes. Add the pieces of fish; cover and cook until tender when flaked with a fork, about 8 minutes. Sprinkle with salt and pepper.

2. Meanwhile, cook the pasta in plenty of boiling salted water until al dente, or firm to the bite, 8 to 10 minutes; drain. Toss spaghetti with about ½ cup of the tomato sauce. Arrange on a platter and spoon the sauce with the fish over the top.

309 PENNE WITH STEAMED VEGETABLES AND FRESH TOMATOES
Prep: 15 minutes   Cook: 10 minutes   Serves: 4

1 cup broccoli florets
1 cup cauliflower florets
1 cup fresh green beans,
   trimmed and cut into
   2-inch lengths
½ cup sliced carrots
2 medium tomatoes, cut into
   ¼-inch dice
½ cup fresh corn kernels (cut
   from 1 medium ear)

¼ cup chopped red onion
1 tablespoon olive oil
¼ cup chopped fresh basil
   leaves
   Salt and freshly ground
   black pepper
8 ounces penne or other
   tubular pasta
   Grated Parmesan cheese

1. Steam the broccoli, cauliflower, green beans, and carrots on a rack set over 1 inch simmering water, covered, 5 minutes. Combine the tomatoes, corn, red onion, olive oil, basil, salt and pepper to taste; reserve separately.

2. Cook the penne in plenty of boiling salted water until al dente, or firm to the bite, about 10 minutes. Spoon out ¼ cup of the pasta cooking liquid; stir into tomatoes. Drain pasta.

3. In a large bowl toss the steamed vegetables, tomato mixture, and pasta. Serve with cheese, if desired.

---

310   SALAD OF PENNE AND CHICKEN WITH SPINACH-BUTTERMILK DRESSING

Prep: 20 minutes   Let stand: 3–24 hours   Cook: 20 minutes
Serves: 4

Buttermilk, almost too thick and creamy to be downed by the glass, makes a terrific sauce ingredient. At only 99 calories per cup it sure beats sour cream, which adds up to almost 400 calories per cup. The sauce can be prepared a day ahead; it thickens upon standing and the flavors have a chance to develop.

Dressing

- ½ cup cooked chopped (squeezed dry) spinach
- ¼ cup chopped Italian flat-leaf parsley
- ¼ cup packed dill sprigs plus a few stems, chopped
- 1 scallion, trimmed and cut into ½-inch lengths

- 1 small garlic clove, minced
- 1 anchovy fillet, chopped
- 1 tablespoon fresh lemon juice
- ½ teaspoon salt
- 1 cup buttermilk
- 2 tablespoons olive oil (optional)

- 1 onion slice
- 1 bay leaf
  Salt
- 1 pound boneless, skinless chicken cutlets

- 12 ounces penne
- 2 cups small cherry tomatoes
- ½ cup sliced red onion

1. For the dressing, combine the spinach, parsley, dill, scallion, garlic, anchovy, lemon juice, and salt in a food processor or blender; process until very finely chopped. Add the buttermilk and olive oil, if using; purée until blended. Transfer to a jar and store in the refrigerator until ready to use. Let stand several hours or overnight; sauce will thicken.

2. Heat about 1 inch of water, the onion, bay leaf, and a pinch of salt in a skillet to simmering. Add the chicken; cover and simmer over low heat until tender, about 10 minutes; cool in broth. Cut chicken into pieces about the same size as the penne. Reserve the broth for other use.

3. Cook the penne in plenty of boiling salted water until al dente, or firm to the bite, about 10 minutes; drain. Rinse with cool water. Combine the pasta, chicken, cherry tomatoes, and onion in a large bowl. Add the dressing; toss just to coat.

Pasta profile

A 5-ounce serving of cooked pasta contains:
210 calories   7 grams protein   41 grams carbohydrate   1 gram fat

311 PENNE WITH STEAMED VEGETABLES AND RICOTTA

Prep: 10 minutes   Cook: 15 minutes   Serves: 4

1 small (about 4 ounces) zucchini, pared and julienned (¼ x 2 inches)
1 small (about 4 ounces) yellow summer squash, pared and julienned (¼ x 2 inches)
1 small carrot, pared and julienned (¼ x 2 inches)
4 ounces Chinese snow peas or green beans, trimmed and cut into 2-inch lengths, if necesssary
1 tablespoon olive oil

1 garlic clove, crushed
  Salt and freshly ground black pepper
8 ounces penne or other tubular pasta
1 container (15 ounces) low-fat ricotta cheese
2 tablespoons fresh lemon juice
½ teaspoon grated lemon zest
2 tablespoons chopped Italian flat-leaf parsley
  Grated Parmesan cheese

1. Steam the vegetables on a rack set over 1 inch simmering water, covered, until tender, about 5 minutes. Transfer to a bowl, and while still hot, add the oil, garlic, salt and pepper to taste; toss to blend.

2. Meanwhile, cook pasta in plenty of boiling salted water until al dente, or firm to the bite, about 10 minutes; drain.

3. In a large bowl, stir ricotta, lemon juice and zest, and parsley together. Add the pasta; stir to blend. Add the vegetables; toss. Season to taste with black pepper and Parmesan.

312 PENNE WITH HERBED RICOTTA AND FRESH TOMATOES

Prep: 20 minutes   Drain: 1 hour   Cook: 10 minutes   Serves: 4

1 container (15 ounces) low-fat ricotta cheese
1 tablespoon minced fresh basil with stems
½ teaspoon grated lemon zest
1 small garlic clove, crushed
½ teaspoon salt
¼ teaspoon coarsely ground black pepper

1 pound firm ripe plum tomatoes
12 ounces penne or other tubular pasta
2 tablespoons julienne strips fresh basil leaves
  Fruity olive oil

1. Place ricotta in a sieve set over a bowl; drain in refrigerator 1 hour. Discard liquid. Combine ricotta with the minced basil, lemon zest, garlic, salt, and black pepper; set aside.

2. Halve the tomatoes lengthwise; scoop out the seeds and pulp. Cut the tomato flesh into ¼-inch lengthwise strips.

3. Cook the penne in plenty of boiling salted water until al dente, or firm to the bite, about 10 minutes. Ladle out ¼ cup of the pasta cooking liquid; reserve. Drain the pasta.

4. In a large bowl, toss the pasta with ¼ cup pasta cooking liquid, ricotta, tomatoes, basil strips, and 1 to 2 tablespoons olive oil until blended.

313 MACARONI WITH CHICKEN AND ASPARAGUS

Prep: 10 minutes   Cook: 10 minutes   Serves: 4

2 tablespoons olive oil
8 ounces asparagus, trimmed and cut into ½-inch diagonals
1 scallion, cut into thin diagonals
2 boneless and skinless chicken breasts, each 6 ounces, cut into ½-inch strips
1 teaspoon fresh thyme leaves, or ¼ teaspoon dried

Salt and freshly ground black pepper
12 ounces tubular macaroni like mostaccioli, ziti, or ziti rigati
2 tablespoons fresh lemon juice
1 tablespoon thinly sliced green scallion tops
Parmesan cheese shavings

1. Heat oil in a medium skillet; add asparagus and scallion; stir-fry 2 minutes. Add chicken; sprinkle with half the thyme leaves and salt and pepper to taste; cover and cook over low heat until cooked through, about 5 minutes.

2. Meanwhile, cook the pasta in plenty of boiling salted water until al dente, or firm to the bite, about 15 minutes; drain.

3. Toss the chicken and asparagus, pasta, lemon juice, scallion tops, and remaining thyme leaves. Serve with shavings of Parmesan cheese.

Variation:

314 PASTA WITH CHICKEN AND TRICOLOR PEPPERS

Substitute ½ *each* large green, red, and yellow bell peppers, cut into ⅛-inch strips, for the asparagus.

Chapter 17

Tortellini, Manicotti, Ravioli, and Other Stuffers

Filled pastas are among the most satisfying of dishes. We know a child who survived two weeks in Italy by ordering Tortellini in Broth at *every* meal, and to this day (she is now an adult) still loves the same dish.

Fortunately, fresh (and frozen) tortellini and ravioli, filled with various combinations of chicken, cheese, prosciutto, spinach, beef, and/or veal, are now more readily available than ever before.

The dried pasta shapes for stuffing, like manicotti and jumbo seashells, have been with us for a while and are as popular as ever. Like lasagne, they are a food for all tastes and times. The recipes can be assembled a day ahead and baked just before serving; and the consensus seems to be that leftovers are almost better than the original dish. The flavors in the recipes are fairly evenly divided between the traditional combinations, like Vegetable-Filled Shells with Tomato Sauce, and a few more unusual combinations, like Manicotti Stuffed with Beef and Porcini.

315   SPINACH-STUFFED MANICOTTI WITH RED PEPPER BÉCHAMEL SAUCE

Prep: 30 minutes   Bake: 45 minutes   Serves: 4

1 package (10 ounces) frozen chopped spinach
2 tablespoons olive oil
1 cup chopped onion
1 teaspoon chopped garlic
1 container (15 ounces) ricotta cheese

1 cup coarsely shredded mozzarella cheese
½ cup grated Parmesan cheese
1 egg, beaten
Pinch of grated nutmeg
Salt and pepper
8 manicotti shells

Red Pepper Béchamel Sauce
3 tablespoons butter
3 tablespoons all-purpose flour
2 cups milk
1 egg

1 jar (7 ounces) roasted red peppers, drained, rinsed, and blotted dry
Salt and pepper

1. Cook the spinach according to package directions; drain and cool. Squeeze or press with the back of a spoon to extract as much moisture as possible. Squeeze the mass of spinach in a triple thickness of paper towels to blot.

2. Heat the oil in a medium skillet; add the onion; sauté until tender, about 5 minutes. Add the garlic; sauté 1 minute. Stir in the spinach; stir over medium heat to cook off any excess moisture.

3. In a large bowl, stir the ricotta, ½ cup of the mozzarella, the Parmesan cheese, egg, nutmeg, and salt and pepper to taste until blended. Stir in the spinach mixture until blended; set aside.

4. Cook the manicotti in plenty of boiling salted water until barely cooked, about 7 minutes. Carefully lift from the water with a slotted spoon and place in a bowl of cool water. Let stand until ready to use.

5. To make the béchamel, melt the butter in a medium saucepan over low heat; gradually stir in the flour until smooth; cook, stirring constantly, about 3 minutes. Gradually add the milk, stirring over medium heat, until sauce is thickened and boiling, about 10 minutes. Beat the egg in a small bowl; gradually whisk the hot sauce into the egg.

6. Meanwhile, purée the roasted peppers in a food processor. Gradually add the hot béchamel sauce to the food processor until thoroughly blended. Add salt and pepper to taste.

7. Heat the oven to 350°F. Lightly butter a 9 x 13-inch baking dish. Carefully lift the manicotti shells from the water, one by one; blot dry. Carefully fill the shells, dividing the spinach filling evenly. Arrange the filled manicotti in a row in the baking dish. Stir the remaining ½ cup mozzarella into the béchamel and pour over the stuffed manicotti.

8. Cover with foil and bake 30 minutes; uncover and bake until sauce is bubbly, about 15 minutes. Let stand at least 10 minutes before serving.

316 MANICOTTI STUFFED WITH BEEF AND PORCINI

Prep: 10 minutes   Soak: 20 minutes   Bake: 45 minutes   Serves: 4

1 ounce dried porcini
1 cup water
2 tablespoons olive oil
.1 cup chopped onion
½ cup minced pared carrot
1 teaspoon minced garlic
1 pound lean ground beef
   Salt and pepper
1 container (15 ounces) ricotta
   cheese

1 cup shredded mozzarella
   cheese
¼ cup chopped Italian flat-leaf
   parsley
6 tablespoons grated
   Parmesan cheese
   Pinch of ground nutmeg
8 manicotti shells

Porcini Béchamel Sauce
   Milk
3 tablespoons butter
3 tablespoons all-purpose
   flour

½ teaspoon salt
   Coarsely ground black
   pepper

1. Combine the dried porcini and 1 cup of water in a small saucepan. Cover and heat to simmering. Let stand, covered, 20 minutes. Drain through a fine sieve lined with a piece of dampened paper towel set over a 2-cup liquid measuring cup; reserve liquid. Rinse any grit from the mushrooms; blot dry; finely chop; set aside.

2. Heat the oil in a large skillet; add the onion and carrot; sauté until tender, about 5 minutes. Stir in the garlic; sauté 1 minute. Add the ground beef; sauté, stirring and breaking up with a fork, just until it loses its pink color. Add the chopped porcini and season with salt and pepper.

3. In a large bowl, stir the ricotta, ½ cup of the mozzarella, parsley, and 3 tablespoons of the Parmesan together until blended. Sprinkle with the nutmeg. Add the sautéed meat mixture; stir to blend.

4. Cook the manicotti in plenty of boiling salted water until just barely tender, about 7 minutes. Carefully lift the manicotti shells, one by one, from the pan with a slotted spoon and set in a bowl of cool water. Let stand until ready to fill.

5. To make the béchamel, add enough milk to the reserved porcini liquid to equal 2 cups. Heat the butter in a saucepan until melted. Gradually whisk in the flour until smooth; cook, stirring constantly, about 3 minutes. Gradually whisk in the milk and porcini liquid mixture; cook, stirring constantly over medium heat, until sauce thickens and boils, about 10 minutes. Stir in the remaining ½ cup mozzarella and season with salt and pepper to taste.

6. Heat oven to 350°F. Lightly butter a 9 x 13-inch baking dish. Carefully drain the manicotti shells; blot dry with paper toweling. Using a teaspoon, carefully fill the shells, distributing the meat and cheese filling evenly among the shells. Arrange in a row in the baking dish. Pour the béchamel sauce over the manicotti. Sprinkle with the remaining 3 tablespoons Parmesan.

7. Cover dish with foil and bake 30 minutes; uncover and bake until top is browned and sauce is bubbly, about 15 minutes. Let stand at least 10 minutes before serving.

---

317 SAUSAGE-STUFFED SHELLS WITH CHUNKY PEPPER-TOMATO SAUCE

Prep: 30 minutes   Bake: 45 minutes   Serves: 4

Sauce

3 tablespoons olive oil
1 cup lengthwise onion slices
1 medium red bell pepper, cut into thin strips
1 medium green bell pepper, cut into thin strips

1 garlic clove, minced
1 can (28 ounces) peeled Italian plum tomatoes, with juice
Salt and freshly ground black pepper

---

12 large seashell-shaped pasta

Filling

1 pound sweet Italian sausage, removed from casings
1 cup chopped mushrooms
¼ cup chopped onion
2 tablespoons finely chopped parsley

Salt and freshly ground black pepper
1 egg, beaten
1 cup ricotta cheese
1 cup shredded mozzarella cheese
¼ cup grated Parmesan cheese

1. For the sauce, heat the oil in a medium skillet; add the onion and green and red peppers; sauté, stirring, over medium heat until tender and peppers begin to brown, about 8 minutes. Add the garlic, sauté 1 minute. Add the tomatoes; stir, breaking up tomatoes with the side of a spoon. Simmer sauce uncovered, stirring occasionally, until reduced and slightly thickened, about 20 minutes. Season with salt and pepper.

2. Cook shells in plenty of boiling salted water until barely tender, about 7 minutes. Lift from water with a slotted spoon and let stand in a bowl of cool water until ready to use.

3. For the filling, brown the sausage in a medium skillet; drain off the fat. Add the mushrooms and onion; cover and cook over low heat until vegetables are tender, about 5 minutes. Cook, uncovered, until edges begin to brown, about 5 minutes. Add parsley; season with salt and pepper. Combine the egg, ricotta, mozzarella, and Parmesan in a large bowl. Fold in the sausage mixture until blended.

4. Heat the oven to 350°F. Lightly butter a 9 x 13-inch baking dish. Drain the shells and invert on paper towels to dry. Fill the shells, distributing the filling evenly. Arrange in rows in the baking dish. Spoon the sauce over the top. Cover and bake 30 minutes. Uncover and bake 15 minutes. Let stand 10 minutes before serving.

318   CHEESE RAVIOLI WITH SHRIMP AND TOMATO-CREAM SAUCE

Prep: 15 minutes   Cook: 25 minutes   Serves: 4

2 tablespoons butter
1 small garlic clove, crushed
1 can (14 ounces) Italian-style peeled plum tomatoes with juices
1 cup heavy cream
8 ounces medium shrimp, shelled, deveined, and coarsely chopped

6 large basil leaves, torn into pieces
   Salt and freshly ground black pepper
1 pound fresh or frozen cheese-filled ravioli

1. Heat butter in a medium skillet; add garlic; sauté 1 minute. Add the tomatoes; cook, stirring and breaking up tomatoes with the side of a spoon, until mixture is slightly reduced and thickened, about 10 minutes.

2. Meanwhile, boil the cream in a medium saucepan, stirring and adjusting heat to prevent boiling over, until reduced by half. Add to the reduced tomato sauce. Stir in the shrimp; simmer over low heat 5 minutes. Stir in the basil. Season with salt and pepper.

3. Cook the ravioli in plenty of boiling salted water until tender; drain. Place on a platter or divide among four serving dishes and spoon some of the sauce on each.

319   SPINACH RAVIOLI WITH FRESH AND SUN-DRIED TOMATO SAUCE

Prep: 10 minutes   Cook: 25 minutes   Serves: 4

Use either spinach- or cheese-filled spinach pasta ravioli. The red sauce looks great on the green spinach pasta.

2 tablespoons olive oil
¼ cup chopped onion
1 small garlic clove, crushed
1 can (14 ounces) Italian-style peeled plum tomatoes with juices
¼ cup slivered sun-dried tomatoes packed in olive oil, drained and blotted dry

   Freshly ground black pepper
1 pound fresh or frozen cheese- or spinach-filled spinach ravioli
   Grated Parmesan cheese

1. Heat the oil in a medium skillet. Stir in the onion; sauté until tender, about 5 minutes. Stir in the garlic; sauté 1 minute. Add the tomatoes; cook, stirring to break up the tomatoes with the side of a spoon, until sauce is thickened and slightly reduced, about 10 minutes. Stir in the sun-dried tomatoes; simmer 5 minutes. Add pepper.

2. Cook the ravioli until tender; drain. Place on platter and spoon sauce over top. Sprinkle with grated cheese.

320   CHICKEN-STUFFED SHELLS WITH SPINACH BÉCHAMEL SAUCE

Prep: 30 minutes   Bake: 45 minutes   Serves: 4

Try this versatile recipe with turkey; or omit the prosciutto and try a combination of half turkey and half baked ham.

Spinach Béchamel Sauce

3 tablespoons butter	1 teaspoon fresh lemon juice
3 tablespoons all-purpose flour	1 teaspoon salt
2 cups milk, heated	Pinch of nutmeg
1 package (10 ounces) frozen chopped spinach, cooked, drained, and squeezed dry	Grinding of black pepper

12 large seashell-shaped pasta

Filling

3 teaspoons butter	2 tablespoons chopped parsley
3 teaspoons finely chopped shallots	1 container (15 ounces) ricotta cheese
1 cup chopped mushrooms	1 egg, beaten
3 slices prosciutto, finely chopped	¼ cup grated Parmesan cheese
2 cups cooked shredded chicken	

1. For the sauce, heat the butter in a small saucepan; gradually stir in the flour; cook, stirring, until smooth, about 3 minutes. Gradually stir in the milk; cook, stirring, until smooth and thick, about 10 minutes. Purée the spinach with half of the béchamel in a food processor. Add the remaining béchamel and lemon juice. Season with salt, nutmeg, and pepper; reserve.

2. Cook the pasta shells in plenty of boiling salted water until barely cooked, about 7 minutes; drain. Let stand in a bowl of cool water until ready to use.

3. For the filling, heat the butter in a medium skillet; add the shallots and mushrooms; sauté until tender, about 10 minutes. Add the prosciutto; sauté 2 minutes. Stir in the chicken and parsley. In a large bowl, combine the ricotta, egg, and Parmesan cheese; fold in chicken mixture until blended.

4. Heat oven to 350°F. Lightly butter a 9 x 13-inch baking dish. Drain the pasta and invert on paper towels to blot dry. Fill shells with chicken mixture, distributing evenly. Arrange in the baking dish. Pour the béchamel over the top. Sprinkle with some Parmesan.

5. Cover with foil and bake 30 minutes. Uncover and bake until browned and bubbly, about 15 minutes. Let stand at least 10 minutes before serving.

321   SPINACH TORTELLINI IN PARMESAN CREAM SAUCE

Prep: 5 minutes   Cook: 10 minutes   Serves: 4

2 cups heavy cream
½ cup grated Parmesan cheese
2 tablespoons butter, softened

1 package (9 ounces) spinach (either meat- or cheese-filled) tortellini

1. Heat cream to boiling in a saucepan, adjusting heat to prevent cream from boiling over, until reduced to 1 cup, about 10 minutes. Stir in Parmesan cheese.

2. Meanwhile, cook the tortellini in plenty of boiling salted water according to package directions, usually about 7 minutes; drain. Toss with butter.

3. Distribute the tortellini evenly among 4 serving plates; spoon sauce over each dish.

322   MANICOTTI STUFFED WITH EGGPLANT AND BEEF WITH BOLOGNESE SAUCE

Prep: 30 minutes   Drain: 1 hour   Bake: 45 minutes   Serves: 4

1 eggplant, about 1 pound
Salt
Vegetable oil
1 pound lean ground beef
½ cup chopped onion
½ cup chopped green bell pepper
½ cup chopped red bell pepper
1 garlic clove, crushed
½ teaspoon salt
⅛ teaspoon ground black pepper

1 egg, beaten
1 cup ricotta cheese
1 cup shredded mozzarella cheese
¼ cup grated Parmesan cheese
8 manicotti shells
2 cups Tomato Sauce, Bolognese Style (page 160)
8 ounces mozzarella cheese, sliced

1. Trim the eggplant. Cut into 1-inch lengths about ¼ inch thick. Toss with 2 teaspoons salt. Place in a colander set over a bowl. Weight eggplant with a saucer and place something heavy on the saucer. Let stand 1 hour.

2. Rinse the eggplant in cool water; drain; squeeze dry. Wrap in several layers of paper towel and press to absorb as much moisture as possible. Heat 1 inch of vegetable oil in a medium skillet; fry the eggplant, half at a time, until golden. Drain on paper towels.

3. Sauté the beef in a medium skillet; drain off any fat. Add the onion, peppers, and garlic. Cover and cook over low heat until vegetables are tender, about 5 minutes. Sauté uncovered, stirring, until the vegetables begin to brown, about 5 minutes. Add the eggplant. Season with salt and pepper. In a large bowl, combine the egg, ricotta, mozzarella, and Parmesan cheeses; fold in the ground beef mixture until blended.

4. Cook the manicotti in plenty of boiling salted water until barely tender, about 7 minutes. Lift from the water with a slotted spoon and place in a bowl of cool water until ready to use.

5. Heat the oven to 350°F. Lightly butter a 9 x 13-inch baking dish. Drain the manicotti; blot dry with paper towels. Fill with the eggplant mixture, distributing evenly. Arrange in the baking dish. Pour the bolognese sauce over and top with the slices of mozzarella cheese.

6. Cover with foil and bake 30 minutes; uncover and bake until browned and bubbly, about 15 minutes. Let stand 10 minutes before serving.

---

323   MANICOTTI STUFFED WITH SPINACH AND FETA CHEESE

Prep: 30 minutes   Bake: 45 minutes   Serves: 4

For a stuffing, frozen chopped spinach is a perfectly acceptable convenience food. Drain it very well by placing in a sieve and pressing on the spinach with the back of a large spoon. Blot with paper towels to remove additional liquid.

2 cups Quick Chunky Tomato Sauce (page 142) or a good quality prepared tomato sauce	8 manicotti shells

Filling

2 tablespoons olive oil	1 egg, beaten
1 cup chopped onion	8 ounces feta cheese, crumbled
6 ounces mushrooms, chopped (about 2 cups)	1 cup shredded mozzarella cheese
1 garlic clove, minced	
1 package (10 ounces) frozen chopped spinach, cooked, drained, and squeezed dry	

1. Make the Quick Chunky Tomato Sauce.

2. Cook the manicotti in plenty of boiling salted water until barely cooked, about 7 minutes. Carefully lift from the water with a slotted spoon and place in a bowl of cool water until ready to use.

3. For the filling, heat the oil in a medium skillet; add the onion and mushrooms and sauté, stirring, until tender and beginning to brown, about 5 minutes. Add the garlic; sauté 1 minute. In a large bowl, combine the spinach, egg, feta, and mozzarella cheese. Add the mushroom mixture and stir to blend.

4. Heat the oven to 350°F. Lightly butter a 9 x 13-inch baking dish. Drain the manicotti shells; blot dry with paper towels. Carefully fill the shells with the spinach mixture, dividing evenly. Arrange in a row in the baking dish. Spoon the tomato sauce over the top.

5. Cover with foil and bake 30 minutes; uncover and bake 15 minutes. Let stand at least 10 minutes before serving.

324 THREE-CHEESE-STUFFED MANICOTTI WITH RED PEPPER BÉCHAMEL SAUCE

Prep: 30 minutes   Bake: 45 minutes   Serves: 4

The bits of sun-dried tomato in the stuffing are pretty as well as delicious. Pancetta is a cured but unsmoked bacon. Slab bacon that has been blanched in boiling water to remove some of the smokiness can be substituted.

Red Pepper Béchamel Sauce (page 183)

8 manicotti shells

Filling
- **1 thick slice pancetta, minced**
- **2 tablespoons olive oil**
- **2 cups ricotta cheese**
- **1 cup shredded mozzarella cheese**
- **2 tablespoons grated Parmesan cheese**
- **1 egg, beaten**
- **2 tablespoons finely chopped parsley**
- **2 tablespoons slivered sun-dried tomatoes packed in oil, blotted dry**
- **Pinch of ground cloves**

1. Make the Red Pepper Béchamel Sauce.

2. Cook the manicotti shells in plenty of boiling salted water until barely cooked, about 7 minutes. Lift from the boiling water and place in a bowl of cool water until ready to use.

3. For the filling, sauté the pancetta in olive oil until golden brown. Drain on paper towels; discard fat in pan. In a large bowl, combine the ricotta, mozzarella, Parmesan, egg, parsley, tomatoes, cloves, and pancetta until blended.

4. Heat oven to 350°F. Lightly butter a 9 x 13-inch baking dish. Drain the manicotti; carefully blot dry with paper towels. Fill the manicotti, distributing the filling evenly. Arrange in rows in the prepared baking dish. Pour the Red Pepper Béchamel Sauce over the top. Cover and bake 30 minutes; uncover and bake until sauce is bubbly on top, about 15 minutes. Let stand 10 minutes before serving.

325 TORTELLINI IN TOMATO AND ANCHOVY CREAM

Prep: 5 minutes   Cook: 20 minutes   Serves: 4

2 cups heavy cream
1 can (14 ounces) Italian-style plum tomatoes with juices, cut up with scissors

2 teaspoons anchovy paste
1 pound spinach tortellini or tortelloni
Coarsely ground black pepper

1. Heat cream to boiling in a large saucepan; boil, adjusting heat to keep from boiling over, until reduced to 1 cup, about 10 minutes.

2. In a medium skillet, heat the tomatoes, stirring and mashing with the back of a large spoon, until liquid cooks off and sauce is reduced and thickened. Stir in anchovy until blended. Gradually stir in the cream until blended.

3. Meanwhile, cook the tortellini in plenty of boiling salted water according to package instructions, usually about 7 minutes; drain.

4. Divide tortellini among four bowls; top with sauce. Sprinkle with black pepper.

326 TORTELLINI IN BROTH

Prep: 5 minutes   Cook: 10 minutes   Serves: 4

4 cups chicken broth (use lightly salted homemade broth or half canned broth and half water)

1 package (9½ ounces) chicken and prosciutto or cheese-filled spinach or plain tortellini
Grated Parmesan cheese

1. Heat the broth to simmering; cover; keep warm.

2. Cook the tortellini in plenty of boiling salted water according to package directions, usually about 7 minutes. Drain. Add to the broth; simmer 2 minutes.

3. Ladle into bowls, distributing the tortellini evenly. Sprinkle with grated cheese.

327   VEGETABLE-FILLED SHELLS WITH TOMATO SAUCE

Prep: 10 minutes   Drain: 30 minutes   Bake: 45 minutes   Serves: 6

This filling uses much of late summer's bounty. Make the quick and easy fresh tomato sauce to spoon over each serving. The fresh sauce is so delicious you might want to double the recipe to be sure you will have plenty on hand. This is an especially festive party dish.

8 ounces zucchini, shredded	2 cups ricotta cheese
1 teaspoon salt	2 cups shredded mozzarella
18 large seashell-shaped pasta	cheese
2 tablespoons butter	1 egg, beaten
2 cups chopped (¼-inch	¼ cup chopped fresh basil
pieces) broccoli	leaves
1 cup chopped mushrooms	¼ cup grated Parmesan cheese
½ cup diced carrot	2 cups Quick Chunky Tomato
¼ cup chopped scallions	Sauce (page 142)
Salt and freshly ground	
black pepper	

1. Toss the zucchini with the salt; transfer to a colander set over a bowl. Place a saucer on top of the zucchini and weight with something heavy. Let stand 30 minutes. Rinse with cool water; drain and squeeze dry. Blot with paper towels to remove excess moisture.

2. Cook the pasta shells in plenty of boiling salted water until barely cooked, about 7 minutes. Transfer with a slotted spoon to a bowl of cool water and let stand until ready to use.

3. Melt the butter in a medium skillet; add the zucchini, broccoli, mushrooms, carrot, and scallions; sauté until vegetables are crisp-tender, about 5 minutes. Season with salt and pepper. In a large bowl, combine the ricotta, 1 cup of the mozzarella, egg, basil, and Parmesan cheese; add the vegetables; stir to blend.

4. Heat oven to 350°F. Lightly butter a 9 x 13-inch baking dish. Drain the shells; carefully invert on paper towels to blot dry. Fill the shells with the stuffing mixture, distributing evenly. Arrange in the prepared baking dish. Cover with foil and bake 30 minutes. Uncover and sprinkle each shell with some of the remaining 1 cup shredded mozzarella. Bake, uncovered, 15 minutes, or until cheese is browned and bubbly.

5. Serve the stuffed shells with some of the tomato sauce spooned over each serving.

Chapter 18

Pasta and Eggs

This chapter was inspired by a wonderful scrambled egg and pasta dish, called Pasta alla Mama, I enjoyed at Hugo's, a popular hangout in West Hollywood. After spending a few days in Los Angeles wining and dining with the best of them, and eating just a little too much wasabi on my raw "cooked" tuna steak, I was thrilled to see what looked like my favorite comfort food, pasta, on the menu. Pasta alla Mamma is a medley of soft scrambled eggs and delicate homemade pasta fragrant with herbs and garlic, and, I think, one of the most comforting foods I have ever eaten. Thank you, Hugo's, for sharing four recipes with us: three variations of Pasta alla Mamma and a hearty Pasta alla Pappa rendition. In addition, we have included a few other rustic family-style egg and pasta combinations. The frittatas were invented from a cupful of leftover cooked spaghetti, and although we have suggested just three variations, there are dozens more. In Italy frittata is often served cold, cut into thin wedges as part of an antipasto or light luncheon. The Rigatoni with Sausage, Peppers, and Eggs was inspired by my mamma's Sunday morning special: scrambled sausage, peppers, and eggs.

328   HUGO'S PASTA ALLA MAMMA
Prep: 5 minutes   Cook: 5 minutes   Serves: 2

Make this dish in small batches, which produces a much creamier product. Too much hot fettuccine cooks the egg just that much faster. At Hugo's, each serving is, of course, made to order. Also the restaurant makes up its own seasoned salt mixture, which they say is similar to commercially blended seasoned salt. Hugo's uses fresh tagliatelle, a ribbon pasta, just a little wider than fettuccine. Fresh fettuccine would be a suitable substitute.

3 tablespoons butter
1 garlic clove, crushed
2 tablespoons chopped
    parsley
   Pinch *each* of dried basil and
    oregano
6 ounces fresh fettuccine

4 eggs, beaten
¼ cup grated Parmesan cheese
   Seasoned or plain salt (see
    headnote)
   Freshly ground black
    pepper

1. Melt the butter in a large heavy skillet; add the garlic; sauté 1 minute. Off heat, stir in the parsley, basil, and oregano.

2. Meanwhile, cook fettuccine in plenty of boiling salted water until al dente, about 2 minutes; drain.

3. Add the pasta to the skillet; stir well. Pour eggs and cheese over the pasta; sprinkle with salt to taste; stir continuously until eggs coat pasta and begin to set in a few places. Serve at once. Sprinkle generously with black pepper.

329   CHICKEN AND SUN-DRIED TOMATO PASTA ALLA MAMMA
Prep: 10 minutes   Cook: 10 minutes   Serves: 2

3 tablespoons butter
4 ounces boneless and
    skinless chicken breast,
    cut into small slivers
1 small garlic clove, crushed
2 tablespoons finely chopped
    parsley
   Pinch *each* dried basil and
    oregano

6 ounces fresh fettuccine
4 eggs, beaten
¼ cup grated Parmesan cheese
   Seasoned or plain salt
1 tablespoon finely slivered
    sun-dried tomatoes
    packed in oil, blotted dry
   Freshly ground black
    pepper

1. Heat butter in a large heavy skillet over medium heat. When foam subsides, stir in the pieces of chicken; sauté, stirring, until cooked through, about 3 minutes. Add the garlic; sauté 1 minute. Add the parsley, basil, and oregano.

2. Meanwhile, cook the fettuccine in plenty of boiling salted water until al dente, or firm to the bite, 2 minutes; drain.

3. Add the pasta to the skillet and stir to blend. Pour eggs and cheese over the pasta; sprinkle with salt to taste; stir continuously until eggs coat pasta and begin to set in a few places. Sprinkle with sun-dried tomatoes. Serve at once, sprinkled with black pepper.

---

330   SPAGHETTI FRITTATA
Prep: 5 minutes   Cook: 25 minutes   Serves: 4

This dish is quick, delicious, and economical, a wonderful way to use up that small amount of leftover spaghetti. Other pasta shapes (elbows, tubetti, or fettuccine) can also be used. A few variations are listed, but the possibilities are endless. And for a quick and easy variation on the variations, the eggs can be scrambled with the spaghetti and other flavoring ingredients until soft-set rather than allowed to cook into a pancake-shaped frittata.

2 tablespoons butter or olive
   oil
½ cup chopped onion
1 garlic clove, crushed
2 cups (approximately)
   leftover spaghetti, cut
   into 1-inch lengths

6 large eggs
½ cup grated Parmesan cheese
2 tablespoons chopped Italian
   flat-leaf parsley
   Pinch of salt and grinding of
   coarsely ground black
   pepper

1. Heat butter in a heavy, preferably nonstick, 10-inch skillet. Stir in onion; sauté over low heat until tender and golden, about 5 minutes. Stir in garlic; sauté 1 minute. Stir in spaghetti until coated and heated through.

2. Beat eggs, cheese, and parsley together. Season with salt and pepper. Add to hot skillet; cook, covered, over medium-low heat until top begins to set and the edges are lightly browned when the frittata is gently lifted with a small spatula, about 12 minutes. Place a large round plate over the skillet and, with hands protected with oven mitts, invert the frittata onto the platter. Slide the frittata back into the skillet so the top can be browned. Cook, uncovered, over low heat, 5 minutes.

3. Slide the cooked frittata back onto the platter. Let stand a few minutes before cutting into wedges to serve.

Variations:

---

331   ASPARAGUS AND HAM FRITTATA

Sauté 1 cup thin diagonal slices of asparagus with the onion; stir in ½ cup slivered lightly smoked fully cooked ham.

---

332   ITALIAN SAUSAGE AND RED BELL PEPPER FRITTATA

Cook 6 ounces Italian sweet sausage, casings removed and crumbled, until lightly browned; drain off all the fat. Add 1 medium red bell pepper,

Variations continue on next page

Variations continued

seeded and cut into thin strips. Cook, stirring, over medium heat until tender and edges begin to brown. Add the sausage mixture to the sautéed onion and garlic along with the spaghetti.

---

333 ARTICHOKE HEARTS AND FONTINA FRITTATA

Cook 1 package (9 ounces) frozen artichoke hearts according to package directions; drain well; coarsely chop. Add artichokes and ½ cup coarsely shredded Italian Fontina (or mozzarella) cheese with the spaghetti.

---

334 EXOTIC MUSHROOM PASTA ALLA MAMMA
Prep: 10 minutes   Cook: 10 minutes   Serves: 2

Many exotic mushrooms are now being cultivated on mushroom farms and will soon be more readily available in markets across the country. Oyster, shiitake, and cremini mushrooms are now being grown on both the east and west coasts. Chanterelle are only found in the wild, but if available are wonderful in this dish.

4 **tablespoons butter**	**Pinch** *each* **dried basil and**
2 **cups chopped, trimmed**	**oregano**
mushrooms (use shiitake	6 **ounces fresh fettuccine**
caps, chanterelle, oyster,	4 **eggs, beaten**
and/or cremini)	3 **tablespoons grated**
1 **small garlic clove, crushed**	**Parmesan cheese**
2 **tablespoons finely chopped**	**Seasoned or plain salt**
parsley	**Freshly ground black**
	pepper

1. Heat butter in large heavy skillet; when foam subsides, add the mushrooms. Sauté, stirring, until tender, about 5 minutes. Add the garlic; sauté 1 minute. Add the parsley, basil, and oregano.

2. Meanwhile, cook the fettuccine in plenty of boiling salted water until al dente, or firm to the bite, about 2 minutes; drain.

3. Add the fettuccine to the skillet; stir to blend. Add the eggs and the cheese; sprinkle with salt to taste. Stir continuously until eggs coat the pasta and begin to set in a few places. Serve at once. Sprinkle with black pepper.

335 GARDEN VEGETABLE PASTA ALLA MAMMA

Prep: 15 minutes   Cook: 10 minutes   Serves: 2

4 tablespoons butter
2 cups combined cut-up (¼- to
   ½-inch pieces) fresh green
   beans, carrots, asparagus,
   and scallions
1 small garlic clove, crushed
2 tablespoons chopped
   parsley

Pinch of dried basil and
   oregano
6 ounces fettuccine
4 eggs, beaten
¼ cup grated Parmesan cheese
Seasoned or plain salt
Freshly ground black
   pepper

1. Heat the butter in a large heavy skillet. When the foam subsides, stir in the prepared vegetables. Sauté, stirring, over low heat until crisp-tender, about 5 minutes. Add the garlic; sauté 1 minute. Stir in the parsley, basil, and oregano.

2. Meanwhile, cook the fettuccine in plenty of boiling salted water until al dente, or firm to the bite, about 2 minutes; drain.

3. Add fettuccine to the vegetables. Add the eggs and cheese; sprinkle with salt to taste. Stir continuously until the egg coats the fettuccine and begins to set in a few places. Serve at once sprinkled with black pepper.

336 RIGATONI WITH SAUSAGE, PEPPERS, AND EGGS

Prep: 10 minutes   Cook: 20 minutes   Serves: 4

1 pound Italian sweet
   sausage, removed from
   casing
3 medium green bell peppers,
   quartered and cut into
   1-inch strips
1 medium onion, quartered
   aud cut into thin
   lengthwise slices

4 ounces mushrooms,
   trimmed and quartered
2 garlic cloves, bruised with
   the side of a knife
12 ounces rigatoni or other
   large tubular pasta
2 eggs, beaten
¼ cup grated Parmesan cheese

1. Brown sausage meat in a large skillet, stirring and breaking up pieces with the side of a fork; drain off excess fat. Add the peppers, onions, mushrooms, and garlic. Cook, covered, over low heat until the peppers are tender and the onion begins to turn golden, about 15 minutes.

2. Meanwhile cook the rigatoni in plenty of boiling salted water until al dente, or firm to the bite, about 15 minutes; drain.

3. Beat the eggs and cheese together. Remove the skillet from the heat. Stir in the egg mixture, stirring constantly until egg is creamy and coating the sausage. Pour over the pasta and toss well. Serve with additional Parmesan sprinkled on top.

337 BACON AND SAUSAGE PASTA ALLA PAPPA

Prep: 10 minutes   Cook: 10 minutes   Serves: 2

Pasta alla Pappa is, of course, a heartier, more rustic version of Pasta alla Mamma.

2 strips bacon, cooked, drained, and crumbled

2 links well-seasoned Italian sausage, casings removed, crumbled, browned, and drained

3 tablespoons butter

1 small garlic clove, crushed

2 tablespoons chopped parsley

Pinch *each* dried basil and oregano

6 ounces fresh fettuccine

4 eggs, beaten

¼ cup grated Parmesan cheese

Seasoned or plain salt

Freshly ground black pepper

1. Cook the meats; set aside. Melt the butter in a large heavy skillet. Add the garlic; sauté 1 minute. Add the cooked bacon and sausage, parsley, basil, and oregano.

2. Meanwhile, cook the fettuccine in plenty of boiling salted water until al dente, or firm to the bite, about 2 minutes; drain.

3. Add the fettuccine to the skillet; stir to blend. Add the eggs and cheese; sprinkle with salt to taste. Stir continuously until the eggs coat fettuccine and begin to set in a few places. Serve immediately sprinkled with freshly ground black pepper.

Chapter 19

The Asian Connection

The Chinese, historians tell us, have been eating pasta since 1700 B.C. Marco Polo evidently did enjoy noodles on his tour through Asia, but recent debates seem to indicate that he did not, in fact, introduce them to the Italians, who had been consuming their own form of pasta since Roman times. Asian egg noodles made with wheat are freshly made and sold in oriental markets. (Spaghetti can be substituted for these sometimes hard-to-find noodles.) Noodles are also made from mung bean starch and rice in various shapes from thin threads to broad flat ribbons. Following are just a few Asian-inspired noodle dishes from the classic Wonton Soup to an old family favorite: Noodle Pancake with Stir-fried Broccoli and Tamari Walnuts.

338 NOODLES WITH SOY DRESSING AND SPRING VEGETABLES

Prep: 15 minutes   Cook: 5–7 minutes   Serves: 4

½ cup thinly sliced scallions
½ cup shredded pared carrot
1 small cucumber, pared and cut into 1-inch julienne
1 cup packed trimmed small sprigs fresh watercress
¼ cup light soy sauce
2 tablespoons oriental sesame oil
2 tablespoons peanut or other vegetable oil
2 tablespoons rice vinegar

1 tablespoon Chinese black vinegar (or a flavorful red wine vinegar)
1 teaspoon hot chili-flavored oriental sesame oil
1 teaspoon sugar
1 teaspoon grated fresh gingerroot
½ teaspoon crushed garlic
12 ounces fresh Chinese egg noodles or thin spaghetti

1. Place the scallions, carrot, cucumber, and watercress in a small bowl; wrap with plastic and refrigerate until ready to serve.

2. Whisk the soy sauce, sesame oil, peanut oil, rice vinegar, black vinegar, chili oil, sugar, gingerroot, and garlic together; set aside.

3. Cook the noodles until al dente, or firm to the bite, about 5 minutes; drain. Rinse with cool water; drain well. Place noodles on a clean kitchen towel and shake to blot excess moisture.

4. Immediately toss noodles with the dressing. Just before serving, add the raw vegetables and toss just once with chopsticks. Serve cold.

339 NOODLE PANCAKE WITH STIR-FRIED BROCCOLI AND TAMARI WALNUTS

Prep: 20 minutes   Cook: 15 minutes   Serves: 4–6

Tamari Walnuts
1 tablespoon peanut oil
½ cup shelled walnuts

1 tablespoon tamari

---

8 ounces fresh Chinese egg noodles or thin spaghetti
2 teaspoons oriental sesame oil
2 tablespoons rice vinegar
1 tablespoon hoisin sauce
1 tablespoon plus 1 teaspoon soy sauce or tamari
2 teaspoons sugar
2 teaspoons cornstarch

¼ teaspoon salt
6 tablespoons peanut oil
1 teaspoon minced fresh gingerroot
1 teaspoon minced garlic
¼ teaspoon crushed dried red pepper
1 bunch (about 1 pound) broccoli, trimmed and cut into 1-inch pieces

1. To make the tamari walnuts, heat the oil in a medium skillet; add walnuts; stir-fry until fragrant, about 10 seconds. Sprinkle with tamari; stir-fry until coated and crisp, about 20 seconds. Do not overcook. Spoon onto a plate to cool.

2. Cook the noodles in plenty of boiling salted water until al dente, or firm to the bite, about 5 minutes; drain. Rinse with cold water; drain again. Place noodles on a clean kitchen towel; shake towel to blot excess moisture. Toss the noodles with 1 teaspoon of the sesame oil; set aside.

3. In a small bowl, stir the remaining teaspoon sesame oil, rice vinegar, hoisin sauce, soy sauce, sugar, cornstarch, and salt until smooth; set aside.

4. Select two large heavy skillets or a skillet and a wok. Heat 3 tablespoons of the peanut oil in each skillet. Add the noodles to the skillet, arranging them in a uniform layer. Cover and cook over medium-high heat 5 to 6 minutes, shaking skillet occasionally to prevent sticking. To the second skillet or wok, add the ginger, garlic, and red pepper; stir-fry 20 seconds. Add the broccoli; stir-fry until coated with the oil and seasonings; cover and cook over medium heat until crisp-tender, about 4 minutes. Add the sauce mixture; stir to coat. Stir-fry over medium heat until thickened, about 3 minutes.

5. When the noodle pancake is browned and crisped on one side, carefully invert onto a platter or a flat lid and slide the pancake, crisped side up, into the skillet. Brown the other side, covered, over medium-high heat, 3 minutes.

6. To serve, transfer the noodle pancake to a platter; spoon the broccoli mixture on top and sprinkle with tamari walnuts.

---

340   NOODLES WITH HOT SESAME SAUCE
Prep: 10 minutes   Cook: 5 minutes   Serves: 4

- 8 ounces fresh Chinese noodles or thin spaghetti
- 1 tablespoon plus 1 teaspoon oriental sesame oil
- 3 tablespoons strong freshly brewed tea
- 2 tablespoons soy sauce
- 2 tablespoons oriental sesame paste
- 1 tablespoon peanut oil
- 1 tablespoon chili paste with garlic
- 1 tablespoon Chinese rice wine or dry sherry
- 1 teaspoon honey
- 1 teaspoon grated fresh gingerroot
- 1 tablespoon fresh coriander (cilantro)
- 1 tablespoon sliced scallion tops

1. Cook the noodles in plenty of boiling salted water until al dente, or firm to the bite, about 5 minutes; drain. Rinse with cold water; drain again. Place noodles on a clean kitchen towel; shake towel to blot excess moisture. Toss the noodles with 1 teaspoon sesame oil; set aside.

2. Whisk the remaining 1 tablespoon sesame oil, tea, soy sauce, sesame paste, peanut oil, chili paste, wine, honey, and ginger until smooth. Toss with the cooked noodles. Sprinkle with the coriander and scallion; toss once.

341   NOODLES WITH PEANUT SAUCE

Prep: 15 minutes   Cook: 5 minutes   Serves: 4

6 tablespoons warm water
6 tablespoons creamy peanut
  butter
3 tablespoons oriental sesame
  paste
3 tablespoons Chinese rice
  wine or dry sherry
3 tablespoons white rice
  vinegar
2 tablespoons light soy sauce
1 tablespoon hot chili-
  flavored oriental sesame
  oil

1 tablespoon minced fresh
  gingerroot
2 garlic cloves, crushed
3 teaspoons oriental sesame
  oil
8 ounces fresh Chinese
  noodles or thin spaghetti
1 scallion, trimmed and sliced
  thin
¼ cup coarsely chopped fresh
  coriander (cilantro)

1. In the bowl of a food processor or with a whisk, blend the water, peanut butter, sesame paste, wine, rice vinegar, soy sauce, chili-flavored sesame oil, ginger, garlic, and 2 teaspoons of the sesame oil until smooth.

2. Cook the noodles in plenty of boiling salted water until al dente, or firm to the bite, about 5 minutes; drain well; rinse with cold water and drain again. Pat dry with paper toweling. In a large bowl, toss noodles with remaining 1 teaspoon sesame oil.

3. Add the peanut mixture to the noodles; toss with chopsticks until blended. Sprinkle with the scallions and coriander; toss just once and serve.

342   JAPANESE NOODLE SALAD

Prep: 15 minutes   Cook: 4–5 minutes   Serves: 4

1 egg
2 teaspoons oriental sesame
  oil
  Pinch of salt
1 package (5.1 ounces) dried
  Japanese curly noodles
  (chuka soba)
3 tablespoons sweet rice
  vinegar (mirin)
2 tablespoons light soy sauce

1 tablespoon peanut oil
1 teaspoon grated fresh
  gingerroot
½ cup slivered cooked ham
¼ cup shredded carrot
1 scallion, trimmed and cut
  into thin diagonal slices
1 tablespoon sesame seeds,
  toasted in a skillet 1
  minute

1. Whisk egg, 1 teaspoon of the sesame oil, and pinch of salt until blended. Heat a small nonstick skillet over medium heat until a drop of water evaporates immediately upon contact; add egg. Cook until set, about 2 minutes. Transfer to a plate; cool. Cut into ¼-inch strips; reserve.

2. Cook the noodles in plenty of boiling salted water until al dente, or firm to the bite, about 4 minutes. Drain. Rinse well with cold water; drain again.

3. In a large bowl, whisk the vinegar, soy sauce, peanut oil, ginger, and remaining 1 teaspoon sesame oil. Add the noodles, ham, carrot, scallions, sesame seeds, and reserved egg strips; toss and serve.

Variation:

343   JAPANESE NOODLE SALAD WITH SHRIMP

Substitute ½ cup chopped cooked shrimp for the ham.

344   CHINESE-STYLE VEGETABLE AND NOODLE SOUP
Prep: 10 minutes   Soak: 30 minutes   Cook: 15 minutes   Serves: 6

If you have a handful of fresh or dried Chinese egg noodles and a few pieces of Chinese-type vegetables, this is an easy freeform recipe to assemble. If using the dried Chinese egg noodles, which are sold in a solid block of tangled threads of egg noodles, stir constantly with a chopstick while cooking so they will cook evenly.

4 dried shiitake mushrooms	½ cup thinly sliced carrot coins
6 cups light chicken broth (use homemade or half canned and half water)	¼ cup chopped red bell pepper
	½ package dried Chinese egg noodles (about 3 ounces)
1 slice (¼ inch) fresh gingerroot	Salt
12 ounces Chinese cabbage, rinsed and cut into ¼-inch slices (about 2 cups)	1 tablespoon rice vinegar
	1 teaspoon soy sauce
	½ teaspoon hot chili-flavored oriental sesame oil
½ cup Chinese snow peas, trimmed and cut into ¼-inch diagonal slices	1 scallion, trimmed and cut into ⅛-inch diagonal slices
½ cup (¼ × 1-inch pieces) broccoli stems	

1. Place mushrooms in a small saucepan; add about 2 cups water and heat, covered, to boiling. Let stand 30 minutes; drain; cut off and discard stems; cut caps into ⅛-inch strips.

2. Simmer broth and ginger, covered, 10 minutes. Stir in cabbage, snow peas, broccoli, carrots, and red pepper. Let stand, uncovered.

3. Cook the noodles in plenty of boiling salted water until al dente, or firm to the bite, about 3 minutes. Drain; rinse immediately to prevent sticking.

4. Add mushrooms and noodles to broth and vegetables; reheat, stirring. Season with salt, vinegar, soy sauce, and sesame oil. Ladle into bowls and sprinkle with scallions.

345   NOODLE PANCAKE WITH BEEF AND VEGETABLE STIR-FRY

Prep: 20 minutes   Cook: 20 minutes   Serves: 4–6

8 ounces fresh Chinese noodles or thin spaghetti

1 teaspoon oriental sesame oil

Marinade

1 tablespoon peanut oil
1 tablespoon Chinese rice wine or dry sherry
1 tablespoon soy sauce
1 tablespoon honey

2 teaspoons cornstarch
1 teaspoon minced fresh gingerroot
1 teaspoon minced garlic

1 pound flank steak, cut into ¼-inch slices, each slice halved crosswise
5 tablespoons peanut oil
1 teaspoon minced fresh gingerroot
1 teaspoon minced garlic
½ cup diagonally sliced trimmed scallions

4 ounces fresh snow peas, trimmed
1 cup sliced trimmed mushrooms
½ cup red bell pepper, seeded and cut into ½-inch squares
½ teaspoon hot chili-flavored oriental sesame oil

1. Cook the noodles in plenty of boiling salted water until al dente, or firm to the bite, about 5 minutes; drain. Rinse with cold water; drain again. Place noodles on a clean kitchen towel and blot excess moisture. Toss the noodles with 1 teaspoon sesame oil; set aside.

2. Whisk together the marinade ingredients. Add the beef; set aside.

3. Select two large heavy skillets or a skillet and a wok. Heat 3 tablespoons of the peanut oil in the large skillet; add the spaghetti, arranging in a uniform layer. Cover and cook over medium-high heat, shaking the pan occasionally to prevent sticking, until browned and crisped, about 5 minutes. Carefully invert the skillet onto a platter or a flat lid; slide the pancake, browned side up, back into the skillet. Brown the other side, covered, over medium-high heat, 3 to 4 minutes.

4. Heat 1 tablespoon of the peanut oil in the other skillet or wok until hot enough to sizzle a pinch of ginger. Add the ginger, garlic, and scallions; stir-fry 1 minute. Add the snow peas, mushrooms, and red bell pepper; stir-fry until crisp-tender, about 3 minutes. Transfer with a slotted spoon to a bowl. Add remaining 1 tablespoon peanut oil to skillet; heat over high heat. Add the flank steak and marinade and the hot chili oil to the skillet; stir-fry 3 minutes. Add the reserved vegetables; stir-fry to blend, about 1 minute.

5. When the noodle pancake is well browned and crisped on both sides, slide onto a platter; spoon the beef mixture on top and serve at once.

Variations:

346 NOODLE PANCAKE WITH VEGETABLE STIR-FRY

Combine marinade ingredients but omit the flank steak; set aside. Add 1 cup broccoli florets, ½ cup green bell pepper strips, and ¼ cup sliced water chestnuts to the vegetables in step 4. Add the marinade ingredients to the stir-fried vegetables; stir-fry until mixture is fragrant and coats the vegetables.

347 NOODLE PANCAKE WITH SHRIMP AND VEGETABLE STIR-FRY

Substitute 1 pound shelled and deveined medium shrimp for the flank steak.

348 WONTON SOUP
Prep: 30 minutes   Cook: 20 minutes   Serves: 6

Wonton wrappers are available frozen in many markets.

Filling

¼ pound lean ground pork
2 tablespoons minced scallions
1 tablespoon minced water chestnuts

1 teaspoon grated fresh gingeroot
1 teaspoon soy sauce
½ teaspoon oriental sesame oil
Pinch of salt

12 wonton wrappers, defrosted
7 cups light homemade chicken broth, or half canned and half water
1 thin slice fresh ginger

1 cup torn trimmed and rinsed spinach leaves
½ cup shredded cooked chicken or slivered baked ham (or ¼ cup each)

1. Combine the filling ingredients; stir to blend. Lay the wonton wrappers out on the counter. Divide the filling evenly among the wrappers, placing a rounded half teaspoonful just below the center of each. Moisten the edges and fold: fold the bottom section over the filling, fold over the sides, then roll into a cylinder.

2. Heat the broth and ginger to boiling; reduce the heat. Cook the wontons, 3 or 4 at a time, in the simmering broth, about 4 minutes, until all have been cooked.

3. Just before serving, add the wontons to the soup along with the spinach and shredded chicken and/or ham. Heat to simmering before serving.

349 NOODLES WITH RICE VINEGAR AND RAW VEGETABLES

Prep: 15 minutes   Cook: 5–7 minutes   Serves: 4

¼ cup peanut oil
2 tablespoons rice vinegar
1 tablespoon lime juice
2 teaspoons oriental sesame oil
1 teaspoon grated fresh gingerroot
½ teaspoon salt
¼ teaspoon hot chili-flavored oriental sesame oil

12 ounces fresh Chinese flat noodles or linguine
1 medium carrot, pared and cut into 2 x ⅛-inch julienne
1 cucumber, pared, seeded, and cut into 2 x ⅛-inch julienne
2 tablespoons chopped coriander (cilantro)
1 teaspoon black sesame seeds

1. Whisk the peanut oil, vinegar, lime juice, sesame oil, gingerroot, salt, and chili oil together.

2. Cook the noodles in plenty of boiling salted water 5 minutes; stir in the carrots. Cook until noodles are al dente, or firm to the bite, and the carrots are crisp-tender, about 2 minutes longer; drain well. Rinse with cold water to cool quickly; drain again. Place the noodles on a clean kitchen towel and shake towel to blot excess moisture.

3. Immediately toss noodles and carrots with the dressing, cucumber, and coriander. Sprinkle with sesame seeds. Serve at room temperature or slightly chilled.

350 SINGAPORE NOODLES

Prep: 30 minutes   Soak: 15 minutes   Cook: 10 minutes   Serves: 4

These are basically rice noodles with stir-fried beef and vegetables. The flavors in this dish are a combination of Chinese and Indonesian.

1 pound lean beef (top round or sirloin)
8 ounces (¼ inch wide) rice noodles (called mi-fun, rice sticks, or rice vermicelli)
¼ cup peanut oil
1 teaspoon minced fresh gingerroot
½ teaspoon minced garlic
1 long thin carrot, pared and cut into thin diagonal slices

1 scallion, trimmed and cut into thin diagonal slices
½ red bell pepper, sliced in ⅛-inch strips
2 ounces Chinese snow peas, trimmed and halved diagonally
⅓ cup light soy sauce
1 teaspoon chili paste with garlic
1 teaspoon ground cumin
1 teaspoon ground coriander

1. Wrap the beef in foil and place in the freezer for 30 minutes to firm meat. Cut into thin slightly diagonal strips; cut each strip into 1-inch lengths; set aside.

2. Soak the rice noodles in boiling water to cover until swollen and translucent, about 15 minutes; drain.

3. Heat 2 tablespoons of the oil in a large heavy skillet or wok; add the ginger and garlic; stir-fry 2 minutes. Add the carrot, scallion, red bell pepper, and snow peas; stir-fry until crisp-tender, about 3 minutes. Scrape out of skillet onto a side dish.

4. Heat the remaining 2 tablespoons oil in the skillet; add the beef; stir-fry, over high heat, just until it begins to lose its pink color, about 2 minutes. Meanwhile, combine the soy sauce, chili paste, cumin, and coriander in a small bowl. Add to the skillet; stir to coat beef; add the noodles and reserved vegetables. Stir with a chopstick just until blended and heated through.

351   EBONY NOODLES
Prep: 15 minutes   Soak: 15 minutes   Cook: 5 minutes   Serves: 6

6 large dried shiitake
   mushrooms
1 package (4 ounces) bean
   threads (also called sai
   fun, cellophane noodles,
   glass noodles, or mung
   bean noodles)

5 ounces fresh spinach
2 tablespoons coarsely
   shredded radish
2 tablespoons thin diagonal
   slices green scallion tops
2 tablespoons minced pickled
   gingerroot

Dressing
⅓ cup tamari
¼ cup rice vinegar
2 tablespoons sugar
1 tablespoon vegetable oil

2 teaspoons oriental sesame
   oil
1 garlic clove, crushed

2 tablespoons toasted sesame
   seeds

1. In a small bowl, soak the mushrooms in boiling water 15 minutes; cut off and discard woody stems. Blot mushrooms with paper toweling and cut into ⅛-inch strips.

2. Meanwhile, place the bean threads in a bowl; pour boiling water over and let stand until swollen and translucent, about 10 minutes. Drain well; rinse with cold water; fluff with chopsticks.

3. Wash the spinach well; place in a saucepan and cook, covered, over low heat with just the liquid left clinging to the leaves until barely limp, about 3 minutes. Add cold water to the saucepan to plump the spinach; drain in a strainer, shaking to remove excess moisture; set aside.

4. In a large bowl, combine the mushrooms, spinach, noodles, radishes, scallion, and pickled ginger. Combine the dressing ingredients in a large jar; shake well to combine and dissolve the sugar. Toss with the noodle mixture. Sprinkle with the sesame seeds.

352   SOBA NOODLE SALAD

Prep: 10 minutes   Soak: 15 minutes   Cook: 5 minutes   Serves: 4

4 dried shiitake mushrooms
1 package (5.1 ounces) dried
     Japanese curly noodles
     (chuka soba)
1 long thin carrot, pared and
     cut into ⅛ × 2-inch pieces

1 scallion, trimmed and cut
     into very thin diagonals
½ cup julienne strips unpared
     European or seedless
     cucumber
¼ cup julienne strips radish

Dressing

2 tablespoons fresh lemon
     juice
2 tablespoons soy sauce

4 tablespoons peanut oil
1 teaspoon grated gingerroot
1 small garlic clove, crushed

1. Soak the shiitake in boiling water to cover 15 minutes. Cut off and discard the woody stems. Blot caps dry with paper toweling and cut into thin slices.

2. Cook the noodles and the carrots in plenty of boiling salted water until al dente, or firm to the bite, about 4 minutes. Drain; rinse with cold water and drain again.

3. Combine the dressing ingredients and whisk to blend.

4. Toss mushrooms, noodles and carrots, scallion, cucumber, and radish strips with the dressing until blended. Serve cold or at room temperature.

353   CHINESE-STYLE SOUP WITH CELLOPHANE NOODLES AND TINY MEATBALLS

Prep: 20 minutes   Cook: 15 minutes   Serves: 6–8

Meatballs

½ pound lean ground pork
1 tablespoon soy sauce
1 tablespoon Chinese rice
     wine or dry sherry
2 teaspoons cornstarch
     dissolved in 2
     tablespoons water

1 tablespoon minced scallions
½ teaspoon grated fresh
     gingerroot
1 small garlic clove, crushed
     Pinch of sugar
1 to 2 tablespoons ice water

2 ounces cellophane noodles
     (also called sai fun, bean
     threads, or glass noodles)
1 thin slice fresh gingerroot

6 cups light homemade
     chicken stock, or half
     canned broth and half
     water
1 scallion, trimmed and cut
     into thin diagonal slices

1. Combine all the ingredients for the meatballs; mix very lightly with a chopstick; do not overwork the mixture. With wet hands, shape into tiny meatballs about ½ inch in diameter; set aside on a platter; refrigerate until ready to cook.

2. Place the nöodles in a bowl and cover with boiling water. Let stand until the noodles swell, about 5 minutes.

3. Add the slice of ginger to the broth; heat the broth to boiling. Reduce to a slow simmer. Carefully lower the meatballs into the broth. Cover and cook over low heat 5 minutes.

4. Drain the noodles and cut into short lengths with scissors. Add to the broth. Ladle hot soup into bowls and sprinkle each with scallion slices.

The Asian Noodle Connection

Egg Noodles: Available fresh in oriental markets; substitute spaghetti if unavailable
Bean Threads, Sai fun, Cellophane Noodles, Glass Noodles: Made from mung bean starch and water; sold dried in small packages
Rice Noodles, Rice Sticks, Rice Vermicelli: Made from rice flour and water; thin sticks or broad flat ribbons

Chapter 20

Desserts, Puddings, and Breakfast Dishes

The desserts and puddings in this chapter, with names like Pineapple-Noodle Pudding with Meringue Topping, Lemon-Scented Pastina Soufflé, and Ricotta and Apricot Noodle Pudding with Crunchy Walnut Topping, have a variety of intriguing flavors and textures and are just a little less heavy than the classic rendition of noodle pudding. At least half the recipes in this chapter were inspired by the old-fashioned and homey Jewish kugel, a noodle pudding that is often, by way of tradition, too sweet and heavy. In some recipes, elbow macaroni takes the place of bulky noodles and the cottage cheese custard is replaced by a lighter milk and egg custard, as in the Tiny Elbows in Baked Custard. The result is a thoroughly delectable cross between baked custard and noodle pudding with a lovely crust of ground nutmeg on top. Orzo, the rice-shaped pasta that is one of my favorites, is wildly successful as a rice substitute and especially good in Chocolate and Coconut Orzo Pudding. Most of these concoctions are desserts, but I have been known to enjoy a comforting spoonful or two at breakfast, not to mention a few snacks here and there. Let your appetite and mood be your guide.

354   RICOTTA AND APRICOT NOODLE PUDDING WITH CRUNCHY WALNUT TOPPING

Prep: 15 minutes   Bake: 35 minutes   Serves: 8

8 ounces egg noodles	1 cup half-and-half
1 container (15 ounces) ricotta cheese	1 teaspoon vanilla extract
	½ teaspoon ground cinnamon
3 eggs	½ cup diced dried apricots
⅓ cup sugar	2 tablespoons cold butter cut into ¼-inch pieces

Crunchy Walnut Topping

½ cup fine dry bread crumbs	¼ cup finely chopped walnuts
¼ cup packed light brown sugar	⅛ teaspoon ground cinnamon
	3 tablespoons butter, melted

1. Cook the noodles in plenty of boiling salted water until al dente, or firm to the bite, about 12 minutes; drain; rinse with cool water.

2. Beat the ricotta, eggs, and sugar until light. Stir in the half-and-half, vanilla, and cinnamon until blended. Fold the noodles, ricotta mixture, apricots, and butter until thoroughly blended.

3. Heat oven to 350°F. Generously butter a 10-inch pie dish. Transfer the noodle mixture to the prepared pie plate.

4. For the topping, combine the bread crumbs, light brown sugar, walnuts, and cinnamon in a small bowl. Add the butter and mix thoroughly with a fork. Sprinkle over the top of the noodles.

5. Baked until top is golden and custard is set, about 35 minutes. Let cool slightly at room temperature before serving.

355   PASTINA WITH BUTTER, CREAM, AND CINNAMON SUGAR

Prep: 5 minutes   Cook: 15 minutes   Serves: 2

This is a dessert pudding, although it makes a nourishing breakfast dish as well. Add a tablespoon of raisins, diced dried apples, or dried apricots for added texture and flavor.

½ cup pastina	1 tablespoon butter
1 cup heavy cream	⅛ teaspoon cinnamon
¼ cup sugar	

1. Cook pastina in plenty of boiling salted water until al dente, or firm to the bite, about 10 minutes; drain. Return to saucepan.

2. Add the cream and 2 tablespoons of the sugar; stir over low heat until hot and thickened, about 2 minutes. Stir in butter. Spoon into bowls. Combine the remaining sugar and cinnamon and sprinkle over top of pudding, to taste.

356 LEMON-SCENTED PASTINA SOUFFLÉ
Prep: 20 minutes   Bake: 35 minutes   Serves: 6

2 cups milk
⅓ cup pastina
1 cup sugar
2 tablespoons butter
1 teaspoon grated lemon zest

1 teaspoon vanilla extract
4 eggs, separated, at room
   temperature
Pinch of salt

1. In a large saucepan, scald milk. Gradually stir in the pastina. Cook, stirring frequently and adjusting heat to prevent scorching, until thickened and the pastina is tender, about 15 minutes. Stir in ½ cup of the sugar until dissolved; add the butter, lemon zest, and vanilla.

2. Beat egg yolks with remaining ½ cup sugar until light and foamy; set aside. Beat the whites until foamy; add a pinch of salt. Gradually beat the remaining ¼ cup sugar into the whites until whites are glossy but not dry.

3. Heat the oven to 350°F. Generously butter a 10-inch square baking dish. Fold the yolks into the pastina until thoroughly blended. Gently fold the whites into the mixture until blended.

4. Transfer to prepared baking dish. Set baking dish in a large baking pan. Add 1 inch of hot water. Bake until top is puffed and golden and pudding is set, about 35 minutes. Cool slightly before serving. Good served warm or at room temperature.

357 COUSCOUS, DRIED FRUIT, AND HONEY PUDDING
Prep: 10 minutes   Let stand: 15 minutes   Serves: 4

Experiment with the various dried fruit mixtures available in handy snack packs for this pudding. Some even contain shavings of coconut and nuts. This pudding is more a breakfast or snack food than something to eat after a meal.

1¼ cups couscous
½ cup mixed finely chopped
   dried fruits (pineapple,
   papaya, apricots, dates,
   raisins)
3 tablespoons finely chopped
   pecans, almonds, or
   hazelnuts

3 cups milk
2 tablespoons honey
½ teaspoon vanilla extract
2 tablespoons sugar
¼ teaspoon ground cinnamon
   Heavy cream

1. Combine the couscous, mixed dried fruits, and pecans; set aside.

2. Scald the milk; stir in the honey and vanilla. Add the couscous mixture; stir once. Cover and let stand until all the milk is absorbed, about 15 minutes.

3. To serve, spoon into bowls. Combine the sugar and cinnamon in a separate bowl. Drizzle puddings with cream and sprinkle with cinnamon sugar.

358   CHOCOLATE AND COCONUT ORZO PUDDING

Prep: 5 minutes   Cook: 25 minutes   Serves: 4–6

4 cups milk
½ cup orzo
¼ cup packed light brown
   sugar
1 cup semisweet chocolate
   chips

⅓ cup flaked coconut
½ teaspoon vanilla extract
   Pinch of salt
   Heavy cream

1. In a large heavy saucepan, scald the milk. Gradually stir in the orzo and cool, stirring frequently and adjusting the heat to prevent milk from boiling over and scorching, until mixture is thickened and the orzo is tender to the bite, about 20 to 25 minutes.

2. Stir in the sugar until dissolved. Add the chocolate and the coconut; stir, off heat, until the chocolate is melted. Add the vanilla and salt. Let cool at room temperature. Serve spooned into dessert bowls with cold heavy cream drizzled on top.

359   PINEAPPLE-NOODLE PUDDING WITH MERINGUE TOPPING

Prep: 15 minutes   Bake: 25 minutes   Serves: 8

8 ounces wide egg noodles
1 package (8 ounces) cream
   cheese
¼ cup packed light brown
   sugar
3 eggs
1 teaspoon vanilla extract
1 teaspoon grated lemon zest

1 can (8 ounces) crushed
   unsweetened pineapple,
   with juice
1 cup half-and-half
3 egg whites
   Pinch of salt
¼ cup granulated sugar

1. Cook the noodles in plenty of boiling salted water until al dente, or firm to the bite, about 12 minutes; drain; rinse with cool water.

2. Beat cream cheese and sugar until light and creamy. Gradually beat in the eggs, one at a time. Add the vanilla and lemon zest.

3. Heat the oven to 350°F. Generously butter a shallow 2-quart baking dish. Fold the noodles, cream cheese mixture, pineapple, and half-and-half until thoroughly blended. Spoon into the prepared baking dish.

4. Beat the egg whites until foamy; add the salt; beat until soft peaks form. Gradually beat in the sugar, 1 tablespoon at a time, until whites are glossy but not dry. Carefully spread the meringue over the top of the noodles.

5. Bake until meringue is golden and the custard is set, about 25 minutes. Cool at room temperature. To serve, cut into squares.

360   CLASSIC NOODLE PUDDING
Prep: 15 minutes   Bake: 25 minutes   Serves: 6–8

Add a handful of raisins to this pudding if you like.

8 ounces wide egg noodles
4 tablespoons butter, melted
1 container (16 ounces) small
 curd creamed cottage
 cheese
¾ cup sugar

4 eggs
1 teaspoon vanilla extract
½ teaspoon ground cinnamon
¼ teaspoon almond extract
 Pinch of nutmeg

Topping
4 tablespoons butter
2 tablespoons sliced
 unblanched almonds

½ cup fine dry bread crumbs

1. Cook the noodles in plenty of boiling salted water until al dente, or firm to the bite, about 10 minutes; drain. Toss with the butter; set aside.

2. Beat the cottage cheese and the sugar until light and fluffy. Beat in the eggs, one at a time, beating well after each addition. Add the vanilla, cinnamon, almond extract, and nutmeg. Fold in the noodles.

3. Heat the oven to 350°F. Lightly butter a 2-quart shallow baking dish. Spread the noodle mixture in the dish.

4. To make the topping, melt the butter in a medium skillet; stir in the almonds; sauté 1 minute. Off heat, add the bread crumbs; stir to blend. Sprinkle over the pudding. Bake until pudding is set, about 25 minutes.

361   TINY ELBOWS IN BAKED CUSTARD
Prep: 15 minutes   Bake: 55 minutes   Serves: 6–8

Try this recipe with any small shaped macaroni. The custard is very delicate. Freshly ground whole nutmeg makes a delicately flavored crust on top.

½ cup raisins
1 cup tiny elbow macaroni
2 tablespoons butter
4 eggs
¾ cup sugar

4 cups milk, scalded
1 teaspoon vanilla extract
 Ground nutmeg, preferably
 fresh

1. Plump the raisins in boiling water to cover; let stand 10 minutes; drain.

2. Meanwhile, cook the elbows in plenty of boiling salted water until al dente, or firm to the bite, about 10 minutes; drain. Toss with butter; set aside.

3. Beat the eggs and sugar until light and fluffy. Gradually stir in the milk. Add the vanilla.

4. Heat oven to 350°F. Lightly butter a 2-quart shallow baking dish. Spread the raisins and the elbows in the dish. Pour the custard mixture over the macaroni; sprinkle the top lightly with nutmeg. Carefully set the dish in a larger baking pan. Add 1 inch of hot water to the baking pan. Bake until custard is set, about 55 minutes.

362   ORZO SAUCEPAN PUDDING
Prep: 5 minutes   Cook: 25 minutes   Serves: 4

The flavorings in this pudding are easily varied: add grated lemon or orange zest; use lemon extract instead of vanilla; add 2 tablespoons raisins, dried currants, or minced candied orange or minced dried apricots. This is a rich and creamy dessert or breakfast dish. Serve with chilled heavy cream poured over the top, if desired.

3½ **cups milk**	½ **cup orzo**
⅓ **cup sugar**	½ **teaspoon vanilla extract**

1. Combine the milk and sugar in a small heavy saucepan. Scald milk, stirring, over medium-low heat. Stir in the orzo. Cook, stirring frequently and adjusting heat to prevent milk from boiling over and scorching, until the mixture is very thick and orzo is tender to the bite, 20 to 25 minutes. Off heat, stir in the vanilla.

2. Pour mixture into a large bowl or four individual custard cups. Cool slightly. Serve warm or at room temperature.

363   ORZO LEMON AND CUSTARD PUDDING
Prep: 5 minutes   Cook: 25 minutes   Serves: 4

4 **cups milk**	2 **tablespoons raisins**
⅓ **cup sugar**	½ **teaspoon grated lemon zest**
½ **cup orzo**	½ **teaspoon vanilla extract**
1 **large egg, beaten**	**Grated nutmeg**

1. In a large heavy saucepan, scald the milk and sugar over medium-low heat. Stir in the orzo and cook, stirring frequently and adjusting heat to prevent milk from boiling over and scorching, until mixture is thickened and orzo is tender to the bite, about 20 to 25 minutes.

2. Meanwhile, beat the egg in a medium bowl. Stir the raisins, lemon zest, and vanilla into the pudding until blended. Gradually add the hot pudding to the beaten egg, stirring constantly with a spoon so that egg doesn't curdle. Sprinkle with nutmeg.

3. Cool slightly at room temperature. Serve warm. Pudding will thicken and set upon cooling.

364 PASTINA WITH MAPLE SYRUP AND DATES
Prep: 10 minutes   Cook: 25 minutes   Serves: 4

3 cups milk
½ cup pastina
¼ cup maple syrup

2 tablespoons butter, softened
¼ cup chopped pitted dates
½ teaspoon vanilla extract

1. Scald milk in a medium saucepan. Stir in the pastina; cook, stirring frequently and adjusting heat to prevent scorching, until pastina is tender and the mixture is thickened, about 20 minutes.

2. Add the maple syrup, butter, dates, and vanilla. Spoon into small custard cups and cool slightly before serving.

365 CARAMELIZED APPLE-CINNAMON NOODLE PUDDING
Prep: 15 minutes   Bake: 55 minutes   Serves: 8

1 cup elbow macaroni or other
  small macaroni shape
  (tubetti or small shells)
2 tablespoons butter
2 cups cut-up pared apples (¼-
  to ½-inch pieces)
2 tablespoons light brown
  sugar
2 tablespoons golden raisins

¼ teaspoon ground cinnamon
1 cup small curd creamed
  cottage cheese
½ cup sugar
3 eggs
2 cups milk, scalded
1 teaspoon vanilla extract
  Pinch of nutmeg

1. Cook the macaroni in plenty of boiling salted water until al dente, or firm to the bite, about 10 minutes; drain.

2. Heat the butter in a medium skillet; when the foam subsides, stir in the apples; sprinkle with the brown sugar. Sauté, stirring, until apples are glazed and slightly caramelized. Stir in raisins and cinnamon.

3. Beat the cottage cheese and the sugar until fairly smooth. Beat in the eggs, one at a time, beating well after each addition. Stir in the milk and the vanilla.

4. Heat oven to 350°F. Lightly butter a 2-quart shallow baking dish. Fold the macaroni and the apples together; spread in the baking dish. Carefully pour in the custard mixture. Sprinkle top with nutmeg. Set the dish in a larger baking pan and add 1 inch of hot water. Bake until set, about 55 minutes.

Index

Index

About the Author

Marie Simmons, former food editor of *Cuisine*, regular contributor to *Woman's Day, Bon Appétit*, and *Good Food*, and coauthor (with Barbara Lagowski) of *Good Spirits: Alcohol-Free Drinks for All Occasions*, began her pasta education as a child under the loving guidance of her Italian mother and grandmother. She lives with her husband, daughter, cat, and dog in Brooklyn and Sag Harbor, New York.